Talk to the World™

A Manual for Students and
Teachers of Conversational English

Talk to the World: A Manual for Students
and Teachers of Conversational English

LanguagePower Publications
1402 North Albert Street
St. Paul, Minnesota 55108

© 1994 Edward Voeller.
All rights reserved. Protected under the Berne Convention. Published in 1994.

No part of this book may be used or reproduced, stored in a retrieval system, or transmitted in any form or by any means, electronic, mechanical, photocopying, recording or in any manner whatsoever without the prior written permission of the copyright holder, except in the case of brief quotations embodied in critical articles and reviews.
Printed in the United States of America

99 98 97 96 95 94   5 4 3 2 1

Book design: LanguagePower Publications, St. Paul, Minnesota

Cataloging-in-Publication Data

Voeller, Edward.
    Talk to the world: a manual for students and teachers of conversational English.

      Includes teaching/study notes, appendix, index.
      1. English language—Text-books for foreign speakers.
2. English language—Study and teaching—Foreign speakers. 3. English language—Conversation and phrase books. 4. English language—Grammar. I. Title
    PE1128.V64 1994   428.24   94- 75328
    ISBN 0-9640278-5-2

Talk to the World™

A Manual for Students and Teachers of Conversational English

by
Edward Voeller

LanguagePower™
Publications

Saint Paul, Minnesota

Contents

Acknowledgements	vii
Introduction	ix
Abbreviations	xviii
Dialogues	1
Teaching/Study Notes	253
Appendix	327
1 Major intonation patterns	327
2 Pronunciation: -s suffix	328
3 Pronunciation: -ed suffix	328
4 verb + *to* verb	329
5 verb + obj + *to* verb	329
6 noun + *to* verb	329
7 verb + *(that-)*clause	329
8 verb + ind obj + *(that-)*clause	330
9 noun + *(that-)*clause	330
10 verb + verb *-ing*	330
11 verb + ind obj + d obj **or** verb + d obj + *to* ind obj	331
12 verb + ind obj + d obj **or** verb + d obj + *for* indo obj	331
13 verb + *(that-)*clause + subjunctive	331
14 verb + verb-*ing* **or** verb + *to* verb	332
15 verb + obj + noun	332
16 verb + obj + compl adj or noun	332
17 verb + obj + compl	332
18 verb + obj + verb	332
19 High-frequency regular verbs	333
20 High-frequency irregular verbs	335
21 Two-word verbs	337
22 Nouns: count and noncount	340
23 Quantifiers	344
24 Expressions with *be*	344
25 Idioms and Expressions	346
26 Adjectives requiring *more* and *less* in the comparative and *most* and *least* in the superlative	351
27 Common past participles used as adjectives	352
Dialogue Index	355
Expression Index	359
Grammar Index	365

Acknowledgements

This manual would not have been possible without the help of hundreds of my students who, over a number of years, provided the sample populations on which I could test, and retest, the dialogues from which those included in this manual have been selected. To my students I owe a great deal of gratitude, and I hope this book is worthy of the patience and cooperation they offered me.

I am also indebted to colleagues at Hokkaido University and to friends in Japan and in the United States, who offered advice regarding grammar and usage, read portions of the manuscript, or made useful comments on the format.

Although a book of this kind is the result of the cummulative pedagogic and second-language experiences of the writer, I need to single out Earl Stevick's *Adapting and Writing Language Lessons* (Washington D.C.: Foreign Service Institute, 1971) as having had particular influence on my ideas about second-language learning and teaching. While I acknowledge the contribution which I believe portions of that important book have had on my approach in this manual, I am also responsible for any misinterpretations of Mr. Stevick's intentions in that work.

This book was predominately written on family time, and I am fortunate and grateful for the patience with which my wife and children have borne the burden of this project.

Edward Voeller

Introduction

Dialogues in the Foreign Language Classroom

Of all the devices or formats for teaching and learning the conversational skills of another language, dialogues are perhaps the most recurrent. Hardly a foreign-language textbook appears that does not include yet more sets of exchanges between **A** and **B** asking for directions to a tourist attraction, ordering a meal at a restaurant, or making self-introductions. Nor are dialogues a recent phenomenon; they comprise the entire volume of the earliest extant textbook for learning a foreign language, James Bellot's *Familiar Dialogues,* published in 1586, and historical linguists tell us that dialogues in the foreign-language classroom have a tradition that goes back centuries earlier than that.

Dubious Dialogues

Their ubiquity notwithstanding, the utility of dialogues can vary considerably. Tourists are familiar with the inefficient exchanges offered in little phrase books for travelers, and foreign-language learners held hostage to a school language requirement frequently lose interest in the target language when they are confronted with the lengthy and overloaded dialogues that introduce lessons in many foreign-language textbooks.

In addition, critics of the format argue that dialogues are often better models of the written than the spoken language, which is characterized by redundancy, ungrammatical usage, slang, hesitation, and meaningful and unmeaningful utterances replacing pauses in speech. The written language, in contrast, contains a wider variety of structures and patterns and a greater range of vocabulary. Some detractors also say that dialogues do not accurately represent the spoken language because intonation and stress are absent from a written exchange. This criticism ignores the role of the teacher, in the classroom or on a recording, who can supply these features of the spoken language; and while *er...* and *uhm...* may or not be unique to

Introduction

English, pause and hesitation are characteristic of all languages. In any event, pause and hesitation do not characterize all short exchanges.

A legitimate criticism of dialogues is that those found in textbooks are frequently inappropriate in length. A dialogue consisting of a single exchange between a waiter and a customer, for example, is not long enough to effectively present a new grammar structure or unfamiliar vocabulary in a meaningful linguistic, social, and cultural context.

More frequently, however, textbook dialogues are too long. They often contain an unrealistic number of unfamiliar vocabulary items and structures, or the utterances may be too long and the number of exchanges too many, making the dialogue unmanageable for both student and teacher. Dialogues are too often used in textbooks to summarize a lesson, or to introduce all the new points of a lesson. The result is invariably a long and contrived set of exchanges that are both unnatural and too broad in their range of grammar and vocabulary.

Many textbook dialogues are also often inappropriate in style—usually too informal—for a particular group of students. Other dialogues, aiming at a broad audience, and including many structure patterns and a broad range of vocabulary, combine levels of style, resulting in a mixture of formal and colloquial speech in a single conversation.

Finally, even when a textbook provides what might be defined as an appropriate dialogue in terms of content and context, the dialogue's utility often ends with its use as a model for repetition and mimicry of the spoken language. Many dialogues do not offer opportunities for substitution and creative practice; they are not significantly variable, and offer only limited opportunities for the replacement of lexical items.

Durable Dialogues

Whatever the criticism of dialogues, they are a feature of second-language pedagogy that over the years has survived an onslaught of trends that have come and gone in the foreign-language classroom. What explains the durability of a format that is often loathed by learners, occasionally misused by teachers, and sometimes abused by lesson writers? Dialogues are, of course, conversation—the goal of the learner in many instances, but although that may account for their pervasiveness, it does not in itself qualify dialogues as teaching or learning devices any more than having the control of a native speaker over a language qualifies one to teach it.

Good dialogues are not merely frozen, immobile models of speech; they are conversation that is controlled and graded to suit the level and experience of the

Introduction

learner. Dialogues can offer examples of how the language works at any level, while presenting essential structures and vocabulary in relevant cultural and social contexts, and thus providing the social formulas for communication as well as the linguistic. This is the advantage that dialogues have as examples of speech over the transcribed authentic conversation of two native speakers.

Additionally, a good dialogue should be obviously portable or adaptable—it should provide opportunities for manipulation and communicative practice. A good dialogue is also a realistic model of the spoken language, natural and authentic in content, relatively brief and to the point, and it contains a reasonable number of unfamiliar words. The appropriate dialogue focuses on one major structure or a limited number of minor ones, or it reviews structures which are familiar to the student, and it is written so that the student can manipulate basic structures and vocabulary items leading to the internalization of patterns in social and cultural contexts.

New patterns are learned more rapidly when the student has a good model conversation and opportunities to use it in both artificial and real communication. Good dialogues provide these opportunities to develop oral language skills, a boast that cannot be made by drills or exercises alone.

▼   ▼   ▼

Talk to the World™

Talk to the World introduces no new theories regarding foreign language acquisition. Its intention is to provide, for students whose goal is the mastery of conversational usage, a carefully graded corpus of appropriate dialogues which can be manipulated and used in meaningful and creative ways. The dialogues in the following pages have been written on the assumption that the special needs of students of conversational English include focused practice with high-frequency grammar patterns and vocabulary in socially and culturally relevant situations. Beyond the role of the dialogue as a model, the dialogues have as their purpose here to provide guided conversation practice, from simple manipulation to communicative performance in numerous expression categories, such as describing an object or a person, and making polite requests.

Talk to the World is intended for learners ranging from real and false beginners to those at upper intermediate levels, with the recognition that a student's language background should be the ultimate criterion for determining the appropriate level of

Introduction

a dialogue. The dialogues in this collection may be used along with the suggestions for practice and communication in the **Teaching/Study Notes** as the main course in many classes, but some teachers will want to supplement the dialogues with additional activities designed to meet the special needs of their students.

Talk to the World can be used with large classes or classes as small as one-to-one tutorial sessions. The manual may supplement courses which emphasize the four language skills, and students and teachers may find Talk to the World a useful grammar reference. Some persons may find the manual helpful for learning conversational English on their own with the aid of a tape recorder.

Format

Talk to the World comprises 250 variable dialogues of from two to four exchanges in length. Each dialogue is supplemented with lexical and/or structural substitutions that can be used to form three additional dialogues based on the original. After practice with the model and the substitutions provided, students create their own dialogues based on the model by devising their own substitutions. In this way the student proceeds from controlled conversation to more communicative activity. Both structures and vocabulary are high-frequency items that characterize spoken English. Grammar has been very carefully graded and reviewed throughout the book, and vocabulary has likewise been consistently reentered.

The grammar and expression contents of a particular dialogue are listed below the dialogue at the bottom of the page. Not all the structures contained in a dialogue are necessarily indicated here, however; those grammatical items which are not included have been introduced in one or more of the preceding dialogues. Dialogue 31, for example, includes *yes/no*-questions with *be* in the simple present tense. This pattern is not indicated under *Grammar,* however, because it has been introduced and dealt with in one or more previous dialogues, and students who need to practice this pattern should turn to that grammatical structure in the dialogues that precede dialogue 31. *Expression* identifies the linguistic/social performance categories (notions and functions), the broad activities which are used to exemplify the structure and vocabulary in the dialogue, and which serve to provide the basic performance skills to the learner.

The dialogues are additionally supplemented with both **Teaching/Study Notes** and extensive appendixes. The **Teaching/Study Notes** provide explanations of usage where necessary, comments on the formality or level of the language, notes on the substitutions, suggestions for practicing the grammar in the dialogue, and teaching and learning suggestions for communicative activities. The **Appendix** provides supplementary sources of high-frequency vocabulary and grammar patterns that students may wish to refer to when they create their own substitutions or variations

Introduction

of the dialogues. Major intonation patterns and pronunciation guides are included among the lists of noncount nouns, verb patterns, quantifiers, vocabulary, expressions with *be*, and useful idioms.

The dialogues are indexed for convenient reference according to title, expression, and grammar content. The indexes are a convenient way to select a dialogue of the appropriate level for particular students by referring to the desired grammar and expression category.

Teaching and Learning with *Talk to the World*

Repetition, manipulation, and creative or communicative practice characterize the learning procedure for each dialogue. After a dialogue has been presented, and students are thoroughly familiar with the new sounds, vocabulary items, and structure, they work in pairs to manipulate the essential features of the dialogue. This step typically requires the student to attend to other features of the dialogue as well, such as agreement in number and person, and proper tense. When the manipulative activities have been completed, students work in pairs to create their own variations of the dialogue. The appendixes provide lists of vocabulary, grammar patterns, and idioms that students may want to draw upon when creating their own variations of the dialogues.

Finally, to help keep the manual relevant to students of varied cultural and linguistic backgrounds, proper names of persons and places have in most cases been omitted, and are to be provided by the student. Buildings, cities, and characters in the dialogues, for example, can take names that are familiar to the learner.

The Dialogue

A and B exchanges in the dialogues are identified by number. These numbers correspond to the numbered substitutions provided for each dialogue, and to the numbered notes in the **Teaching/Study Notes**.

The portions of a dialogue which are underlined, are those for which substitutions have been provided. When two underlined portions of a dialogue obviously require the same substitution, the substitution is sometimes noted only once where it is initially required.

Students should be aware that substitutions may affect portions of the dialogue that are not underlined. The substitution of a plural noun for a singular form, for example, may require an adjustment for agreement with a verb that is not underlined. The student is required to consider the entire dialogue when changing specified portions of the dialogue. Also, it is advisable that the substitutions be used in the order in which they occur on the page.

Introduction
8 These Things

Students may want to choose names for A and B, and substitute proper nouns for dashes in the dialogue.

A: _____   Are <u>these</u> <u>--C--'s shoes</u>? ①
B: _____   No. <u>Those</u> are <u>--D--'s</u>. ②
            Are these things <u>--D--'s</u> too? ③
            <u>The camera</u> is <u>--D--'s</u>, but <u>the magazine</u> is <u>--C--'s</u>. ④

Line numbers in the dialogue correspond to the numbered lines in the substitutions and in the Teaching/Study Notes.

Three substitutions are provided here for the underlined portions of the dialogue.

▼ 1 ▼ 2 ▼ 3

▼ 1	▼ 2	▼ 3
① these/--C--'s books	① this/Mr. ------'s dictionary	① these/--C--'s bags
② those/--D--'s	② that/Mrs. ------'s	② those/--D--'s
③ --D--'s	③ Mrs. ------'s	③ --D--'s
④ the umbrella/--D--'s/the coat and hat/--C--'s	④ the notebook/Mrs. ------'s/the briefcase/Mr. ------'s	④ the jacket/--D--'s/the hat/--C--'s

The grammar structures and the categories of expression that are the focus of the lesson are listed at the bottom of the page.

Grammar: wo: s + *be* + compl (n: pl); *be*: simple pres tense; yes/no-ques: simple pres tense (*be*); *these/those*: dem adj/pron (pl); n: pl; n: poss *'s*; *but*: conj; *too*: adv
Expression: indicating ownership/possession

Talk to the World

Introduction
Teaching/Study Notes

> *Circled numbers in the Teaching/Study Notes refer to dialogue line numbers.*

8 Sorting Things Out

① Note that *these* and *those* are the plural forms of *this* and *that*. ❖ See **Appendix 2** for the pronunciation of the possessive *'s*. The *s* is omitted when the name or noun is in its plural form. ▶ the <u>teachers' books</u>, the <u>Smiths' house</u>
② <u>No</u>. **OR** <u>No, they aren't</u>.
③ <u>Are these things --D--'s too</u>? **OR** <u>Are these --D--'s things too</u>?
④ The conjunction *but* introduces contrasting information in this dialogue.
Practice Make sentences with *but*. ▶ T: <u>The camera is the student's. The bag isn't the student's</u>. S: <u>The camera is the student's, but the bag isn't</u>. **OR** T: <u>The camera is the student's. The bag is the teacher's</u>. S: <u>The camera is the student's, but the bag is the teacher's</u>.
Communication Holding objects belonging to three or four students, the teacher asks the rest of the class questions about ownership. ▶ T: <u>Is this --C--'s</u>? S: <u>No, it isn't. It's --D--'s</u>. **OR** <u>Yes, it is</u>. ❖ The teacher holds up an object belonging to one student. The other students guess who the owner of the object is. ▶ S: <u>Is it --C--'s</u>? T: <u>No, it isn't</u>. S: <u>Is it --D--'s</u>? T: <u>Yes, it is</u>.

▼   ▼   ▼

Suggestions for Using *Talk to the World*

Using dialogues to their maximum potential involves three general procedures: presentation, practice, and creative or communicative use.

Presentation

In order to maintain the interest and motivation of students, dialogues should be presented with judicious variety when they are used regularly in the classroom. Some teachers prefer to have their students listen to a reading or a recording, or watch a dramatization of the conversation before they see a printed version of it. This is so that students rely on their ears to learn new sounds rather than an imperfect transcription of the sounds. Visual aids are useful at the listening stage to help students distinguish the roles in the dialogue. One technique is alternately pointing to two stick figures drawn on the blackboard, or to two persons in an illustration or photograph; a dramatization or a reading of the dialogue prepared by two students also provides visual effect. It is important to keep any presentation

Introduction

lively and interesting, and to use natural speed, stress, and intonation when modeling a dialogue, and to include contracted forms whenever possible.

Once students have heard the dialogue three or four times, it may be appropriate for them to look at the printed version. Be sure that the meaning of the exchanges is clear. Provide the meanings of any unfamiliar words, and ask students questions which might indicate whether or not they understand the situation and the conversation. Students might be asked, for example, to identify the roles of speakers **A** and **B**, or give one or more likely situations or contexts for the dialogue.

For some students, a dialogue as a dictation is an effective presentation; immediate feedback on listening comprehension ability is provided when students see the printed version.

Practice

When students understand the dialogue and can conceptualize the situation, they are ready to practice the exchanges, beginning with repetition, first as a group, and then individually. In this procedure, too, variation is desirable so that it does not become tedious. One approach is to have half of the class take the role of speaker **A** and the other half speaker **B**. Repetition is important at this stage because it encourages fluency and facilitates recall of the dialogue. Lengthy sentences are easier to recall and repeat with accurate stress and intonation if the "backward buildup" technique is used. Beginning at the end of a sentence, have students repeat small sections of the utterance until the whole sentence can be said naturally.

Check pronunciation, stress, and intonation by having individual students repeat a line after it has been modeled. Work through all the lines of the dialogue in this manner, a process that should not take too long if the dialogue selected is the proper level for the student.

It may be desirable to have students memorize a dialogue. With the teacher assuming the role of speaker **A** and the class as speaker **B**, test group recall with books closed. Repeat this procedure, exchanging roles when appropriate, until a strong response is elicited from the class. At this point most of the students will be able to recite the dialogue on an individual basis. Assign **A** and **B** roles to the best students, and have them recite the dialogues from memory.

As a class activity, have the students replace the underlined portions of the dialogue with one or more of the substitutions provided. When students feel comfortable with the dialogue—and understand that when substitutions are used, small changes for verb tense or agreement may have to be made in portions of the dialogue that are not underlined—they are ready to practice the substitutions in pairs. Choose several

Introduction

pairs of students to demonstrate—with books closed if it is desirable—the variations of the dialogue provided. Correct the students' pronunciation, and sentence stress and intonation when necessary.

Creative Use

In the final procedure students use the dialogues creatively by working in pairs and devising original substitutions. Humorous and interesting, but grammatical, idiomatic, and logical variations should be encouraged. If the dialogue lends itself to this activity, advanced students might be capable of changing the setting of the dialogue. A conversation involving a complaint at a department store, for example, might be changed to a scene at a travel agency involving a dissatisfied client. Finally, some students might enjoy presenting their dialogues in front of the class.

▼ ▼ ▼

Additional Activities with Dialogues

• Use puppets or pictures to demonstrate or present a dialogue.

• Students are given a dialogue in which the lines are out of proper sequence. Students unscramble the dialogue and practice it.

• Restate a recently learned dialogue. Keep the meaning essentially the same.

• Students continue a dialogue they have learned in the class by adding one or more additional sets of exchanges.

• Students are given only the first pair of exchanges of a dialogue, they are required to write one or two additional exchanges.

• Pairs of students get only the A or B roles of a dialogue. They are required to write the lines for the missing role.

• Students work in pairs to create a dialogue from a picture, a photograph of two prominent persons, or a cartoon without captions.

• Students must devise an appropriate dialogue for a given situation: exchanging money at a bank, for example, or giving directions to a familiar place.

• One student writes the first A exchange of a dialogue, and passes it to the next student who writes the subsequent B exchange. This process continues until everyone has contributed A or B exchange to the dialogue.

Abbreviations

adj	adjective	**p**	past
adv	adverb/adverbial	**part**	participal/participial
affirm	affirmative	**pass**	passive
art	article	**pfct**	perfect
cl	clause	**phr**	phrase
compar	comparative	**pl**	plural
compl	complement	**poss**	possessive
con	connective	**pres**	present
cond	conditional	**pron**	pronoun
conj	conjunction	**quant**	quantifier
cont	continuous	**ques**	question
contr	contraction	**refl**	reflexive
dem	demonstrative	**reg**	regular verb
det	determiner	**rel**	relative
d obj	direct object	**s, subj**	subject
fut	future	**S**	student
ger	gerund	**sing**	singular
imper	imperative	**subord cl**	subordinate clause
ind obj	indirect object	**super**	superlative
infin	infinitive	**t**	tense
insep	inseparable verb	**T**	teacher
irreg	irregular verb	**v**	verb
n	noun	**vi**	intransitive verb
neg	negative	**vt**	transitive verb
obj	object	**wo**	word order

Symbols in Teaching/Study Notes

❖ separates unrelated items.
▶ introduces an example or sample answers; examples are also underlined.
OR indicates alternatives to lines in the dialogues and in examples.

Dialogues

1 What Is It? Guess!

A: _____ Is it <u>a necklace</u>? ①

B: _____ No, it's not <u>a necklace</u>. ②

Is it <u>a watch</u>? ③

<u>A watch</u>? No, it isn't <u>a watch</u>. ④

Uhm, . . . is it <u>a bracelet</u>? ⑤

Yes, it is! ⑥

Oh! It's <u>a bracelet</u>. Thank you very much! ⑦

Happy Birthday! ⑧

▼❶ ▼❷ ▼❸

① a book	① a calculator	① an alarm clock
③ a computer game	③ a camera	③ an album
⑤ a CD player	⑤ an FM radio	⑤ an electric razor

Grammar: wo: s + *be* + compl (n: sing); *be*: simple pres tense; *no, not*: neg; contr: *be, not*; *yes/no-ques*: simple pres tense *(be)*; *it*: subj pron; *a/an*: art; *thank you*

Expression: identifying objects; expressing gratitude/negation

2 Downtown

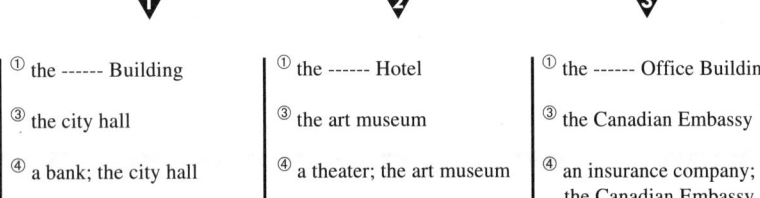

A: _____ Excuse me. Is this <u>the ------ Building</u>? ①

B: _____ Yes, it is. ②

And . . . is that <u>the post office</u>? ③

No, that's <u>a library</u>. <u>The post office</u> is over there. ④

Oh, . . . thank you very much. ⑤

That's all right. ⑥

▼❶ ▼❷ ▼❸

① the ------ Building | ① the ------ Hotel | ① the ------ Office Building
③ the city hall | ③ the art museum | ③ the Canadian Embassy
④ a bank; the city hall | ④ a theater; the art museum | ④ an insurance company; the Canadian Embassy

---

Grammar: wo: s + *be* + compl (n: sing, adv); *be:* simple pres tense; *no:* neg; contr: *be;* yes/no-ques: simple pres tense *(be);* short reply: *be; this:* dem pron (sing); *the/a/an:* art; *over there:* adv of place; *it:* subj pron

Expression: finding places; asking for/giving directions; expressing location/position

Talk to the World

3 At Airport Customs

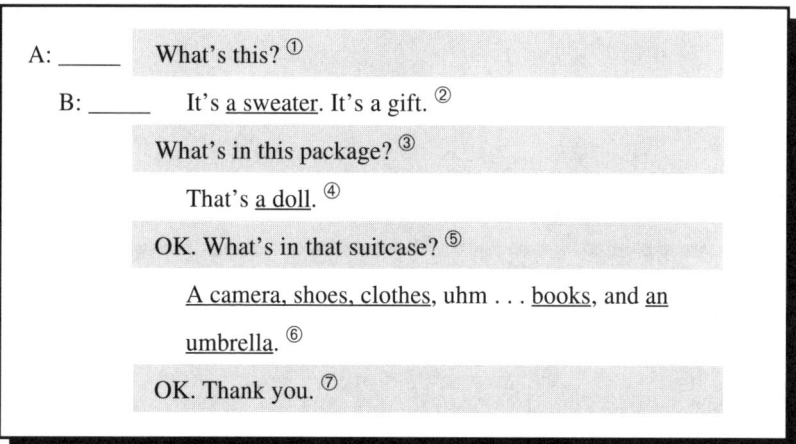

A: ____ What's this? ①
B: ____ It's <u>a sweater</u>. It's a gift. ②
What's in this package? ③
That's <u>a doll</u>. ④
OK. What's in that suitcase? ⑤
<u>A camera, shoes, clothes</u>, uhm . . . <u>books</u>, and <u>an umbrella</u>. ⑥
OK. Thank you. ⑦

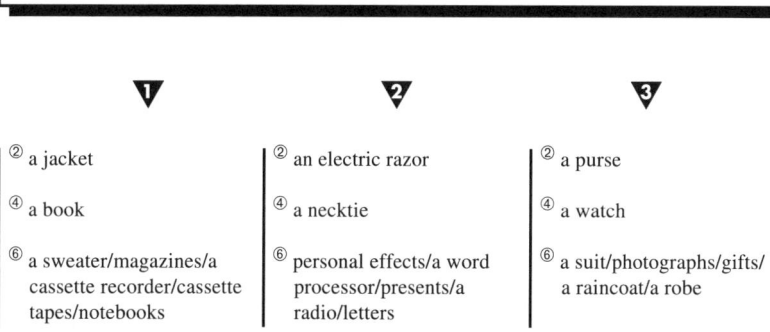

② a jacket

④ a book

⑥ a sweater/magazines/a cassette recorder/cassette tapes/notebooks

② an electric razor

④ a necktie

⑥ personal effects/a word processor/presents/a radio/letters

② a purse

④ a watch

⑥ a suit/photographs/gifts/a raincoat/a robe

Grammar: wo: s + be + compl (n: sing, adv); be: simple pres tense; contr: be; n: pl; what: wh-ques, simple pres tense (be); a/an: art; this, that: dem pron/adj (sing); and: conj; in: prep of place; adv of place; it: subj pron
Expression: identifying objects

Talk to the World

4 Window Shopping

A: _____ That's <u>nice</u>. ①

B: _____ What's <u>nice</u>? ②

That <u>dress</u>. ③

Oh, that. Yes, that *is* <u>a nice dress</u>. ④

▼ ▼ ▼

① beautiful | ① pretty | ① unusual
③ jacket | ③ scarf | ③ purse
④ a beautiful jacket | ④ a pretty scarf | ④ an unusual purse

Grammar: wo: s + be + compl (adj); be: simple pres tense; contr: be; what: wh-ques, simple pres tense (be); adj: be + adj, adj + n; that: dem adj/dem pron (sing); a/an: art
Expression: admiring something; paying a compliment

Talk to the World

5 From China

A: ____ Are <u>you and Mr. ------</u> from <u>China</u>? ①
B: ____ Yes, <u>we</u> are. ②
Are <u>you</u> from <u>Beijing</u>? ③
No, <u>we</u>'re from <u>Harbin</u>. ④
Oh. ⑤

▼1 ▼2 ▼3

① ------ and ------/California	① Mrs. ------/Canada	① you/Australia
② they	② she	② I
③ they/Los Angeles	③ she/Toronto	③ you/Sydney
④ they/San Francisco	④ she/Vancouver	④ I/Melbourne

Grammar: wo: s + be + compl (adv); be: simple pres tense; contr: be; yes/no-ques: simple pres tense (be); short reply: be; I, you, he, she, we, they: subj pron; adv of place; from: prep of place; and: conj

Expression: requesting/providing personal information; expressing geographic location; indicating national origin

Talk to the World

6 Hello!

A: _____ Hello, --B--! ①

B: _____ Hello, --A--. How are you? ②

I'm fine, thanks. How are you and --C--? ③

We're fine. How's --D--? ④

She's fine. ⑤

▼1

① --B--
② --A--
③ you
④ I; --C--
⑤ he

▼2

① --B--
② --A--
③ --C-- and --D--
④ they; --E-- and --F--
⑤ they

▼3

① --B--
② --A--
③ --C--
④ he; --D--
⑤ she

Grammar: wo: s + be + compl (adj); be: simple pres tense; contr: be; how: wh-ques, simple pres tense (be); adj: be + adj; subj pron; and: conj
Expression: greeting someone; opening a conversation

Talk to the World

7 Austrian

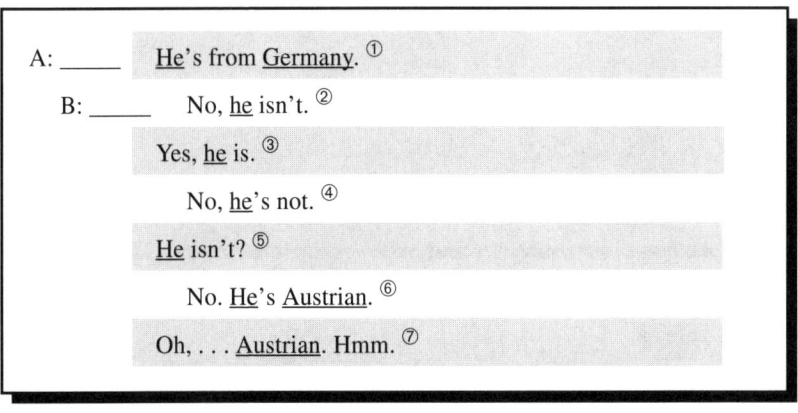

A: _____ He's from Germany. ①
B: _____ No, he isn't. ②
Yes, he is. ③
No, he's not. ④
He isn't? ⑤
No. He's Austrian. ⑥
Oh, ... Austrian. Hmm. ⑦

▼1

① she/the United States
⑥ Canadian

▼2

① they/France
⑥ Swiss

▼3

① he/Thailand
⑥ Malaysian

Grammar: wo: s + be + compl (adv); be: simple pres tense; no, not: neg; contr: be, not; yes/no-ques, intonation: simple pres tense (be); short reply: be; subj pron; adj: be + adj, adj of nationality; adv of place; from: prep of place

Expression: expressing disagreement; indicating national origin; correcting/contradicting someone; expressing negation

8 These Things

A: _____ Are these --C--'s shoes? ①
B: _____ No. Those are --D--'s. ②
Are these things --D--'s too? ③
The camera is --D--'s, but the magazine is --C--'s. ④

▼ 1

① these/--C--'s books

② those/--D--'s

③ --D--'s

④ the umbrella/--D--'s/the coat and hat/--C--'s

▼ 2

① this/Mr. ------'s dictionary

② that/Mrs. ------'s

③ Mrs. ------'s

④ the notebook/ Mrs. ------'s/ the briefcase/Mr. ------'s

▼ 3

① these/--C--'s bags

② those/--D--'s

③ --D--'s

④ the jacket/--D--'s/the hat/ --C--'s

Grammar: wo: s + be + compl (n: pl); be: simple pres tense; yes/no-ques: simple pres tense (be); these/those: dem adj/pron (pl); n: pl; n: poss 's; but: conj; too: adv
Expression: indicating ownership/possession

Talk to the World

9 Where's the Hotel?

A: _____ Excuse me. Where's <u>the Grand Hotel</u>? ①

B: _____ It's <u>across from the city hall</u>. ②

Thanks. Uhm, . . . where's <u>the city hall</u>? ③

It's <u>behind the public library</u>. And <u>the public library</u> is <u>right down this street</u>. OK? ④

Thanks a lot. ⑤

▼1 ▼2 ▼3

① the Japanese Embassy	① the police station	① the ------ Theater
② next to the ------ Building	② opposite ------ High School	② beside the hospital
③ the ------ Building	③ ------ High School	③ the hospital
④ in back of the stadium; the stadium/up this street	④ kitty-corner from the train station; the train station/down that way	④ next to the hotel; the hotel/just around the corner

Grammar: wo: s + be + compl (adv); be: simple pres tense; where: wh-ques, simple pres tense (be); adv of place; across from, behind, beside, in back of, kitty-corner from, next to, opposite: prep of place; the: art; adv of direction

Expression: expressing direction; expressing location/position; finding places; asking for/ giving directions

10 That's My Bag

A: _____ Is this <u>your bag</u>? ①
B: _____ No. <u>My bag</u> is <u>blue</u>. ②
There's <u>a blue bag</u>. ③
Yes. That's <u>my bag</u>. ④

▼ **1**

① ------'s camera bag

② his camera bag/black

▼ **2**

① our carry-on bag

② our carry-on bag/tan

▼ **3**

① Mr. & Mrs. ------'s suitcase

② their suitcase/white

Grammar: wo: s + be + compl (adj); be: simple pres tense; yes/no-ques: simple pres tense (be); my, your, his, her, our, their: poss adj; adj: be + adj, adj + n; this, that: dem pron; there: adv of place

Expression: indicating ownership/possession; identifying/describing objects; colors; claiming things

11 In Your Shirtpocket

A: _____ Where are the passports? ①

B: _____ They're in my purse. Where's the camera? ②

Right there. On the suitcase. ③

How about the tickets? ④

The tickets? In your shirtpocket. ⑤

▼1 ▼2 ▼3

① the travelers checks

② on the table; my carry-on bag

③ Next to the suitcase.

④ the map

⑤ In your hand.

① the car keys

② on top of the refrigerator; the house key

③ Under my camera bag.

④ the guidebook

⑤ In my carry-on bag.

① my purse

② by the door; the umbrella

③ On the floor by the chair.

④ my sunglasses

⑤ In my purse.

Grammar: how about + n, where: wh-ques, simple pres tense (be); right there: adv of place; by, in, next to, on, on top of, under: prep of place; n: pl
Expression: expressing location/position; finding things

Talk to the World

12 Yours or Hers?

A: _____ Is this <u>yours or --C--'s</u>? ①
B: _____ It's <u>--C--'s</u>. ②
Are <u>these</u> <u>hers</u> too? ③
<u>The magazines</u>? Yes. ④

▼**1**

① ------'s or ours
② ours
③ these/ours
④ The pens?

▼**2**

① ------'s or yours
② mine
③ this/yours
④ The cassette recorder?

▼**3**

① yours or --C-- and --D--'s
② --C-- and --D--'s
③ those/theirs
④ The notebooks?

Grammar: yes/no-ques, or-ques: simple pres tense (be); mine, yours, his, hers, ours, theirs: poss pron; n: poss 's; n pl; *too* adv
Expression: indicating ownership/possession; claiming things

Talk to the World

13 Everybody's Things

A: _____ Are <u>my gloves</u> in the suitcase? ①

B: _____ <u>Your gloves</u>? Yes, <u>they</u> are. ②

How about <u>------'s</u>? ③

<u>His</u> are in the suitcase too. ④

▼1

① ------'s camera

③ yours and mine

④ ours

▼2

① our passports

③ the children's

④ theirs

▼3

① your cap

③ ------'s

④ hers

Grammar: yes/no-ques: simple pres tense *(be)*; short reply: *be;* how about + n: wh-ques; poss adj; poss pron; n: pl

Expression: indicating ownership/possession; finding things

Talk to the World

14 Suggestions

A: _____ Does ----- have <u>a tennis racket</u>? ①
B: _____ Yes, she does. ②

Does she have <u>a watch</u>? ③

Yes. She has two <u>watches</u>. ④

How about <u>a radio</u>? ⑤

She has <u>a radio</u>. ⑥

Does she have <u>a photo album</u>? ⑦

No, she doesn't have <u>a photo album</u>. That's a good idea. Thanks for the suggestion. ⑧

▽1

① a good purse
③ a cassette recorder
⑤ a nice sweater
⑦ a bracelet

▽2

① a camera
③ a silk scarf
⑤ a hair dryer
⑦ a ring

▽3

① a pearl necklace
③ a TV
⑤ a calculator
⑦ a pendant

Grammar: wo: s + vt + obj; *have*: simple pres tense; *do*: pro-verb; contr: *do, not; not*: neg; yes/no-ques: simple pres tense *(have)*; short reply: *do; how about* + n: *wh*-ques; subj pron; quant: cardinal numbers; n: pl; *thanks for* + n

Expression: offering suggestions; indicating ownership/possession; expressing gratitude

Talk to the World

15 Fruit and Vegetables

A: _____ <u>Tomatoes</u> <u>were</u> on sale today. ①

B: _____ <u>They</u> <u>were</u>? ②

Yes, but <u>lettuce</u> <u>wasn't</u>. ③

<u>Was</u> <u>lettuce</u> expensive? ④

Yes, <u>it</u> <u>was</u>. ⑤

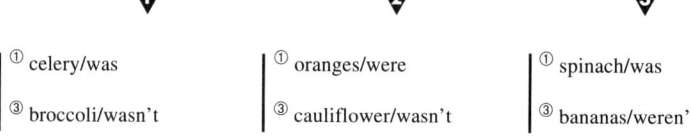

① celery/was

③ broccoli/wasn't

① oranges/were

③ cauliflower/wasn't

① spinach/was

③ bananas/weren't

Grammar: nouns: count vs noncount; n: pl; *be*: simple past tense; *today*: adv of time; adj: *be* + adj
Expression: talking about food; past reference *(be)*

16 Take Ten Guesses

A: _____ Is it <u>a boy</u>? ①

B: _____ No, it isn't. ②

It's <u>a girl</u>. Does <u>she</u> have <u>brown hair</u>? ③

No, <u>she</u> doesn't. ④

Does <u>she</u> have <u>a yellow sweater</u>? ⑤

Yes, <u>she</u> does. ⑥

Is it ------? ⑦

Yes, it is! ⑧

▼ ❶ ▼ ❷ ▼ ❸

① a girl | ① a man | ① a woman

③ a boy; glasses | ③ a woman; long hair | ③ a man; a plaid shirt

⑤ tan pants | ⑤ a red skirt | ⑤ a necktie

⑦ ------ | ⑦ ------ | ⑦ ------

Grammar: wo: s + vt + obj; *have*: simple pres tense; *do*: pro-verb; contr: *do, not; not*: neg; yes/no-ques: simple pres tense *(have)*; short reply: *do;* subj pron; adj: adj + n

Expression: describing people; colors

Talk to the World

17 In the Refrigerator

A: _____ I'm hungry. ①

B: _____ There's some <u>potato salad</u> in the refrigerator. ②

<u>Is</u> there any <u>apple pie</u>? ③

No, there <u>isn't</u> any <u>apple pie</u>, but there <u>are</u> some <u>sandwiches</u>. ④

▼ 1

② pizza
③ cake
④ pudding

▼ 2

② oranges
③ apples
④ apple sauce

▼ 3

② hamburgers
③ orange juice
④ grape juice

Grammar: *there + be:* simple pres tense; contr: *be; yes/no-*ques: *there + be* (simple pres tense); nouns: noncount; *some, any:* quant (adj); n: pl; *not:* neg

Expression: talking about food; expressing quantity

-17- Talk to the World

18 Flour and Eggs

A: _____ Where's <u>the flour</u>? ①

B: _____ It's in the cupboard. ②

Where <u>are</u> <u>the eggs</u>? ③

We don't have any. ④

Do we have any <u>sugar</u>? ⑤

Yes, there'<u>s</u> some in the cupboard. ⑥

▼❶ ▼❷ ▼❸

① the baking powder | ① the salt | ① the cinnamon

③ the vanilla | ③ the milk | ③ the butter

⑤ nuts | ⑤ powdered sugar | ⑤ raisins

Grammar: there + be: simple pres tense; have: simple pres tense; do: pro-verb; contr: do, not; where: wh-ques, simple pres tense (be); yes/no-ques: simple pres tense (have); some, any: quant (adj, pron); nouns: noncount; not: neg

Expression: talking about food; expressing quantity; finding things

19 Photographs

A: _____ Is this --C--? ①
B: _____ No, that's --D--. ②
That's --D--? ③
Yes, that's him. ④
Is this you? ⑤
No, that's not me. That's --E--. ⑥

▼ 1

① --C-- and --D--
② --E-- and --F--
③ --E-- and --F--
④ them
⑤ --G--
⑥ her; --H--

▼ 2

① --C--
② me
③ you
④ me
⑤ --D-- and you
⑥ --D-- and me; --E-- and --F--

▼ 3

① --C-- and --D--
② you and me
③ you and me
④ us
⑤ --E--
⑥ him; --F--

Grammar: yes/no-ques, intonation: simple pres tense (be); me, you her, him, us, them: obj pron; this, that: dem pron
Expression: identifying people

20 For Me?

A: _____ Is this for us? ①
B: _____ No. ②
   For --C--? ③
   No, it's not for him. It's for --D--. ④
   Is it from --E--? ⑤
   No, it's not from her. ⑥
   From --F--? ⑦
   Yes. ⑧

▼ 1

① me
③ --C-- and --D--
④ them; --E-- and --F--
⑤ --G--
⑥ him
⑦ --H-- and --I--

▼ 2

① --C--
③ me
④ you; --D--
⑤ you
⑥ me
⑦ --D--

▼ 3

① you and me
③ --C--
④ her; --D--
⑤ --E-- and --F--
⑥ them
⑦ --G--

Grammar: object pronouns; *for, from:* prep with obj pron
Expression: talking about people

Talk to the World

21 Photo Album

A: _____ Is this --C--? ①
B: _____ No, that's --D--. ②
        Who's he? ③
           He's my mother's cousin. ④
        Who's this? ⑤
           That's a friend. ⑥

▼1

① --C--
② --D--
③ she
④ she/my cousin's wife
⑥ an uncle

▼2

① --C-- and --D--
② --E-- and --F--
③ they
④ they/my friend's children
⑥ my grandfather's sister

▼3

① --C--
② --D--
③ he
④ he/--E--'s husband
⑥ my cousin's daughter

Grammar: *who*: wh-ques, simple pres tense *(be)*; *this, that*: dem pron; poss adj; n: poss 's
Expression: identifying people; talking about relatives

Talk to the World

22 Who Has It?

A: _____ Who has <u>the tennis racket</u>? ①
B: _____ <u>I</u> have <u>it</u>. ②
Oh, do <u>you</u> have <u>the balls</u> too? ③
No. <u>The balls</u> are <u>on the floor in the closet</u>. ④

▼1

① the baseball glove
② ------/it
③ he/the bat
④ the bat/in the car

▼2

① the camera
② mom/it
③ she/the flash unit
④ the flash unit/on the shelf in your room

▼3

① the golf clubs
② ------ and ------/them
③ they/the golf balls
④ the golf balls/in the golf bag

Grammar: wo: s + vt + obj; *have*: simple pres tense; *yes/no*-ques: simple pres tense *(have)*; *who*: *wh*-ques, (subj) with simple pres tense *(have)*; adv of place; *in, on*: prep of place
Expression: expressing location/position; indicating ownership/possession

Talk to the World

23 Spinach

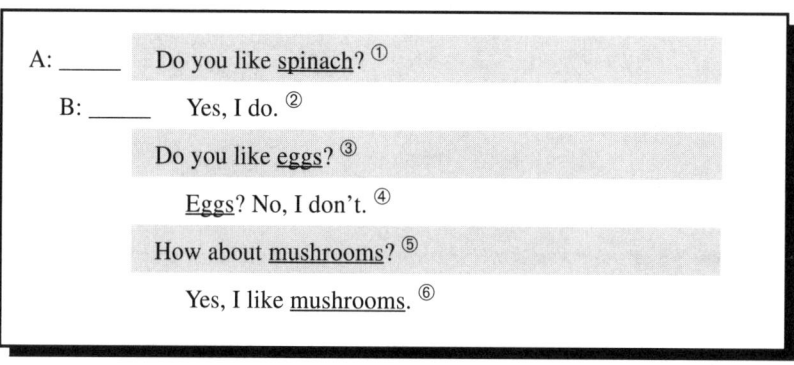

A: _____   Do you like <u>spinach</u>? ①
B: _____   Yes, I do. ②
          Do you like <u>eggs</u>? ③
          <u>Eggs</u>? No, I don't. ④
          How about <u>mushrooms</u>? ⑤
          Yes, I like <u>mushrooms</u>. ⑥

▼1 ▼2 ▼3

① fruit	① beef	① apple pie
③ grapefruit	③ fish	③ pumpkin pie
⑤ peaches	⑤ chicken	⑤ cake

Grammar: wo: s + vt + obj; simple pres tense; *do:* pro-verb; contr: *do, not;* *yes/no*-ques: simple pres tense; short reply: *do;* nouns: noncount
Expression: indicating preferences; talking about food; expressing likes/dislikes

Talk to the World

24 Belongings

A: _____ Is this <u>our suitcase</u>? ①
B: _____ No, that's ------'s. ②
　　　　 Does this belong to <u>him</u> too? ③
　　　　 No, that belongs to <u>us</u>. ④

▼1

① your camera
② --C--'s
③ her
④ --D--

▼2

① --C--'s bag
② ours
③ us
④ --D--

▼3

① my garment bag
② --C-- and --D--'s
③ them
④ Mr. ------

Grammar:　　wo: s + vt + obj; simple pres tense; *yes/no*-ques: simple pres tense; two-word insep v: simple pres tense; obj pron; poss adj; n: poss 's
Expression:　indicating ownership/possession; claiming things

25 Do You Know Him?

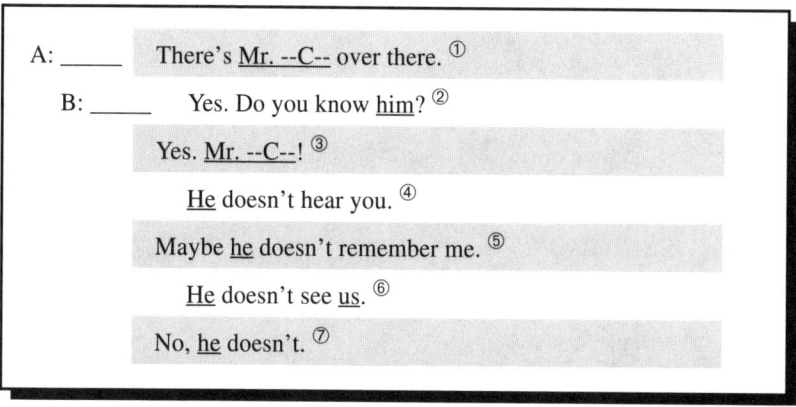

A: _____   There's <u>Mr. --C--</u> over there. ①
B: _____   Yes. Do you know <u>him</u>? ②
            Yes. <u>Mr. --C--</u>! ③
            <u>He</u> doesn't hear you. ④
            Maybe <u>he</u> doesn't remember me. ⑤
            <u>He</u> doesn't see <u>us</u>. ⑥
            No, <u>he</u> doesn't. ⑦

▼1 ▼2 ▼3

① ------
② him
④ he
⑥ he/you

① Mr. & Mrs. ------
② them
④ they
⑥ they/us

① ------
② her
④ she
⑥ she/you

Grammar: wo: s + vt + obj; simple pres tense; contr: *do, not*; *yes/no*-ques: simple pres tense;
            subj pron; obj pron; *maybe:* adv; *do:* pro-verb
Expression: talking about an acquaintance

Talk to the World

26 Occupations

A: _____ He <u>sells cars</u>. ①
B: _____ No, he doesn't. ②
Yes, he does. ③
No, he doesn't. He <u>sells</u> *trucks*. ④
He does? ⑤
Yes, he does. ⑥
Oh. ⑦

▼1

① teaches English
④ teaches *French*

▼2

① drives a taxi
④ drives a *truck*

▼3

① writes novels
④ writes *music*

Grammar: wo: s + vt + obj; simple pres tense; do: pro-verb; yes/no-ques, intonation: simple pres tense; short reply: do; no, not: neg; contr: do, not
Expression: talking about occupations; correcting/contradicting someone; expressing disagreement; expressing negation

27 Where Are You From?

A: _____ Where are you from? ①
B: _____ I'm from Japan. ②
Oh, ... Where in Japan? ③
I'm from Oita. Oita is in the southern part of the country. ④
Near Nagasaki? ⑤
No. East of Nagasaki. ⑥
Oh, I see. ⑦

▼❶ ▼❷ ▼❸

② California	② Brazil	② Canada
④ Eureka; Eureka/northern/ state	④ Porto Alegre; Porto Alegre/southern/ country	④ Winnipeg; Winnipeg/ central/country
⑤ San Francisco	⑤ Sao Paulo	⑤ Toronto
⑥ North of San Francisco.	⑥ Southwest of Sao Paulo.	⑥ West of Toronto.

Grammar: *where*: *wh*-ques, simple pres tense *(be)*; adv of place; *from*: prep of place; adv of direction
Expression: expressing geographic location/geographic direction; indicating national origin

Talk to the World

28 Looking for Things

A: _____ Where's <u>the tape recorder</u>? ①
B: _____ <u>It's right here</u>. ②
Oh, good. Now, where's <u>a cassette</u>? ③
<u>There's one over there</u>. ④
Ah! Great. Thanks. ⑤

▼ **1**

① the coffee
② Here it is.
③ a cup
④ There's one on the table.

▼ **2**

① the dictionary
② It's over there.
③ a pencil
④ Here's one here.

▼ **3**

① the tennis racket
② It's in the closet.
③ a ball
④ There's one right there.

Grammar: *where*: *wh*-ques, simple pres tense *(be)*; *one*: pron; adv of place
Expression: expressing location/position; finding things

Talk to the World

29 At a Bookstore

A: _____ Do you have a guidebook of <u>France</u>? ①
B: _____ Yes, we do. Right here. ②
Does it have <u>a map of Paris</u>? ③
Yes, it does. There's <u>a map of Paris</u> <u>in the front of the book</u>. ④
What's the price of this book? ⑤
It's only ------.* ⑥

* amount of money

▼**1**

① New York

③ a list of restaurants

④ a list of restaurants/on the top of page ten

▼**2**

① Japan

③ a picture of Mt. Fuji

④ a picture of Mt. Fuji/in the back of the book

▼**3**

① Mexico

③ a description of Mexico City

④ a description of Mexico City/in the middle of the book

Grammar: *there + be*: simple pres tense; *have*: simple pres tense; *do*: pro-verb; *yes/no*-ques: simple pres tense *(have)*; short reply: *do*; *what*: wh-ques, simple pres tense *(be)*; *of*: relational prep; adv of place; *only*: adv of degree; *you, we*: impers pron
Expression: expressing cost; describing objects; expressing location/position

-29-   Talk to the World

30 Whose?

A: _____ Is this <u>your pen</u>? ①

B: _____ No, it's not <u>mine</u>. <u>My pen</u> has <u>a blue cap</u>. ②

Whose is it? ③

Maybe it's ------'s. ④

▼ **1**

① --C--'s dictionary

② his; his dictionary/a red cover

④ --D--'s dictionary

▼ **2**

① our suitcase

② ours; our suitcase/a black handle

④ ------'s

▼ **3**

① --C--'s camera

② hers; her camera/a telephoto lens

④ --D--'s

Grammar: whose: wh-ques, simple pres tense (be); mine, yours, his, hers, ours, theirs: poss pron; poss adj; n: poss 's; adj: adj + n; maybe: adv

Expression: indicating ownership/possession; identifying objects; claiming things; colors

Talk to the World

31 Is This Yours?

A: _____ Is <u>this</u> your <u>jacket</u>? ①
B: _____ No. <u>The blue one</u>'s mine. ②
Are <u>these gloves</u> yours? ③
No. <u>Those</u> are mine. <u>The leather ones</u>. ④

▼ ❷ ❸

① that/umbrella
② the red one
③ this purse
④ that; the brown one

① this/hat
② the white one
③ those mittens
④ these; the green ones

① these/boots
② the big ones
③ that briefcase
④ that; the black one

Grammar: *one/ones*: pron; poss adj; poss pron; dem adj/pron; adj + n
Expression: indicating ownership/possession; identifying objects; claiming things

Talk to the World

32 Which One?

A: _____ Which <u>book</u> is <u>--C--'s</u>? ①
B: _____ The <u>two blue ones</u> are <u>hers</u>. ②
          Which <u>ones</u> are <u>yours</u>? ③
          <u>That</u>'s <u>mine</u> there. The <u>big red one</u>. ④

▼ ❷ ❸

① boots/--C--'s

② black ones/his

③ ones/--D--'s

④ those/hers; old brown ones

① tennis balls/--C--'s

② two white ones/hers

③ ones/--D--'s

④ those/his; orange ones

① car/--C-- and --D--'s

② green one/theirs

③ one/yours

④ that/ours; new white one

Grammar: *which* + n: *wh*-ques, simple pres tense *(be)*; *one/ones*: pron; poss pron; adj: adj + adj + n; adj + n

Expression: indicating ownership/possession; identifying objects; claiming things; offering/making a choice; expressing alternatives

Talk to the World

33 What's It Like?

A: _____   What's your <u>new jacket</u> like? ①
B: _____   It's <u>blue</u> and <u>it</u> has <u>tiny gold buttons</u>. ②
　　　　　　How about your <u>new hat</u>? ③
　　　　　　It's <u>brown</u> and it has <u>fur trim</u>. ④

▼

① new shoes	① new gloves	① new skirt
② they/white/they/brown laces	② they/gray wool/they/leather palms	② it/red corduroy/it/large pockets
③ new sweater	③ new coat	③ new blouse
④ green/large wooden buttons	④ brown leather/a hood	④ white/long sleeves

---

Grammar: what...like: wh-ques, simple pres tense (be); adj: be + adj; adj + n; adj + adj + n
Expression: describing objects; talking about clothing

Talk to the World

34 Two Places for Rent

A: _____ The apartment has <u>a swimming pool</u>, and the house doesn't. ①

B: _____ Yes, but the house has <u>a patio</u>. ②
So does the apartment. ③
And the house is <u>near a shopping center</u>. ④
So is the apartment. And the apartment has <u>a large kitchen</u>. ⑤
The house does too. ⑥

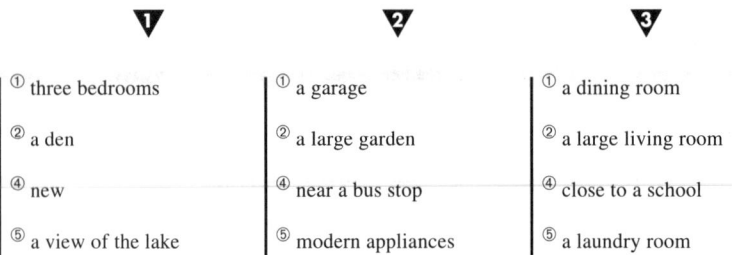

▼1	▼2	▼3
① three bedrooms	① a garage	① a dining room
② a den	② a large garden	② a large living room
④ new	④ near a bus stop	④ close to a school
⑤ a view of the lake	⑤ modern appliances	⑤ a laundry room

Grammar: *have:* simple pres tense; *do:* pro-verb; *but:* conj; *too, so:* rejoinders
Expression: describing objects; making comparisons

Talk to the World

35 Small Talk

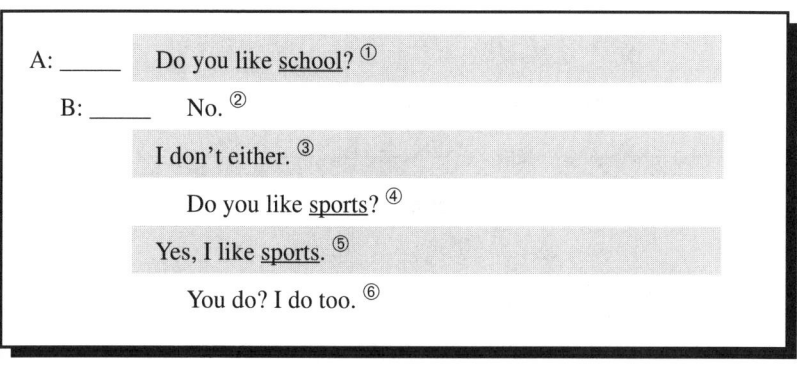

A: _____ Do you like <u>school</u>? ①
B: _____ No. ②
I don't either. ③
Do you like <u>sports</u>? ④
Yes, I like <u>sports</u>. ⑤
You do? I do too. ⑥

▼**1**

① history class
④ English class

▼**2**

① Mr. ------
④ Mrs. ------

▼**3**

① classical music
④ jazz

Grammar: simple pres tense; *do:* pro-verb; *yes/no-*ques: simple pres tense; short reply: *do; too, either:* rejoinders
Expression: expressing likes/dislikes; indicating preferences

Talk to the World

36 A New Restaurant

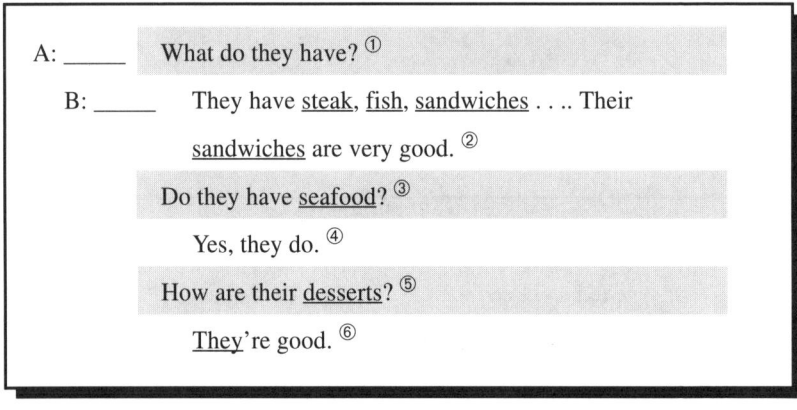

A: _____ What do they have? ①

B: _____ They have <u>steak</u>, <u>fish</u>, <u>sandwiches</u> . . . . Their <u>sandwiches</u> are very good. ②

Do they have <u>seafood</u>? ③

Yes, they do. ④

How are their <u>desserts</u>? ⑤

<u>They</u>'re good. ⑥

▼**1** ▼**2** ▼**3**

② spaghetti/vegetable dishes/chicken; chicken

③ good salads

⑤ service

② hamburgers/chili/salads; salads

③ pizza

⑤ coffee

② lobster/shrimp/salmon; salmon

③ soup

⑤ tomato soup

Grammar: *have:* simple pres tense; *do:* pro-verb; *yes/no*-ques: simple pres tense *(have)*; short reply: *do; what: wh*-ques, simple pres tense *(have); how: wh*-ques, simple pres tense *(be);* nouns: noncount; *very:* adv of degree

Expression: talking about food

37 What Kind?

A: _____ Do you have a car? ①
B: _____ Yes. ②
What kind is it? ③
It's a ------.* ④
Hmm. ⑤
What kind of car do you have? ⑥
I don't have a car. ⑦
Oh. ⑧

* brand name

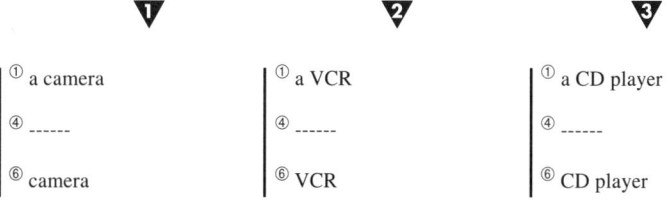

▼1	▼2	▼3
① a camera	① a VCR	① a CD player
④ ------	④ ------	④ ------
⑥ camera	⑥ VCR	⑥ CD player

Grammar: what kind (of): wh-ques, simple pres tense (be, have)
Expression: classifying things; brand names

Talk to the World

38 That Goes Here

A: _____ Where does <u>this</u> go? ①

B: _____ That belongs <u>in the corner next to the TV</u>. ②

Where do <u>these books</u> belong? ③

<u>They</u> go <u>on that shelf</u>. ④

▼1

① this lamp

② next to the plant on top of the TV

③ the stereo

④ it/on the floor between the speakers

▼2

① the painting

② on the wall above the sofa

③ this pan

④ it/in the kitchen under the sink

▼3

① the photo album

② in the bottom drawer on the right side of the desk

③ the end table

④ it/beside the bed

Grammar: wo: s + vi; simple pres tense; *where: wh*-ques: simple pres tense; adv of place; prep of place

Expression: expressing location/position

Talk to the World

39 Lost and Found

A: _____ Are these things yours? ①
B: _____ Yes. Where were they? ②
The keys were under the table in the kitchen. ③
Where was my coin purse? ④
That was on the table behind the toaster. ⑤
Thanks. ⑥

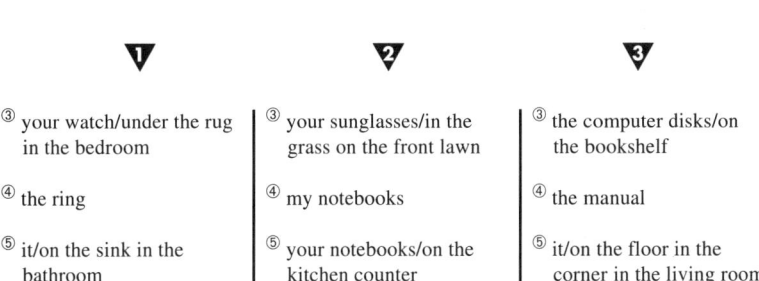

1

③ your watch/under the rug in the bedroom

④ the ring

⑤ it/on the sink in the bathroom

2

③ your sunglasses/in the grass on the front lawn

④ my notebooks

⑤ your notebooks/on the kitchen counter

3

③ the computer disks/on the bookshelf

④ the manual

⑤ it/on the floor in the corner in the living room

Grammar: *be*: simple past tense; *where*: *wh*-ques, simple past tense *(be)*; adv of place; prep of place
Expression: expressing location/position; past reference *(be)*

Talk to the World

40 What Time Is It?

A: _____ Is it <u>2 o'clock</u> yet? ①
B: _____ No, not yet. ②
What time is it? ③
It's almost <u>1:40</u>. What time is <u>your class</u>? ④
It's at <u>2:15</u>. ⑤

▼1

① 10:30

④ 10:10; the meeting

⑤ 10:30

▼2

① 1:15

④ 1 o'clock; your dentist appointment

⑤ 1:30

▼3

① 7:45

④ 7:30; your flight

⑤ 8:15

Grammar: *what time:* wh-ques, simple pres tense *(be);* short reply: *not yet; yet:* adv; adv of time; *at:* prep of time; *almost:* adv of degree
Expression: requesting/indicating the time

Talk to the World

41 Wednesday the 19th

A: _____ When is <u>our flight</u>? ①
B: _____ It's on <u>the 19th of next month</u>. ②
What day is that? ③
That's <u>a Wednesday</u>. ④
Hmm. What's the date today? ⑤
It's <u>the 7th</u>. And today's <u>Friday</u>. ⑥

▼1 ▼2 ▼3

① our final exam | ① your wedding anniversary | ① your birthday

② the 23rd of this month | ② the 4th of January | ② the 16th of December

④ a Saturday | ④ a Sunday | ④ a Thursday

⑥ the 2nd; Saturday | ⑥ the 18th; Tuesday | ⑥ the 1st; Monday

---

Grammar: what day, when: wh-ques, simple pres tense (be); a/the: art; adv of time (dates, days); on: prep of time; quant: ordinal numbers
Expression: discussing scheduled events/activities; days; dates

Talk to the World

42 Schedules

A: _____ What time does your train leave? ①

B: _____ It leaves in two hours. ②

When does it arrive in Paris? ③

It arrives in Paris at 7:30. ④

▼① ▼② ▼③

① your class start | ① the movie begin | ① your plane leave
② starts/ten minutes | ② begins/a half hour | ② leaves/an hour and a half
③ finish | ③ end | ③ arrive in Moscow
④ finishes/4:30 | ④ ends/11 o'clock | ④ arrives in Moscow/9PM

Grammar: wo: s + vi; simple pres tense (future meaning); *when, what time: wh*-ques, simple pres tense; adv of time; *in, at*: prep of time; adv of place
Expression: discussing scheduled events/activities

Talk to the World

43 Two Tours

A: _____ Tour A goes to <u>Bangkok</u> and Tour B goes to <u>Singapore</u>. ①

B: _____ Do both of them go to <u>Japan</u>? ②

Yes. And they both go to <u>Hong Kong</u>. ③

But Tour A <u>is 20 days</u>, and Tour B <u>is 30 days</u>. ④

Right. ⑤

▼1 ▼2 ▼3

▼1	▼2	▼3
① Paris/Madrid	① Rome/Athens	① Oslo/Stockholm
② London	② Germany	② Eastern Europe
③ Geneva	③ Italy	③ Vienna
④ costs $2,800/costs $3,500	④ begins on the 10th/begins on the 14th	④ lasts two weeks/lasts ten days

Grammar: wo: s + vi; simple pres tense; yes/no-ques: simple pres tense; *both (of)*: quant; adv of direction; *to*: prep of direction
Expression: making comparisons; discussing scheduled events/activities; expressing direction

Talk to the World

44 Travel Information

A: _____ Do you have any departures for <u>Honolulu on Sunday morning</u>? ①

B: _____ Yes, we do. There's one <u>at 8:30 and one at 10 o'clock</u>. ②

How about <u>on Monday the 25th</u>? ③

No, there aren't any <u>on the 25th</u>, but there's one <u>on the 26th</u>. It's <u>in the afternoon at 3 o'clock</u>. ④

Hmm. OK. Thank you. ⑤

▼1 ▼2 ▼3

① ------/in the evening of the 3rd	① ------/today	① ------/at around noon tomorrow
② at 6PM	② at 6:20	② at 11:30
③ in the morning on the 4th	③ tonight	③ the day after tomorrow
④ on the 4th/on the 5th; at 9 o'clock in the morning	④ tonight/on Wednesday evening; at 7PM	④ the day after tomorrow/ on Saturday; at 2:30 Saturday afternoon

Grammar: *there + be*: simple pres tense; *have*: simple pres t; *yes/no*-ques: simple pres tense *(have)*; *one*: pron; *any*: quant (adj, pron); adv of time; *on, in, at*: prep of time
Expression: discussing scheduled events/activities; days; dates

Talk to the World

45 How About Jam?

A: _____ Is there any <u>milk</u> <u>in the refrigerator</u>? ①
B: _____ Yes, <u>a little</u>. ②

Do we have any <u>apples</u>? ③

Yes, we have <u>a few apples</u>, but we don't have any <u>oranges</u>. ④

How about <u>jam</u>? ⑤

We have some <u>jam</u>. ⑥

▼1

① sugar/on the shelf
② a little
③ ice cream
④ a little ice cream/coffee
⑤ potatoes

▼2

① sausages/in the freezer
② a few
③ fruit
④ a little fruit/bread
⑤ tea

▼3

① rice/in the cupboard
② a little
③ carrots
④ a few carrots/lettuce
⑤ butter

Grammar: there + be: simple pres tense (vs have); yes/no-ques, simple pres tense (there + be);
            some, any, a few, a little: quant (adj, pron); nouns: noncount
Expression: talking about food; expressing quantity

46 Delicious Cake

A: _____ This cake is delicious. ①
B: _____ Yes, it is, isn't it? ②
The coffee is good too, isn't it? ③
Yes, it is. ④

▼1 ▼2 ▼3

① this class/easy
② it
③ the teacher/nice/she

① that dress/nice
② it
③ the shoes/nice/they

① this party/great
② it
③ the food/terrific/it

Grammar: tag ques (agreement): simple pres tense (be)
Expression: expressing agreement; opening a conversation

47 Her Car

A: _____ ------ has a 1990 Mercedes Benz, doesn't she? ①

B: _____ Yes. ②

That's her car over there, isn't it? ③

No. She has a 1990 Mercedes Benz all right, but that's not her car. Her car has a sun roof. ④

▼ 1

① You have a leather book bag, don't you?

③ That's your book bag, isn't it?

④ My book bag doesn't have pockets on the sides.

▼ 2

① ------'s husband is very tall, isn't he?

③ That's her husband, isn't it?

④ Her husband is bald.

▼ 3

① Your bicycle has a basket, doesn't it?

③ That's your bicycle, isn't it?

④ My bicycle doesn't have fenders.

Grammar: tag ques (confirmation): simple pres tense *(be, have)*; *all right:* adv
Expression: identifying and describing objects/people; confirming information; acknowledging something

48 Is It Expensive?

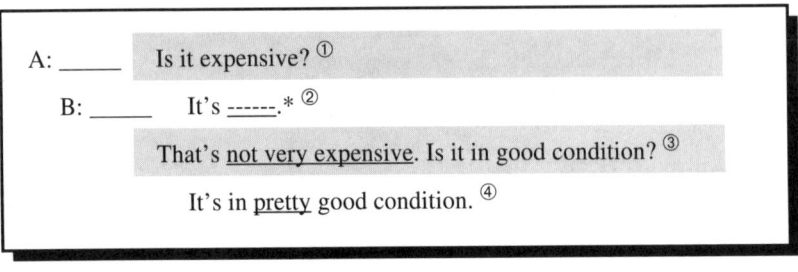

A: _____ Is it expensive? ①
B: _____ It's ------.* ②
That's <u>not very expensive</u>. Is it in good condition? ③
It's in <u>pretty</u> good condition. ④

*amount of money

▼ 1
③ very expensive
④ rather

▼ 2
③ extremely expensive
④ quite

▼ 3
③ kind of cheap
④ really

Grammar: extremely, kind of, not very, pretty, quite, rather, really, very: adv of degree
Expression: making an evaluation; expressing cost

Talk to the World

49 Korea, Not Japan

A: _____ He's from Japan, and he works in New York. ①
B: _____ He's from Korea, not Japan. ②
        He is? ③
        Yes, . . . and he works in Los Angeles, not New York. ④
        No, he doesn't. ⑤
        Yes, he does. ⑥
        No, ... ⑦

1	2	3
① the movie starts at 3 o'clock/it lasts four hours	① his name is --C--/he lives in Tokyo	① she's 20 years old/she has three brothers
② the movie starts at 4 o'clock/3 o'clock	② his name is --D--/--C--	② she's 21/20
④ it lasts three hours/four hours	④ he lives in Osaka/Tokyo	④ she has three sisters/three brothers

---

Grammar: wo: s + vi; simple pres tense; *not:* in rejoinder
Expression: correcting/contradicting someone; expressing disagreement

50 Once in a While

A: _____ What do you do in your free time? ①

B: _____ I <u>take walks in the woods</u>, I <u>bake bread</u>, and I like to <u>read novels</u>. ②

You like to <u>read novels</u>? Do you ever <u>read historical novels</u>? ③

<u>Yes, once in a while; but I usually read mystery novels</u>. ④

▼1

② work on my car/study English/play chess

③ play chess on a computer

④ No, never.

▼2

② play the piano/write letters/go jogging

③ jog on the university campus

④ Yes, I always jog on the university campus.

▼3

② take pictures/go to the pool/work out in the gym

③ work out in the school gym

④ No, I always work out at the Athletic Club.

Grammar: wo: s + vt + obj; simple pres tense (habitual); what: wh-ques, simple pres tense; yes/no-ques: simple pres tense; ever: adv in yes/no-ques; adv of frequency

Expression: expressing frequency; describing customary/habitual activities; talking about pastimes

Talk to the World

51 How Often?

A: _____ Do you ever go abroad on business? ①
B: _____ Yes, but not very often. ②
How often do you go? ③
Oh, . . . once a year or so. How about you? ④
Oh, I go about three or four times a year. ⑤
Oh, really? ⑥

▼1 ▼2 ▼3

① work overtime
② quite frequently
③ work over~
④

①

① skip class
② often
③ skip class
④ around once a week

 rdly ever skip class

 ple pres tense; *ever:* adv in *yes/no*-ques,
 : adv of degree; *every:* deter

Talk to the World

52 Gift Suggestions

A: _____ Does ----- like to cook? How about a cookbook? ①

B: _____ She doesn't like to cook. ②

Does she like tennis? How about a tennis racket? ③

She doesn't like tennis. ④

How about a theater ticket? ⑤

A theater ticket? Good idea! Thanks for the suggestion. ⑥

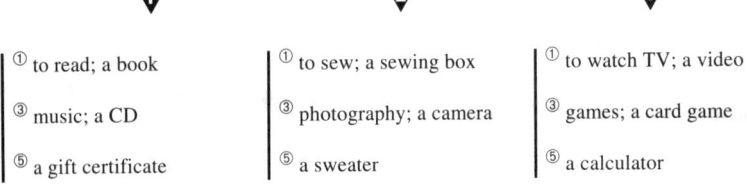

① to read; a book
③ music; a CD
⑤ a gift certificate

① to sew; a sewing box
③ photography; a camera
⑤ a sweater

① to watch TV; a video
③ games; a card game
⑤ a calculator

Grammar: wo: s + vt + obj; simple pres t; yes/no-ques: simple pres t; v(like) + to verb
Expression: indicating preferences; offering suggestions; expressing likes/dislikes

Talk to the World

52 Gift Suggestions

A: _____ Does like <u>to cook</u>? How about <u>a cookbook</u>? ①

B: _____ She doesn't like <u>to cook</u>. ②

Does she like <u>tennis</u>? How about <u>a tennis racket</u>? ③

She doesn't like <u>tennis</u>. ④

How about <u>a theater ticket</u>? ⑤

<u>A theater ticket</u>? Good idea! Thanks for the suggestion. ⑥

▼

① to read; a book

③ music; a CD

⑤ a gift certificate

---

① to sew; a sewing box

③ photography; a camera

⑤ a sweater

---

① to watch TV; a video

③ games; a card game

⑤ a calculator

Grammar: wo: s + vt + obj; simple pres t; *yes/no*-ques: simple pres t; v*(like)* + *to* verb
Expression: indicating preferences; offering suggestions; expressing likes/dislikes

Talk to the World

51 How Often?

A: _____ Do you ever go abroad on business? ①
B: _____ Yes, but not very often. ②
How often do you go? ③
Oh, ... once a year or so. How about you? ④
Oh, I go about three or four times a year. ⑤
Oh, really? ⑥

▼1

① work overtime

② quite frequently

③ work overtime

④ almost every day

⑤ work overtime about twice a week

▼2

① play tennis

② sometimes

③ play

④ about once every two weeks

⑤ play every Friday

▼3

① skip class

② often

③ skip class

④ around once a week

⑤ hardly ever skip class

Grammar: simple pres tense; *how often*: wh-ques, simple pres tense; *ever*: adv in yes/no-ques, simple pres tense; adv of frequency; *or so*: adv of degree; *every*: deter
Expression: expressing frequency

-51- Talk to the World

53 Wants and Desires

A: _____ She wants <u>a new television</u> and he doesn't. ①
B: _____ What does he want? ②

A <u>new stereo system</u>. And he wants <u>to take a trip abroad</u> and she doesn't. ③

What does she want to do? ④

She wants <u>to save the money</u>. ⑤

① a new refrigerator
③ a camera; to take tennis lessons
⑤ to take karate lessons

① a new sports car
③ a dog; to go on a trip
⑤ to stay home

① new furniture
③ a new house; to invest some money
⑤ to spend the money

Grammar: v(*want*) + *to* verb; *what*: *wh*-ques, simple pres tense with v(want) + *to* verb
Expression: expressing desires

-53-

Talk to the World

54 Smile!

A: _____ <u>Stand over there</u>. ①
B: _____ Here? ②
Right. <u>Look natural</u>. ③
OK. ④
<u>Don't look at the camera</u>. ⑤
Hurry! Take the picture. ⑥

▼1

① Sit down over there.
③ Relax.
⑤ Don't squint.

▼2

① Stand next to that bench.
③ Smile.
⑤ Don't move.

▼3

① Sit on the grass.
③ Look at the camera.
⑤ Hold still.

Grammar: imper: affirm, neg; two-word insep v: imper; adv of manner
Expression: directing someone to do something; giving instructions

55 Picnic Plans

A: _____ Who's bringing <u>the salad</u>? ①

B: _____ --C-- is. I'm bringing <u>some orange juice</u>. ②

Well, I'm bringing <u>some sandwiches</u>. ③

Good. ④

What's --D-- bringing? ⑤

Ice cream. ⑥

Great. ⑦

▼ 1

① the grill

② some charcoal

③ a blanket

⑥ A badminton set.

▼ 2

① the hamburger meat

② the buns

③ some potato salad

⑥ A bean salad.

▼ 3

① the cups and plates

② some fruit punch

③ a cake

⑥ Some iced tea.

Grammar: wo: s + vt + obj; cont: pres; *who* (s), *what*: *wh*-ques, pres cont; short reply: cont
Expression: indicating intentions; talking about food

Talk to the World

56 Who Am I Thinking Of?

A: _____ Is she wearing <u>a white blouse</u>? ①

B: _____ No, she isn't. ②

Does she have <u>a blue skirt</u> on? ③

No, she doesn't. ④

Is she wearing <u>brown loafers</u>? ⑤

Yes, she is. ⑥

Are you thinking of ------? ⑦

Yes, I am. ⑧

▼**1**

① a gray jumper

③ a red and white sweater

⑤ black stockings

▼**2**

① plaid slacks

③ a white windbreaker

⑤ a gold necklace

▼**3**

① blue jeans

③ a checked shirt

⑤ tennis shoes

Grammar: cont: pres; *yes/no*-ques: pres cont; short reply: cont; two-word sep verb: *have on*
Expression: describing/identifying people; talking about clothing

Talk to the World

57 To the Kitchen

A: _____ Where are you going? ①
B: _____ To the kitchen. ②
　　　　　To wash the dishes? ③
　　　　　No, not to wash the dishes. ④
　　　　　To set the table? ⑤
　　　　　No. I'm going to the kitchen to eat something. ⑥

▼ 1

② To the store.
③ To get a paper?
⑤ To buy some coffee?
⑥ to the store to get some change

▼ 2

② To the library.
③ To study?
⑤ To return a book?
⑥ to the library to meet a friend

▼ 3

② Downtown.
③ To meet --C--?
⑤ To go to a movie?
⑥ downtown to pay some bills

Grammar:　cont: pres; adv of direction; *to*: prep of direction; clause of purpose with *to* + v; *where*: *wh*-ques, pres cont
Expression:　indicating intentions; indicating purpose; expressing direction

Talk to the World

58 Gossip

A: _____   Guess what! <u>Mr. ------</u> is going to <u>marry his secretary</u>. ①

B: _____   I don't believe it. ②

I'm not kidding. And <u>he</u>'s going to <u>sell his house</u>. ③

Really? ④

And <u>they're</u> going to <u>live in Tahiti</u>. ⑤

Oh, that's just gossip. ⑥

▼1

① ------/quit school

③ she/get a job

⑤ she/take singing lessons

▼2

① ------/resign his position

③ he/go to a trade school

⑤ he/become a carpenter

▼3

① ------/sell her company

③ she/become a doctor

⑤ she/work overseas

Grammar: cont: *be going to* + v
Expression: indicating intentions/plans; expressing surprise

Talk to the World

59 At a Sale

A: _____ Look at that price! Try on <u>that coat</u>. ①

B: _____ <u>It</u>'s cheap, but <u>it</u>'s not my size. ②

Try <u>it</u> on! ③

I don't really like <u>it</u>. I want to try <u>this leather jacket</u> on. ④

I'm going to look for <u>a dress</u>. Look at these prices! ⑤

▼1

① this sweater
④ these suede boots
⑤ a hat

▼2

① that jacket
④ this skirt
⑤ a belt

▼3

① those sandals
④ that raincoat
⑤ an apron

Grammar: imper: affirm; cont: *be going to* + v; two-word sep, insep v
Expression: directing someone to do something; talking about clothing

60 Doing Things

A: _____ It sure is quiet here. Where is everyone? ①

B: _____ --C-- is in her room changing her clothes. ②

What's --D-- doing? ③

She's reading. ④

Where's --E--? ⑤

In her room. ⑥

She's probably working on her science project. ⑦

No, she isn't working on her science project. She's listening to the radio. ⑧

▼1

② in the living room/watching TV

④ doing her homework

⑥ Outside.

⑦ cutting the grass

⑧ washing her car

▼2

② in the cafeteria/having lunch

④ using the computer

⑥ In her office.

⑦ talking on the phone

⑧ looking at a catalogue

▼3

② in the library/doing some research

④ talking to her teacher

⑥ In the language lab.

⑦ studying

⑧ recording a lesson

Grammar: cont: pres; *what:* wh-ques, pres cont; *probably:* adv; *everyone:* pron
Expression: presently occuring activities; expressing probability/speculation; making an assumption

Talk to the World

61 Plans

A: _____ Are you going to <u>study this afternoon</u>? ①
B: _____ No, are you? ②
No. ③
What are you going to do? ④
First I'm going to <u>play tennis</u>, and then I'm going to <u>go to a movie</u>. ⑤

▼ **1**

① go to class/today

⑤ go to the library/go shopping

▼ **2**

① stay home/tomorrow

⑤ go out to eat/go to a party

▼ **3**

① go to the library/on Saturday

⑤ clean my room/wash my car

Grammar: cont: *be going to* + v; *what: wh*-ques, pres cont (*be going to* + v); *yes/no*-ques: cont (*be going to* + v); *first, then:* adv of time
Expression: indicating intentions/plans; describing a sequence of events

Talk to the World

62 Right Now

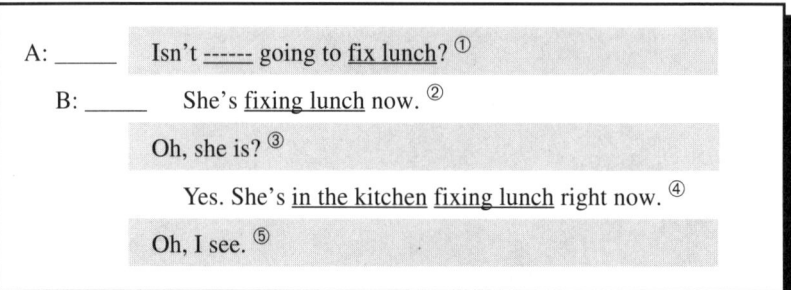

A: _____ Isn't ------ going to fix lunch? ①
B: _____ She's fixing lunch now. ②
Oh, she is? ③
Yes. She's in the kitchen fixing lunch right now. ④
Oh, I see. ⑤

▼ **1**

① ------/do his homework

② doing his homework

④ in his room

▼ **2**

① ------/get ready for school

② getting ready for school

④ upstairs

▼ **3**

① ------/complain about the hotel service

② complaining about the hotel service

④ on the phone

Grammar: cont: pres; cont: *be going to* + v; yes/no-ques: pres cont; adv of place; *now, right now*: adv of time
Expression: indicating intentions; presently occuring activities

Talk to the World

63 Late for Work

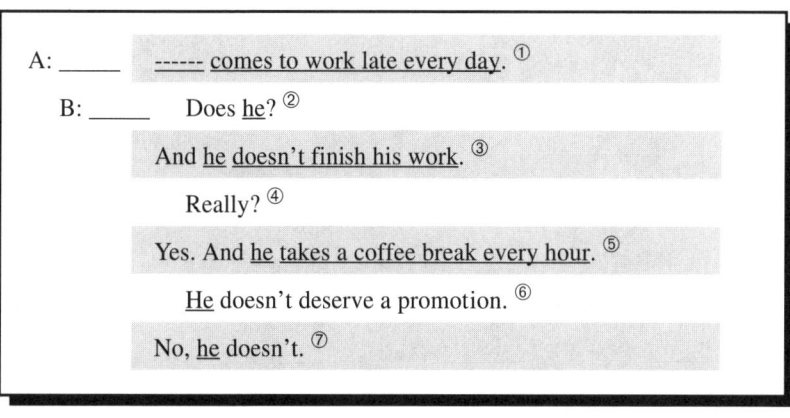

A: _____   ------ <u>comes to work late every day</u>. ①

B: _____   Does <u>he</u>? ②

And <u>he</u> <u>doesn't finish his work</u>. ③

Really? ④

Yes. And <u>he</u> <u>takes a coffee break every hour</u>. ⑤

<u>He</u> doesn't deserve a promotion. ⑥

No, <u>he</u> doesn't. ⑦

▼ 1

① copies his books on the photocopy machine

③ leaves the office early

⑤ doesn't keep his desk clean

▼ 2

① is impolite to customers

③ takes two hours for lunch

⑤ doesn't wear a necktie to work

▼ 3

① talks on the telephone all day

③ takes a half hour for her coffee break

⑤ disturbs everyone in the office

Grammar: simple pres tense (habitual); *really:* adv; *every:* deter
Expression: describing customary/habitual activities

64 By Yourself?

A: _____ I'm going to play tennis. ①
B: _____ By yourself? ②
No, not by myself. ③
Who's going to play with you? ④
_____. ⑤

▼ 1

① --C--/repair her car

② herself

③ herself

④ help her

⑤ --D--

▼ 2

① we/drive to the coast

② yourselves

③ ourselves

④ go with you

⑤ --C-- and --E--

▼ 3

① --C-- and --D--/sing at the party

② themselves

③ themselves

④ sing with them

⑤ --E--

Grammar: *myself, yourself, himself, herself, itself, ourselves, yourselves, themselves:* reflexive pronouns; *by, with:* prep with object
Expression: indicating intentions

Talk to the World

65 Newer Than That

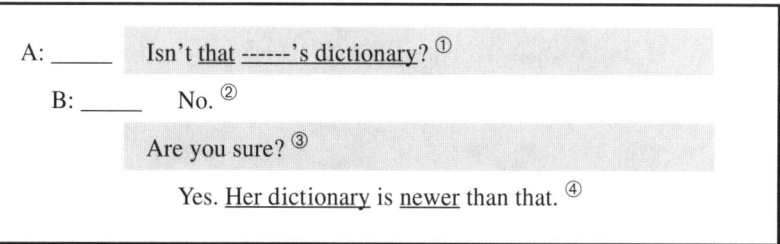

A: _____ Isn't that ------'s dictionary? ①
B: _____ No. ②
          Are you sure? ③
          Yes. Her dictionary is newer than that. ④

① those/------'s skis   ① that/our new teacher   ① that/------'s car
④ his skis/longer   ④ our new teacher/younger   ④ her car/cleaner

Grammar: adj: compar adj + -er + than; yes/no-ques: neg ques simple pres tense (be)
Expression: making comparisions; identifying objects

66 A Difficult Language

A: _____ Is <u>English</u> <u>more difficult</u> than <u>Russian</u>? ①

B: _____ No, <u>Russian</u> is <u>more difficult</u> than <u>English</u>. ②

Is it really? ③

Oh, sure. ④

▼1
① New York/more expensive/Tokyo

▼2
① your car/more economical/your motorcycle

▼3
① your suitcase/heavier/my suitcase

Grammar: adj: compar *more* + adj + *than,* adj + *-er* + *than*
Expression: making comparisons; ranking things

Talk to the World

67 The World's Longest

A: _____   The Nile is the longest river in the world. ①

B: _____   No, it's not. ②

It's not? ③

No, the Amazon River is longer. ④

It is? ⑤

Yes, it is. ⑥

1

① Mt. Logan/the highest mountain in North America

④ Mt. McKinley/higher

2

① Niagra Falls/the widest waterfall in the world

④ Khrone Falls in Laos/ wider

3

① Tokyo/the largest city in the world

④ Mexico City/larger

Grammar: adj: compar adj + -est, adj + -er
Expression: making comparisons

Talk to the World

68 The Most Expensive

A: _____ This restaurant is very expensive. ①
B: _____ Yes. It's the most expensive restaurant in town. ②
Really? Is it more expensive than the Harbor Inn? ③
Oh, yes. Much more expensive. ④

① this hotel/nice

② the nicest hotel around here

③ the Grand Hotel

① that boy/tall

② the tallest boy on our team

③ ------

① that employee/ambitious

② the most ambitious employee in my office

③ you

Grammar: adj: compar adj + -est, most + adj, adj + -er + than, more + adj + than; much: adv of degree
Expression: making comparisons; ranking things

Talk to the World

69 Busy People

A: _____ Are you free this weekend? ①

B: _____ Well, <u>I have a dentist appointment Saturday morning</u>. I'm not free then. ②

How about Saturday evening? ③

<u>I play volleyball Saturday evenings</u>. And I'm going to go on a picnic on Sunday. ④

Well, how about <u>next Sunday</u>? ⑤

Next Sunday? Sure, I'm free <u>next Sunday</u>. ⑥

▼1

② I have a piano lesson Saturday afternoon.

④ I work Saturday evenings. And I'm having company on Sunday.

⑤ on Monday

▼2

② I teach judo Saturday mornings.

④ I have a date Saturday evening. And I'm going to be out of town on Sunday.

⑤ next Saturday evening

▼3

② I have a basketball game Saturday morning.

④ I work at the library Saturday evenings. And I'm going to go out with my wife on Sunday.

⑤ next Sunday afternoon

Grammar: simple pres tense contrasted with pres cont/*be going to* + v; adv of time (days); simple pres tense (future meaning)

Expression: indicating intentions; discussing scheduled events/activities; describing habitual/ customary activities; days

Talk to the World

70 Good Movies

A: _____ Is *The Sound of Music* as good a movie as *Gone With the Wind*? ①

B: _____ Well, *The Sound of Music* is a good movie . . . . ②
But it's not as good as *Gone With the Wind*? ③
Well, no. It's not as good as Gone with the Wind. ④

▼ 1   ▼ 2   ▼ 3

① Mr. ------/good a teacher/ Mrs. ------

② a good teacher

① Chicago/interesting a city/New York

② an interesting city

① Math 201/difficult a course/Math 301

② a difficult course

Grammar: adj: compar (not) as + adj + as, (not) as + adj + n + as
Expression: making comparisons; soliciting an opinion; acknowledging something

71 Size and Shape

A: _____ How <u>large</u> is <u>the desk</u>? ①
B: _____ It's about <u>150 centimeters long and 170 centimeters wide</u>. ②

How old is it? ③

It's <u>two years</u> old. ④

What color is it? ⑤

It's <u>brown</u>. ⑥

Is it in good condition? ⑦

Yes. It's just like new. ⑧

▼ 1   ▼ 2   ▼ 3

① deep/the bookcase	① tall/the refrigerator	① big/the table
② 40 centimeters deep	② 175 centimeters tall	② 150 centimeters by one meter
④ six months	④ a few years	④ one year
⑥ gray	⑥ yellow	⑥ natural wood

Grammar: how + adj, what color: wh-ques;   about, just like;   by: prep with measurements
Expression: describing objects; dimensions; age; colors

Talk to the World

72 A Shopping List

A: _____   We need <u>tea</u>. Get <u>a box of tea bags</u>, <u>some rolls</u> . . . . ①
B: _____   . . . <u>some rolls</u>. OK. ②

And <u>a bunch of bananas</u>, and <u>some grapefruit</u>. And <u>two cans of corn</u>. ③

OK. Is that all? ④

No. Get <u>some ice cream</u> too. ⑤

Anything else? ⑥

And <u>a package of raisins</u>. ⑦

① salt; a box of salt/two cartons of milk	① salad dressing; a bottle of salad dressing/a package of butter	① tuna fish; a small can of tuna fish/a small ham
③ some cheese/a couple of bars of soap; a box of detergent	③ a bag of apples/a couple of tomatoes; two heads of lettuce	③ a jar of instant coffee/ some milk; a tube of toothpaste
⑤ a small bag of flour	⑤ a chocolate cake mix	⑤ some hamburger meat
⑦ a stalk of celery	⑦ a frozen pizza	⑦ an onion

Grammar: nouns: noncount; quant: noncount n quantifiers
Expression: talking about food; expressing quantity

Talk to the World

73 Quantities

A: _____ We don't have enough <u>juice</u>. And we need more <u>coffee</u>. ①

B: _____ How <u>much juice</u> is there? ②

One bottle. ③

How <u>many glasses</u> do we have? ④

We have enough of <u>those</u>. ⑤

▼ 1

① coffee cups; napkins
② many coffee cups
③ six
④ much salad
⑤ that

▼ 2

① bread; tea
② much bread
③ one loaf
④ much ice cream
⑤ that

▼ 3

① chicken; chairs
② much chicken
③ one large plate
④ many rolls
⑤ those

Grammar: *how much/many* + n: *wh*-ques, simple pres tense (have); quant: noncount n quantifiers; *enough (of), more:* quant
Expression: expressing quantity; talking about food

74 Let's Go to a Movie

A: _____ Let's go to a movie. ①

B: _____ Oh, let's not go to a movie again. ②

What do you want to do? ③

I don't know. Let's go out to eat. ④

Go out to eat? Uhm . . . OK. Let's go out to eat then. ⑤

▼ **1**

① visit my parents

④ stay home and watch TV

▼ **2**

① go for a drive

④ play tennis

▼ **3**

① make a cake

④ make a pie

Grammar: *let's (not)* with suggestions
Expression: offering/soliciting/declining suggestions; expressing agreement; making a proposal

Talk to the World

75 Pastimes

A: _____ ------ certainly <u>knits</u> a lot, doesn't <u>she</u>? ①

B: _____ Is <u>she</u> <u>knitting</u> again? ②

Yes, <u>she</u>'s always <u>knitting</u>. ③

<u>Knitting</u> is <u>her</u> favorite pastime. ④

▼1 ▼2 ▼3

| ① practices the piano | ① works on his car | ① jogs

Grammar: cont: pres + *always*; gerund as subj; *always, again*: adv of frequency; *a lot*: adv of degree
Expression: talking about pastimes; describing habitual/customary activities

76 Doing Well

A: _____ How am I doing in <u>English</u>? ①
B: _____ You're <u>doing quite well</u>. ②
How well am I doing in <u>math</u>? ③
You're doing <u>rather poorly</u> in <u>math</u>. ④

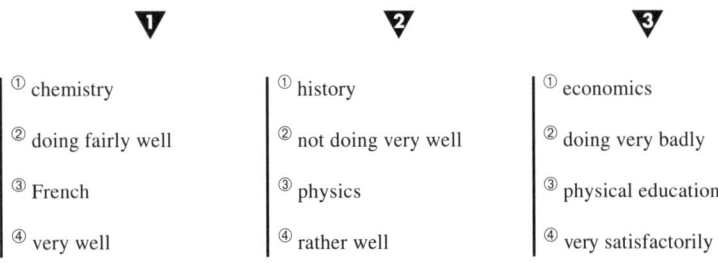

1	2	3
① chemistry	① history	① economics
② doing fairly well	② not doing very well	② doing very badly
③ French	③ physics	③ physical education
④ very well	④ rather well	④ very satisfactorily

Grammar: how + adv: *wh*-ques, pres cont; adv of manner; adv of degree
Expression: making an evaluation

Talk to the World

77 Getting Better

A: _____ How do you feel today? ①
B: _____ Oh, I feel very well. Thank you. ②
How is your <u>leg</u>? ③
My <u>leg</u> feels much better. ④
That's good. ⑤
Yes, it feels much better today. ⑥

▼1 ▼2 ▼3

| ③ back | ③ neck | ③ shoulder

Grammar: *how: wh*-ques, simple pres tense; adv: compar *well, better;* adv of manner; adv of degree
Expression: talking about health; making comparisons

78 A Self-Introduction

A: _____   Hello. My name is --C-- --D--*. ①

B: _____   --E-- --F--*. How do you do? ②

<u>Nice to meet you</u>. ③

Excuse me. What's your <u>last name</u> again? ④

<u>--D--</u>. ⑤

* given and family names

▼ 1   ▼ 2   ▼ 3

1	2	3
② It's a pleasure to meet you.	② Glad to meet you.	② It's nice to meet you.
③ I'm please to meet you.	③ Happy to meet you.	③ Nice to meet you too.
④ first name	④ surname	④ family name

Grammar: *again:* adv in *wh-*ques for confirmation
Expression: confirming information; making self-introductions/introductions; making an acquaintance

Talk to the World

79 Tourist Attractions

A: _____ What's there to see in <u>Honolulu</u>? ①
B: _____ Well, there's <u>the Bishop Museum</u>. That's popular with tourists. ②
Is there <u>a zoo</u>? ③
Yes. There's <u>the Honolulu Zoo</u>. ④
Hmm. ⑤
And there's <u>a botanical garden</u>. ⑥
Sounds interesting. ⑦
Yes, <u>Honolulu</u> is an interesting city. ⑧

▼1

① London
② Buckingham Palace
③ any parks
④ Regent's Park and Hyde Park
⑥ a lot of theaters

▼2

① New York
② Central Park
③ any interesting sights
④ Wall Street and the World Trade Center
⑥ many good restaurants

▼3

① Tokyo
② the Imperial Palace
③ any good museums
④ the Sumo Museum and the Science Museum
⑥ the Kabuki theater

Grammar: *there + be* + infin; *what: wh*-ques, with *there + be* + infin
Expression: offering suggestions

Talk to the World

80 At Dinner

A: _____ Could you please pass <u>the salad</u>? ①

B: _____ Sure. ②

Thanks. Would you pass <u>the salad dressing</u> to me too, please? ③

Here you are. ④

Thank you. ⑤

▼1

① the sugar
③ the cream

▼2

① the bread
③ the butter

▼3

① the salt
③ the pepper

Grammar: wo: s + vt + ind obj + d obj; v + indo obj + do obj **or** v + d obj + *to* + ind obj; *to*: prep with indo obj; *could, would* (in polite requests): modals; obj pron
Expression: making polite requests; talking about food

81 A Request

A: _____   Please <u>show --C-- and --D--</u> <u>the new contract</u>. ①
B: _____   <u>--E--</u> has <u>the new contract</u> right now. ②
           OK. Then please <u>show it to them</u> later. ③
           Sure. ④

▼1
① send/--C-- and me/the new schedule
② --D--/the new schedule
③ send/it/to us

▼2
① mail/--C--/the cassettes
② --D--/the cassettes
③ mail/them/to him

▼3
① give/--C--/my dictionary
② --D--/your dictionary
③ give/it/to her

Grammar: wo: s + vt + ind obj + d obj; v + indo obj + d obj **or** v + d obj + to ind obj; to: prep with indo obj; imper: affirm; obj pron; *sure:* adv; *right now:* adv of time
Expression: making polite requests

82 Why?

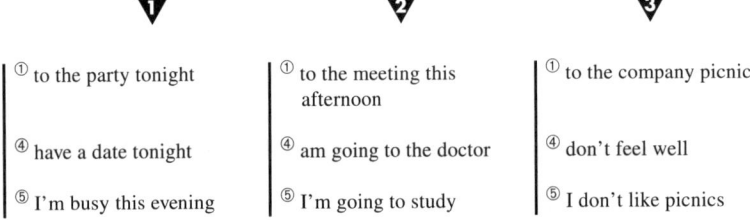

A: _____ Are you going <u>to English class today</u>? ①
B: _____ No, are you? ②
No. Why aren't you going? ③
I <u>have a headache</u>. How come you're not going? ④
Because <u>I have a sore throat</u>. ⑤
That's a good reason. ⑥

▼1

① to the party tonight

④ have a date tonight

⑤ I'm busy this evening

▼2

① to the meeting this afternoon

④ am going to the doctor

⑤ I'm going to study

▼3

① to the company picnic

④ don't feel well

⑤ I don't like picnics

Grammar: cont: pres; *why, how come:* wh-ques, pres cont; *yes/no*-ques: pres cont; *because:* conj; clause of reason

Expression: requesting/stating reasons; asking for/giving excuses

Talk to the World

83 Getting Around

A: _____   How are you going to get <u>to the party tonight</u>? ①
B: _____   I'm going by <u>bus</u>. ②
           How are you getting <u>home</u>? ③
           I'm <u>taking a taxi</u> <u>home</u>. ④

▼**1** ▼**2** ▼**3**

① to the airport	① to work tomorrow	① downtown
② airport limousine	② car	② subway
③ to your hotel	③ to the meeting	③ back
④ getting a ride	④ walking	④ taking the bus

Grammar: *how*: wh-ques, pres cont, *be going to* + v; adv of means; *by*: prep of means; adv of direction; *to*: prep of direction
Expression: discussing transportation

-83-   Talk to the World

84 I Think So Too

A: _____ ------ thinks that <u>this is easy</u>. ①
B: _____ I don't think so. Do you think so? ②
No, I don't think <u>it</u> is. ③
I think <u>it's difficult</u>. ④
I think so too. ⑤

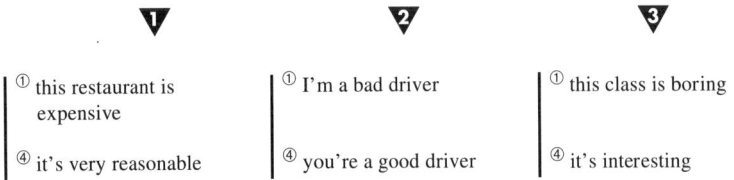

▼1
① this restaurant is expensive
④ it's very reasonable

▼2
① I'm a bad driver
④ you're a good driver

▼3
① this class is boring
④ it's interesting

Grammar: v(think) + that-clause; so: pro-clause
Expression: expressing an opinon; expressing agreement

Talk to the World

85 Predictions

A: _____ You will <u>meet a handsome man next month</u>. ①
B: _____ That's interesting. ②
And you will <u>take a long trip next year</u>. ③
Will I <u>leave the country</u>? ④
No, you won't. ⑤
Is that all? ⑥
No. You will <u>change jobs soon</u>. ⑦

▼1

① get some good news soon

③ get a new job

④ be happy

⑦ live a long time

▼2

① be very successful in your work

③ make a lot of money

④ be rich

⑦ move to a different country

▼3

① get married next year

③ have many children

④ get a good job

⑦ find some money soon

Grammar: *will* (prediction): modal; *yes/no*-ques with modal; adv of time
Expression: anticipating events; making a prediction

86 Offering Help

A: _____   -----, do you want me to <u>mail this letter</u>? ①
B: _____   Yes, <u>mail that</u>, will you please? ②
            Sure. ③
            Thanks. And will you <u>buy some stamps</u> too? ④
            OK. ⑤

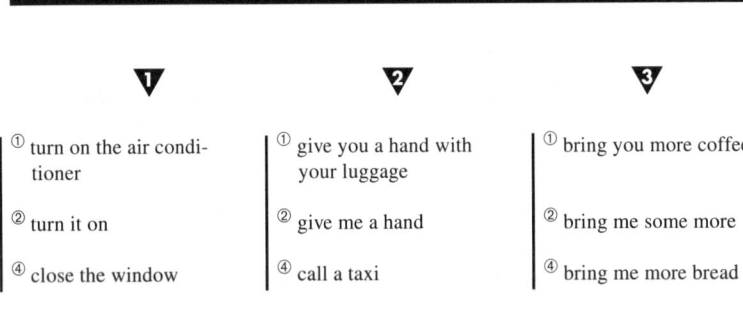

▼1	▼2	▼3
① turn on the air conditioner	① give you a hand with your luggage	① bring you more coffee
② turn it on	② give me a hand	② bring me some more
④ close the window	④ call a taxi	④ bring me more bread

Grammar: v(want) + obj + to + v; will (request): modal; yes/no-ques: modal; imper: affirm;
           will tag ques (request)
Expression: making polite requests; offering/requesting assistance

87 Dining Out

A: _____ I'm going to order <u>the trout</u>. ①
B: _____ Hmm. I think that I'll order <u>the trout</u> too. ②
And I'm going to get <u>some potato salad</u> too. ③
That's a good idea. I think I will too. ④
Aren't you going to order <u>the onion soup</u> too? ⑤
No. Why? ⑥
I am. ⑦

▼1

① the vegetable salad
③ some chicken soup
⑤ a sandwich

▼2

① lasagna
③ an Italian salad
⑤ coffee

▼3

① veal stew
③ the vegetable dish
⑤ some iced tea

Grammar: cont: *be going to* + v in contrast with *will* modal; *yes/no*-ques: pres cont: *be going to* + v; v*(think)* + *that*-clause; contr: *will*; *will* (intention): modal
Expression: talking about food; indicating intentions

88 Hopeful

A: _____ I hope <u>the weather is nice tomorrow</u>. ①
B: _____ I hope so too. I <u>think</u> <u>it will be</u>. ②
I hope <u>it doesn't rain</u>. ③
I <u>don't think</u> <u>it will</u>. ④
I hope <u>not</u>. ⑤

▼ 1

① the test tomorrow is easy

② think/it will be

③ he doesn't ask us about lesson ten

④ don't think/he will

⑤ not

▼ 2

① they still have tickets for Friday evening

② think/they will

③ there are still some good seats

④ think/there will be

⑤ so

▼ 3

① the flight isn't crowded

② don't think/it will be

③ it departs on time

④ think/it will

⑤ so

Grammar: v(hope, think) + that-clause; will (prediction/assurance) modal; so: pro-clause
Expression: expressing a hope; expressing conviction; making a prediction

Talk to the World

89 The Weekend

A: _____ What are you going to do <u>this weekend</u>? ①
B: _____ I'll probably <u>play tennis</u>. Do you have any plans? ②
I'm going to <u>go swimming with ------</u>. ③
Where? ④
I don't know. I think <u>we'll go to the university pool</u>. ⑤

▼1 ▼2 ▼3

① next weekend	① this summer	① on Sunday
② stay home	② go to summer school	② go to my cousin's
③ go for a drive with my family	③ take a trip	③ play golf
⑤ we'll go to a lake up north	⑤ I'll go to Mexico	⑤ I'll play at the local country club

Grammar: *will*: modal contrasted with *be going to* + v, *will* after *think*, *probably*: adv; adv of time; *what*: wh-ques with *be going to* + v
Expression: indicating plans/intentions; expressing probability

90 Keeping Busy

A: _____ What do you plan to do this afternoon? ①
B: _____ I'm going to <u>take a nap</u>. ②
What are you planning on doing this evening? ③
I'm <u>having dinner with a friend</u>. Why? ④
Are you interested in <u>going to a movie</u> some time? ⑤
Sure, but not today. Sorry. I don't have any plans for tomorrow though. ⑥
OK. Good. ⑦

▼1
② play tennis
④ studying for my test
⑤ going shopping with me

▼2
② do some work
④ having company
⑤ visiting ------

▼3
② work in the yard
④ visiting a friend
⑤ coming over to my house

Grammar: cont: pres; cont: *be going to* + v; v(*plan*) + *to* v; v + v-*ing*; *be interested in* + v-*ing*; *though*: adv
Expression: indicating plans/intentions; making a proposal

Talk to the World

91 Starting Tomorrow

A: _____ I'm going to stop <u>smoking</u>. ①
B: _____ You are? ②
Yes, and I'm going to start <u>jogging every day</u>. ③
Good for you. Starting when? ④
Starting . . . <u>tomorrow</u>. ⑤

▼1

① going to bed late every night

③ getting up early

⑤ tonight

▼2

① working overtime every day

③ playing tennis on weekends

⑤ next month

▼3

① eating in the cafeteria

③ bringing my lunch to work

⑤ Monday

Grammar: cont: *be going to* + v; v*(stop, start)* + v-*ing*; adv of time; *starting:* prep
Expression: indicating intentions; expressing determination

Talk to the World

92 Another Roll?

A: _____ Would you like <u>more soup</u>? ①
B: _____ No, thank you. <u>It</u>'s delicious though. ②
        Will you have <u>another roll</u>? ③
        No, thanks. But I'd like <u>more chicken</u>. ④
        Oh, please help yourself. ⑤
        Thank you. ⑥

▼1

① another sandwich
② they
③ another cup of coffee
④ more salad

▼2

① more bread
② it
③ more cheese
④ another piece of ham

▼3

① more tea
② it
③ another piece of cake
④ more ice cream

Grammar: *will, would like* + n (offer): modals; *yes/no*-ques: modal; nouns: noncount; quant: noncount n quantifiers; *more, another*: quant; *though*: adv; contr: *would*
Expression: talking about food; declining offers; offering something

Talk to the World

93 More Salad?

A: _____ Would you care for <u>some more salad</u>? ①
B: _____ Yes, please. ②
    Would you care to have <u>some more bread</u> too? ③
    No, thank you. I don't care for <u>any more bread</u>. ④

▼ **1**

① a roll
③ some more soup
④ any more soup

▼ **2**

① some more ice cream
③ another cup of coffee
④ any more coffee

▼ **3**

① more spaghetti
③ a piece of cheese
④ any cheese

Grammar: would + care for + obj, would + care to + v + obj: (offers) modal; yes/no-ques:
     modal; nouns: noncount; *some more, any more:* quant
Expression: talking about food; accepting/declining offers; offering something

94 Some of Them

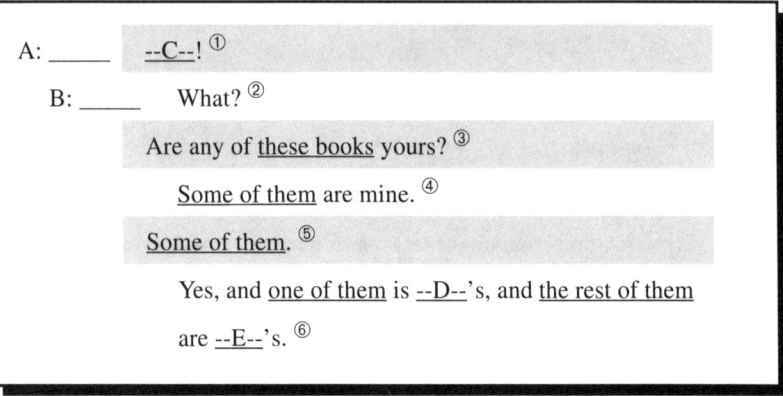

A: _____ --C--! ①

B: _____ What? ②

Are any of <u>these books</u> yours? ③

<u>Some of them</u> are mine. ④

<u>Some of them</u>. ⑤

Yes, and <u>one of them</u> is --D--'s, and <u>the rest of them</u> are --E--'s. ⑥

▼ **1**

③ this stuff

④ part of it

⑥ about half of it/some of it

▼ **2**

③ this equipment

④ a little of it

⑥ some of it/some of it

▼ **3**

③ those students

④ two of them

⑥ a few of them/the rest of them

Grammar: a few of, a little of, any of, half of, one of, part of, some of, the rest of: quant
Expression: expressing quantity; claiming things

Talk to the World

95 Helping Others

A: _____ Would you help me find <u>my pens</u>? ①

B: _____ How many are you looking for? ②

<u>Three</u>. ③

Well, there's <u>one of them</u> . . . <u>on the table</u>. ④

Great. Now, . . . where are <u>the other two</u>? ⑤

There's <u>another</u> <u>over there</u>, and <u>the other one</u> is <u>in your pocket</u>. ⑥

▼**1**

① my notebooks

③ Four.

④ one/on the desk

⑤ the other three

⑥ another one/on the floor/ the others/right there

▼**2**

① the tennis balls

③ Six.

④ three of them/on the chair there

⑤ the others

⑥ two others/in the container here/the other ball/there

▼**3**

① the cassettes

③ Six.

④ one of them/in the tape recorder

⑤ the others

⑥ another/on top of the radio/the other four/on the shelf

Grammar: *another, the other, the others*: quant; v(help) + obj + v
Expression: requesting assistance; finding things; expressing quantity

Talk to the World

96 Feeling Ill

A: _____ Are you OK? You don't look well. ①
   B: _____ I've got <u>a headache</u>. ②
                Well, sit down, relax, and take it easy. ③
                No, I've got to <u>go to the bakery</u>. ④
                Well, OK, but . . . ⑤

▼ 1

② a bad cold

④ return this book to the library today

▼ 2

② a sore throat

④ study for my test

▼ 3

② a pain in my side

④ go to work today

Grammar: have got + n; have got to + v: modal; contr: have
Expression: talking about health; expressing necessity

Talk to the World

97 A Dining Experience

A: _____ How was the dinner? ①
B: _____ It was great. ②
What did you have? ③
I had <u>chicken</u> and <u>fresh vegetables</u>. ④
What did you have to drink? ⑤
<u>Tea</u>. ⑥
What did you have for dessert? ⑦
<u>Apple pie</u>. ⑧

▼1

④ spring rolls/sweet and sour pork

⑥ green tea

⑧ orange sherbet

▼2

④ roast beef/a potato

⑥ coffee

⑧ Camembert cheese

▼3

④ salmon/a salad

⑥ juice

⑧ cake

Grammar: *be, have*: simple past tense; *what: wh*-ques, simple past tense *(have)*; *have + to + v; have + for + n*
Expression: talking about food

98 A Great Trip

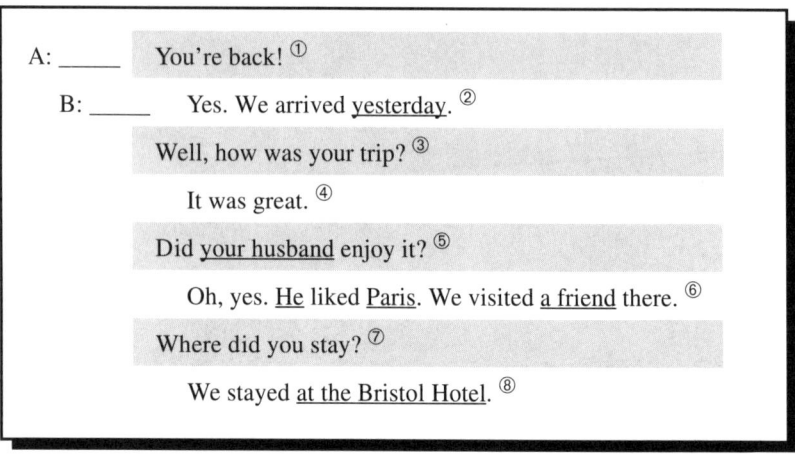

A: _____ You're back! ①
B: _____ Yes. We arrived <u>yesterday</u>. ②
Well, how was your trip? ③
It was great. ④
Did <u>your husband</u> enjoy it? ⑤
Oh, yes. <u>He</u> liked <u>Paris</u>. We visited <u>a friend</u> there. ⑥
Where did you stay? ⑦
We stayed <u>at the Bristol Hotel</u>. ⑧

▼ 1

② this morning
⑤ your children
⑥ New York; my sister
⑧ at my sister's place

▼ 2

② late last night
⑤ your wife
⑥ Bangkok; a university
⑧ at the President Hotel

▼ 3

② the day before yesterday
⑤ your friend
⑥ Cairo; some companies
⑧ with a friend

Grammar: simple past tense (reg v); *where*: *wh*-ques, simple past tense; *yes/no*-ques: simple past tense
Expression: reporting past events/activities

Talk to the World

99 Travel Experiences

A: _____ We had a great time in <u>England</u>. ①
B: _____ Where did you go in <u>England</u>? ②
We went to <u>London</u> and <u>Stratford-upon-Avon</u>. ③
What did you do in <u>London</u>? ④
We <u>went to musuems</u>; we <u>saw a play</u>; and we went shopping. ⑤
What did you buy? ⑥
I bought <u>a coat</u>, and my husband bought <u>some shoes</u>. ⑦

▼1	▼2	▼3
① Japan	① Canada	① India
③ Tokyo/Kyoto	③ Vancouver/Montréal	③ New Delhi/Bombay
④ Kyoto	④ Montréal	④ New Delhi
⑤ went on a tour/saw a tea ceremony	⑤ rode the subway/took a tour of the city	⑤ went to a festival/took pictures
⑦ some food/a painting	⑦ a jacket/a fur hat	⑦ some tea/a sweater

Grammar: simple past tense (irreg) v; *where, what*: *wh*-ques, simple past tense
Expression: reporting past events/activities

Talk to the World

100 The Baby

A: _____ Did you see the baby? ①
B: _____ No. What did he do? ②
He picked up the cup, and then he drank the milk. ③
Did he spill any? ④
No, he didn't. ⑤

③ she lifted the box/she dropped it

④ Did she open it?

③ she stood up/she fell down

④ Did she get hurt?

③ she picked up the bottle/she threw it

④ Did she break it?

Grammar: simple past tense; two-word sep verbs
Expression: reporting past events/activities

101 Who Did It?

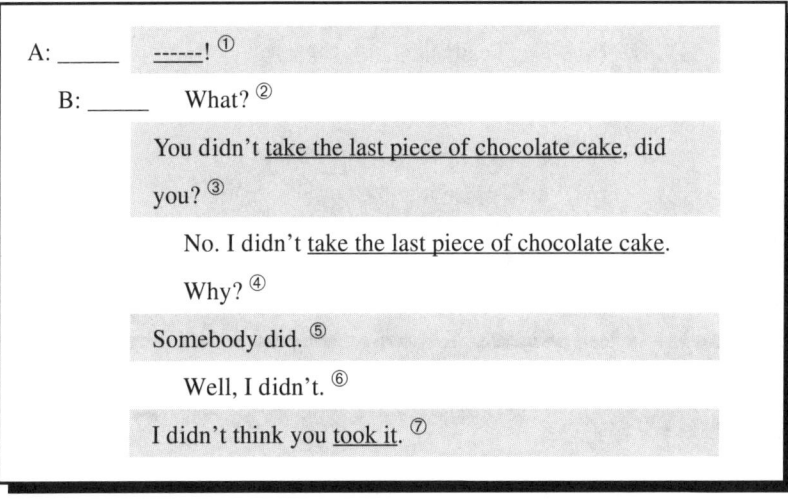

A: _____ ------! ①
B: _____ What? ②
You didn't <u>take the last piece of chocolate cake</u>, did you? ③
No. I didn't <u>take the last piece of chocolate cake</u>. Why? ④
Somebody did. ⑤
Well, I didn't. ⑥
I didn't think you <u>took it</u>. ⑦

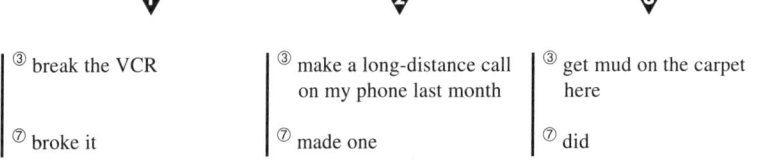

| ③ break the VCR | ③ make a long-distance call on my phone last month | ③ get mud on the carpet here |
| ⑦ broke it | ⑦ made one | ⑦ did |

Grammar: simple past tense; tag ques, simple past tense
Expression: reporting past events/activities; denying something

Talk to the World

102 The What to Whom?

A: _____ Did you <u>give</u> <u>the dictionary</u> to <u>the teacher</u>? ①
B: _____ Did I <u>give</u> the *what* to *whom*? ②
       Did you <u>give</u> <u>the teacher</u> <u>the dictionary</u>? ③
       No, I didn't <u>give</u> <u>it</u> to <u>the teacher</u>. ④
       Well, who did you <u>give</u> <u>it</u> to? ⑤
       To ------. ⑥

▼ 1

① send/the reports/your supervisor

④ send/them/him

▼ 2

① take/the packages/your sister

④ take/them/her

▼ 3

① mail/the books/your friend

④ mail/them/him

Grammar: wo: s + vt + ind obj + d obj; v + ind obj + d obj **or** v + d obj + *to* ind obj; *what* as obj; *whom* as obj of *to*
Expression: clarifying/confirming information

Talk to the World

103 Correcting Someone

A: _____ I'm really looking forward to <u>this summer</u>. ①
B: _____ Why? ②
I'm going to <u>go to Europe</u>. ③
Didn't you just recently <u>go to Europe</u>? ④
No, I <u>went to North Africa</u>, not <u>Europe</u>. ⑤
Oh, I see. ⑥

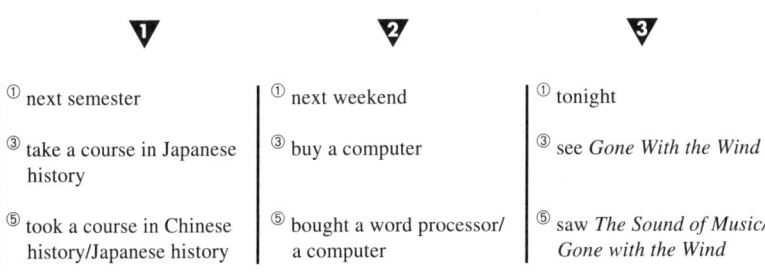

▼ 1	▼ 2	▼ 3
① next semester	① next weekend	① tonight
③ take a course in Japanese history	③ buy a computer	③ see *Gone With the Wind*
⑤ took a course in Chinese history/Japanese history	⑤ bought a word processor/ a computer	⑤ saw *The Sound of Music/ Gone with the Wind*

Grammar: simple past tense (irreg v); *just:* adv; *yes/no*-ques: neg ques with simple past tense; *not:* in rejoinder
Expression: reporting past events/activities; clairifying/confirming information

Talk to the World

104 What Do They Do?

A: _____ How many children does ------ have? ①

B: _____ Mmm . . . let's see. He has one son in the city here; he has <u>another one in New York</u>, and <u>two others in Paris. Four sons.</u> ②

What do they do? ③

<u>One is a student; one is a lawyer;</u> and <u>the other two are doctors.</u> ④

He doesn't have any other children? ⑤

No. There are no others. ⑥

② another in Tokyo/one other in Osaka; Three boys.

④ one is a businessman/the other is a stockbroker

② two more in Europe/three in Canada; Six sons.

④ two are diplomats/the others are teachers

② two in Paris/another two in London; Five sons.

④ two others are in the military/the two others are engineers

Grammar: *another, the other, the others, other, others:* quant; *one:* pron
Expression: talking about occupations

Talk to the World

105 Weight Watcher

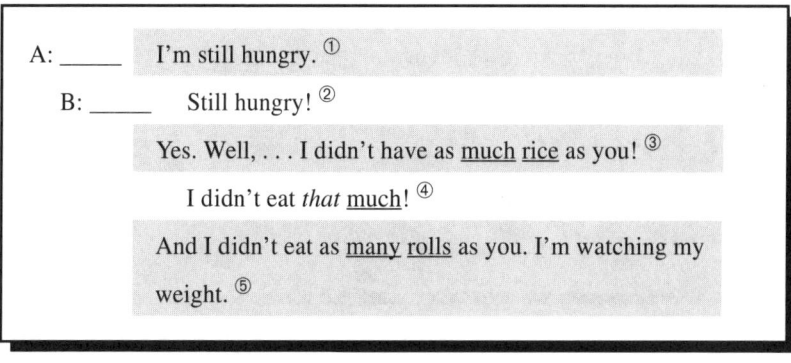

A: _____ I'm still hungry. ①
B: _____ Still hungry! ②
Yes. Well, ... I didn't have as <u>much rice</u> as you! ③
I didn't eat *that* <u>much</u>! ④
And I didn't eat as <u>many rolls</u> as you. I'm watching my weight. ⑤

▼1
③ many/baked potatoes
⑤ much/chicken

▼2
③ much/spaghetti
⑤ many/servings of roast beef

▼3
③ many/pieces of pie
⑤ much/ice cream

Grammar: quant: compar *as much/many* + n + *as;* nouns: noncount; *that:* adv of degree; *still:* adv
Expression: making comparisons; talking about food

Talk to the World

106 Well, I Can!

A: _____ I'm going to <u>cook dinner tonight</u>. ①

B: _____ You're going to <u>cook dinner</u>? ②

Yes. Why? ③

I didn't know you <u>could cook</u>. ④

Well, I <u>can</u>! ⑤

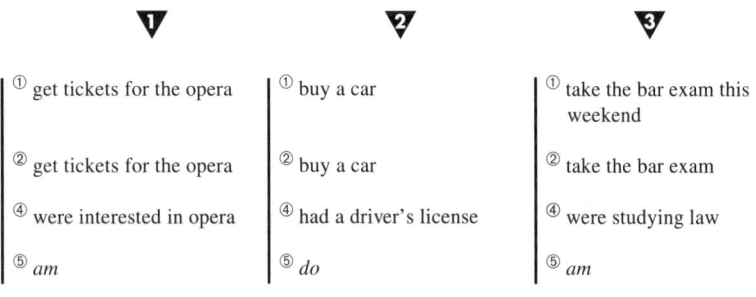

1	2	3
① get tickets for the opera	① buy a car	① take the bar exam this weekend
② get tickets for the opera	② buy a car	② take the bar exam
④ were interested in opera	④ had a driver's license	④ were studying law
⑤ *am*	⑤ *do*	⑤ *am*

Grammar: v*(know)* + *that*-clause: simple past tense; *could* (past of *can*): modal
Expression: indicating intentions; expressing doubt

107 Things to Do

A: _____ What should we do <u>tonight</u>? ①

B: _____ I don't know. What do you want to do? ②

We could <u>visit --C--</u>. ③

<u>Visit --C--</u>? No, I don't want to <u>visit --C--</u>. ④

We could <u>take --C-- to that new pizza restaurant</u>. ⑤

That would be fun. ⑥

Should we do that? ⑦

OK. ⑧

▼1   ▼2   ▼3

▼1	▼2	▼3
① this weekend	① Saturday night	① this summer
③ drive to the lake	③ stay home and watch TV	③ go camping
⑤ go to a play	⑤ visit ------ in the hospital	⑤ go abroad
⑥ That'd be OK.	⑥ That'd be nice to do.	⑥ I'd like that.

Grammar: *would, should, could:* modals
Expression: offering/soliciting suggestions; expressing agreement/alternatives

108 Me Neither

A: _____ I didn't <u>do my English homework for today</u>. ①
B: _____ Neither did I. ②

Did you <u>do your chemistry homework</u>? ③

No. ④

I didn't either. ⑤

▼1

① go to class on Monday

③ go to class on Tuesday

▼2

① have breakfast this morning

③ have lunch today

▼3

① get to class on time today

③ get to class on time yesterday

Grammar: *either, neither:* rejoinders; *yes/no-*ques: simple past tense
Expression: reporting past events/activities

Talk to the World

109 Similar People

A: _____ --C-- is a lot like <u>his father</u>. ①
B: _____ In what way? ②

They're both <u>good at foreign languages</u>, and both of <u>them</u> <u>like to cook</u>. ③

That's true. And <u>they</u> both <u>play the violin</u>. ④

And neither of <u>them</u> <u>likes team sports</u>. ⑤

Yes, but <u>--C-- is patient with people</u>, and <u>his father isn't</u>. ⑥

That's true. ⑦

▼1

① --C--/her sister

③ they/independent/them/ like to be with people

④ they/want to be doctors

⑤ them/cares for small talk

⑥ --C-- is very ambitious/ her sister isn't

▼2

① you/your brother

③ you/interested in other people/you/like to argue

④ we/like to eat sweets

⑤ you/is shy

⑥ I don't like school/my brother does

▼3

① --C--/our teacher

③ they/easy going/them/ like classical music

④ they/enjoy teaching

⑤ them/likes to fail students

⑥ --C-- is impatient/ our teacher isn't

Grammar: *both (of), neither (of)*: quant; *be like:* in compar; *a lot*: adv of degree
Expression: describing people; making comparisons; talking about an acquaintance

-109-   Talk to the World

110 Saturday and Sunday

A: _____ How did you spend your weekend? ①
B: _____ Well, ... Saturday evening I <u>went to a movie</u> .... ②
What did you do on Sunday? ③
I <u>slept late, read a book, and went shopping</u>. What did you do? ④
I <u>stayed home and watched TV all weekend</u>. ⑤

▼1 ▼2 ▼3

② made a pizza

④ had a party at my house

⑤ flew to New York on Saturday and came back on Sunday

② wrote some letters

④ took some pictures and visited a friend

⑤ stayed home and studied Saturday and Sunday

② bought a new car

④ watched *Gone With the Wind* on TV, played tennis, and cut the grass

⑤ threw a party on Saturday and cleaned up the mess on Sunday

Grammar: simple past tense; *how, what: wh*-ques, simple past tense
Expression: reporting past events/activities

111 For You

A: _____   Who <u>painted your room</u> for you? ①
B: _____   --C-- <u>painted it</u> for me ②
           That was nice of him to do that. ③
           Yes, he's nice to me. ④
           Didn't he <u>make you those shelves</u> too? ⑤
           No. --D-- <u>made the shelves</u> for me. ⑥

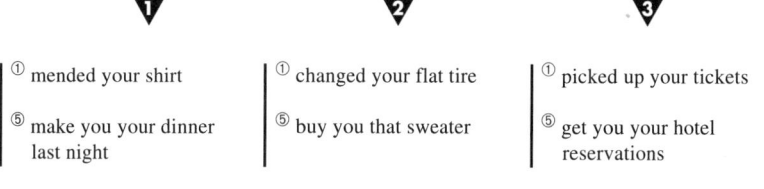

▼ 1	▼ 2	▼ 3
① mended your shirt	① changed your flat tire	① picked up your tickets
⑤ make you your dinner last night	⑤ buy you that sweater	⑤ get you your hotel reservations

Grammar: wo: s + vt + ind obj + d obj; v + ind obj + d obj **or** v + d obj + *for* ind obj; *for*: prep with obj pron; simple past tense; *of*: adj + *of* + obj (+ *to* v); *to*: adj + *to* + obj
Expression: identifying people; talking about an acquaintance

Talk to the World

112 Travel Time

A: _____ How long does it take for you to get <u>to school</u> from your house? ①

B: _____ <u>By car</u>? ②

<u>By bus</u>. ③

It takes <u>about an hour</u> <u>by bus</u>. ④

<u>An hour</u>? ⑤

How much time does it take you to get <u>to school</u>? ⑥

<u>About fifteen minutes on foot</u>. ⑦

▼1

① to the airport

② By taxi?

③ By airport bus.

④ an hour and twenty minutes/by airport bus

⑦ about forty minutes/by car

▼2

① here

② On foot?

③ By car.

④ about ten minutes/by car

⑦ about fifteen minutes/by bicycle

▼3

① downtown

② By bus?

③ By car.

④ twenty-five minutes/by car

⑦ thirty-five minutes/by bus

Grammar: *how much time, how long: wh-*ques, simple pres tense; v + *(for)* + obj + *to* v; adv of means; *by:* prep of means; *to:* prep of direction; adv of direction

Expression: discussing transportation; indicating quantity of time

Talk to the World

113 Last Night

A: _____ What did you do last night? ①
B: _____ First we went to <u>a movie</u>, ... ②
What <u>movie</u> did you go to? ③
<u>Casablanca</u>. ④
Then what? ⑤
Then we <u>had dinner with his parents</u>. ⑥
Did you have a good time? ⑦
Yes. ⑧

▼1
② a coffee shop
④ ------
⑥ went for a drive around the lake

▼2
② a museum
④ ------
⑥ went to a restaurant

▼3
② a bookstore
④ ------
⑥ watched TV at his house

Grammar: what + n: wh-ques, simple past tense; first, then: adv
Expression: reporting past events/activities; describing a sequence of events

Talk to the World

114 Housework

A: _____ Did you help your mother? ①
B: _____ Yes. ②
What did you do? ③
I <u>washed the dishes</u> and <u>took the garbage out</u>. ④
Good. ⑤
What did *you* do? ⑥
Ah, . . . well, I'm going to <u>clean up the yard</u> . . . later on. ⑦

▼1   ▼2   ▼3

④ vacuumed the living room/dusted the furniture
④ made some sandwiches/went to the store
④ washed out the refrigerator/washed the kitchen floor

⑦ clean out the garage
⑦ put in the air conditioner
⑦ hang out the clothes

Grammar: simple past tense; two-word sep v
Expression: reporting past events/activities

115 Guess My Occupation

A: _____ Do you work outdoors? ①
B: _____ Sometimes. ②
Do you work in an office? ③
No. ④
Do you have a college degree? ⑤
No, I don't. ⑥
Do you work with your hands? ⑦
Hmm . . . sort of. ⑧

▼1 ▼2 ▼3

① Do you wear a uniform?
② No.
③ Do you meet the public?
④ Sometimes.
⑤ Do you work alone?
⑥ Yes, usually.
⑦ Do you travel on your job?
⑧ Sometimes.

① Do you use machinery?
② No.
③ Do you work with tools?
④ Sort of.
⑤ Are you a carpenter?
⑥ No.
⑦ Do you work with food?
⑧ No.

① Do you teach something?
② No.
③ Do you sell something?
④ No.
⑤ Are you an artist?
⑥ Kind of.
⑦ Are you a photographer?
⑧ Yes!

Grammar: simple pres tense; *yes/no*-ques: simple pres tense; *sort of, kind of:* adv; adv of frequency
Expression: talking about occupations; describing customary/habitual activities

116 By Coincidence

A: _____ Where are you from? ①
B: _____ Sydney, Australia. ②
Well, ... so are we! Where do you live in Sydney? ③
We live on Main Street. ④
So do we! What a coincidence! We're from the same city, and we live on the same street. ⑤

1

① Where are you going?

② To Rome.

③ so are we! What flight are you taking?

④ Flight 203.

⑤ So are we! We're going to the same city, and we're taking the same flight.

2

① What university did you attend?

② London University.

③ so did I! When did you graduate?

④ I graduated in 1980.

⑤ So did I! We attended the same university, and we graduated in the same year.

3

① When were you in London?

② In September.

③ so was I! Where did you stay?

④ At the Hilton Hotel.

⑤ So did I! We were in London in the same month, and we stayed at the same hotel.

Grammar: the same + n; so in rejoinder; what + n in exclamation
Expression: making comparisons; expressing surprise/coincidence

Talk to the World

117 The Same or Different?

A: _____ I hear you have <u>a new car</u>. ①
B: _____ Yes. <u>It</u>'s almost the same as <u>my old car</u>. ②
Is <u>it</u>? ③
<u>It has a different engine</u>, but <u>the interior is the same</u>. ④
Yes, it does sound like they are similar. ⑤
Well, <u>it</u> is a little bit different from <u>my old car</u>, but they are a lot alike. ⑥

① a new pair of shoes	① a new coat	① a new bicycle
② they/--C--'s shoes	② it/--C--'s coat	② it/my old bicycle
④ the heels are different/ they have the same design on the toe	④ it's the same style/it has different buttons	④ it's the same kind of bicycle/the handlebars are different
⑥ they/--C--'s shoes	⑥ it/--C--'s coat	⑥ it/my old bicycle

Grammar: different (from), the same (as), similar, alike; emphatic do
Expression: making comparisons; describing objects

118 Causes

A: _____ I don't feel well this morning, so I'm not going to go to class. ①

B: _____ You're not going to go to class? ②

No. Are you? ③

No. ④

Why? ⑤

I'm not going to go because I didn't do my homework. ⑥

① I don't like ------/I'm not going to go to her party	① I missed the bus this morning/I didn't go to school	① I don't have any money/ I'm not going on the class trip
⑥ I'm not going to go/I'm busy Saturday evening	⑥ I didn't go to school/I overslept	⑥ I'm not going/I don't like class trips

Grammar: *so:* conj; *because;* clause of reason; clause of result
Expression: requesting/stating reasons; indicating/inquiring about causes; asking for/giving excuses

Talk to the World

119 Too Tired

A: _____   Let's go to a movie. ①
B: _____   No. I'm too tired to go to a movie. ②
           Then let's visit --C--. ③
           Visit --C--? ④
           Yes. Let's visit --C--. ⑤
           No. It's too late now to visit --C--. And besides, I'm too tired. ⑥

▼1

① make a cake
② to make a cake
③ go for a drive
⑥ to go for a drive

▼2

① go for a walk
② to go for a walk
③ go out for dinner
⑥ to go out for dinner

▼3

① play a game
② to play a game
③ go shopping
⑥ to go shopping

Grammar: too + adj + to v; let's with suggestions; besides: adv
Expression: stating reasons; offering suggestions

Talk to the World

120 Where Were You?

A: _____ Where were you at about 10:30 yesterday morning? ①
B: _____ At 10:30? I was <u>at the library studying</u>. ②
Where were you yesterday afternoon? ③
Let's see . . . I was <u>at a restaurant having lunch with a friend</u>. Why? ④
I called you five times yesterday, and nobody answered. ⑤

▼1

② in the gym playing basketball

④ on my way home from school

▼2

② in my office typing

④ at the barbershop getting a haircut

▼3

② outside walking my dog

④ at the bank waiting for a friend

Grammar: cont: past
Expression: reporting past events/activities

Talk to the World

121 A Telephone Conversation

A: _____   I'll be arriving <u>at 1PM</u>. ①

B: _____   OK. Then I'll meet you in the arrival lounge. I'll be <u>waiting next to the rent-a-car counter</u>. ②

OK. I'll look for you there. I'll be <u>carrying a blue suitcase</u>. ③

I'll be <u>wearing a navy blue blazer, and I wear glasses</u>. ④

Good. I'm looking forward to meeting you. ⑤

1

① at noon
② standing at the north exit
③ wearing a gray suit
④ wearing a red shirt

2

① on flight 022
② standing by the information booth
③ carrying a blue carry-on bag
④ holding a newspaper

3

① at 6:30
② waiting by the main entrance
③ wearing sunglasses
④ holding an umbrella

Grammar: *will* (promise/assurance): modal; cont: future
Expression: describing people; indicating future intentions; talking about clothing

Talk to the World

122 Tomorrow

A: _____ Just think. At this time tomorrow we'll be <u>in Honolulu.</u> ①

B: _____ Yes. And we'll be <u>on the beach sipping cool drinks.</u> ②

On the beach sipping cool drinks? ③
Or maybe we'll be <u>playing tennis.</u> ④
Not me. I'll be <u>playing golf!</u> ⑤

▼1

① at the ski resort

② in the lodge sitting in front of the fireplace

④ making new friends

⑤ skiing

▼2

① in the mountains

② hiking on a mountain trail

④ picking mountain flowers

⑤ fishing

▼3

① in Paris

② shopping in a department store

④ sitting at a sidewalk cafe

⑤ visiting the art galleries

Grammar: *will* (prediction): modal; cont: future
Expression: anticipating events; expressing conviction/likelihood

Talk to the World

123 Fond Memories

A: _____ At this time last year we were <u>in Honolulu</u>. ①
B: _____ That's right. It doesn't seem that long ago, does it? ②
<u>We were relaxing on the beach at Waikiki</u>. ③
And <u>you were complaining about the heat</u>. ④
<u>We had a good time</u>. ⑤
Yes, we did. ⑥

▼ 1

① in Switzerland

③ We were freezing on the ski slopes.

④ we were going to parties at the ski lodge

▼ 2

① in New York

③ We were visiting museums.

④ we were trying to find our way around the city

▼ 3

① in school

③ We were studying for exams.

④ you were going to football games every weekend

Grammar: cont: past; *that:* adv of degree
Expression: reporting past events/activities

124 Tomorrow's Activities

A: _____ What shall we do tomorrow? ①
B: _____ I don't know. What would you like to do? ②
Let's <u>go to a movie</u>, shall we? ③
You'd like to <u>go to a movie</u>? That's OK with me. ④

▼1 ▼2 ▼3

| ③ play tennis | ③ go to the beach | ③ stay home

Grammar: shall, would like to: modals; what: wh-ques, with modal; shall: in tag ques with let's; let's in a suggestion
Expression: offering/soliciting suggestions; making plans; expressing agreement

Talk to the World

125 Permission

A: _____ May <u>I ride to school with you</u>? ①
B: _____ Sure. ②

Thanks. Can <u>my friend ride with us</u> too? ③

You can ride to school with me, but I'm afraid I can't let <u>your friend ride with us</u>. ④

That's OK. ⑤

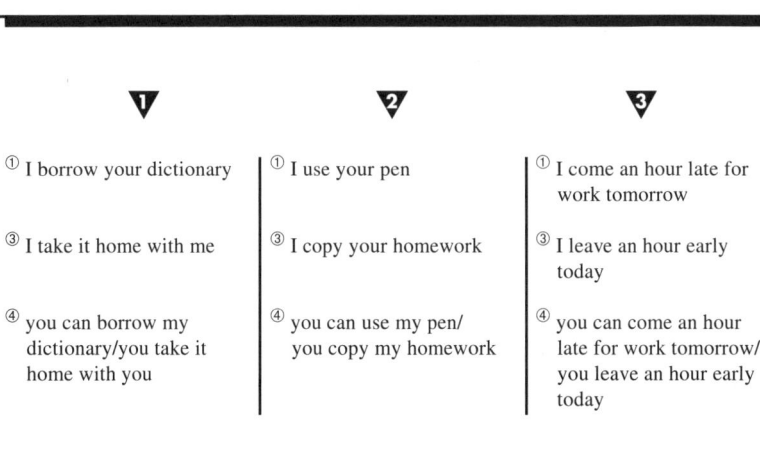

▼1	▼2	▼3
① I borrow your dictionary	① I use your pen	① I come an hour late for work tomorrow
③ I take it home with me	③ I copy your homework	③ I leave an hour early today
④ you can borrow my dictionary/you take it home with you	④ you can use my pen/ you copy my homework	④ you can come an hour late for work tomorrow/ you leave an hour early today

---

Grammar: *can, may* (permission): modals; *let* (allow) + obj + v; *with* (prep) + obj
Expression: requesting/granting/declining permission

Talk to the World

126 Happy to Help

A: _____ Can I help you with <u>the cleaning</u>? ①
B: _____ Oh, . . . thank you, but I think I can manage. ②
OK. ③
But could you help me <u>wash the dishes</u>? ④
Sure. I'd be glad to. ⑤

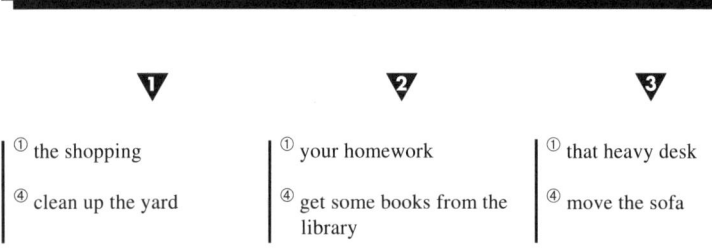

① the shopping
④ clean up the yard

① your homework
④ get some books from the library

① that heavy desk
④ move the sofa

Grammar: *can* (offer), *could* (request), *would* + *be* + adj + *to* v: modals; v (*help*) + obj + v
Expression: requesting/offering/declining assistance

Talk to the World

127 Work to Do

A: _____ Well, do we have anything left to do? ①
B: _____ Did you <u>make hotel reservations</u>? ②
No. ③
Well, then we have to do that. ④
And we have to <u>stop the newspaper</u>. ⑤
That's right. We need to <u>stop the newspaper</u>. ⑥

| ② get the travelers checks | ② arrange the room for the meeting | ② vacuum the carpet |
| ⑤ confirm our flight reservations | ⑤ call the catering service | ⑤ take out the garbage |

Grammar: need to; have to: modal; have + obj + to v
Expression: expressing necessity

128 Popular Sights

A: _____ You can't miss <u>the art museum</u>. That's really interesting. ①

B: _____ Yes, I know. I'm going there. ②

And you have to see <u>the university</u>. ③

<u>The university</u>. Is that a popular tourist attraction? ④

Oh, yes. <u>The university</u> is a must. ⑤

▼1

① the historical museum
③ Lake ------

▼2

① the capitol
③ the new ------ Building

▼3

① ------ Park
③ the new shopping mall

Grammar: *can* (neg form expressing necessity), *have to* (recommendations): modal; n: *a must*
Expression: expressing necessity; making recommendations; urging someone to do something

Talk to the World

129 It Must Be Hers

A: _____ Is this --C--'s jacket or --D--'s? ①

B: _____ That's not --D--'s jacket. His jacket has a hood. ②

Then it must be --C--'s. ③

Yes. It's not --D--'s jacket, so it has to be --C--'s. ④

▼ 1

① purse
② She has a green purse.

▼ 2

① tennis racket
② He doesn't have an aluminum racket.

▼ 3

① camera
② He has a cheap camera.

Grammar: *must* (deduction), *have to* (deduction, certainty): modal; *so:* conj + result clause; yes/no-ques, or-ques with *be*

Expression: identifying/describing objects; expressing certainty/deduction

130 Should and Had Better

A: _____ Are you going to take Chinese or chemistry next term? ①

B: _____ I don't know. What do you think I should do? ②

I think you should take Chinese. ③

Do you? But I'm very bad at foreign languages. ④

Well, then you'd better take chemistry. ⑤

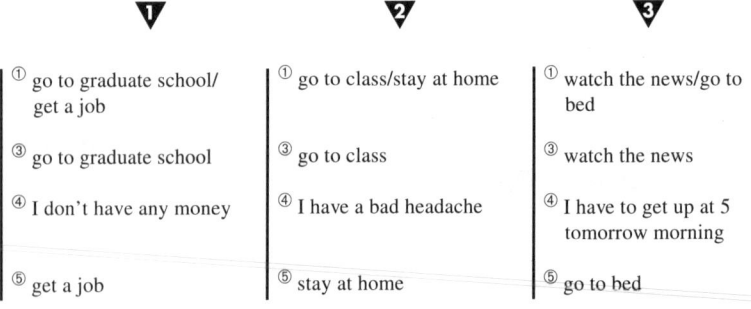

① go to graduate school/ get a job

③ go to graduate school

④ I don't have any money

⑤ get a job

① go to class/stay at home

③ go to class

④ I have a bad headache

⑤ stay at home

① watch the news/go to bed

③ watch the news

④ I have to get up at 5 tomorrow morning

⑤ go to bed

Grammar: *should* contrasted with *had better:* modal; *wh-*ques: *that-*clause
Expression: soliciting/offering advice; making a choice

Talk to the World

131 An Idea

A: _____ I'm going to go to Hawaii this winter. ①
B: _____ That ought to be fun. ②
You ought to come too. ③
I ought to. ④
Why don't you? ⑤
No, I really should save my money. ⑥

1
① study Russian next term
② difficult
③ study it
⑥ take a physics course

2
① see a movie about China this afternoon
② interesting
③ see it
⑥ go to the library and study

3
① go to ------'s party tonight
② exciting
③ go
⑥ go to bed early tonight

Grammar: *should, ought to*: modal
Expression: expressing obligation; expressing likelihood; offering advice

132 Why, Then?

A: _____ Did you get hurt? ①
B: _____ No. ②
         Why are you crying then? ③
         I . . . . ④
         If you didn't get hurt, why are you crying? ⑤
         ------ took my bicycle. ⑥

① Were you in an accident?	① Are those your sunglasses?	① Are you going to eat now?
③ Why were you late for class then?	③ What are you doing with them then?	③ Why are you fixing sandwiches then?
⑤ If you weren't in an accident, why were you late for class?	⑤ If those aren't your sunglasses, what are you doing with them?	⑤ If you aren't going to eat now, why are you fixing sandwiches?
⑥ I overslept.	⑥ ------ lent them to me.	⑥ These sandwiches are for you.

Grammar: *then*; *if*-clause with clause of reason
Expression: requesting/stating reasons; consequences

Talk to the World

133 A Full Schedule

A: _____ ------ is really busy. She <u>jogs every day</u>, she<u>'s taking judo lessons</u>, she . . . ①

B: _____ When does she find time <u>to jog</u>? ②

After she <u>comes home from work</u>. ③

When does she have time <u>to practice judo</u>? ④

She <u>practices judo</u> before she <u>eats breakfast</u>. She's busy! ⑤

1	2	3
① visits her mother every day/is studying for an exam	① is writing a book/is taking dancing lessons	① works part-time at a store/does volunteer work
② to visit her mother	② to write	② to work at the store
③ returns home from school	③ gets up in the morning	③ finishes her classes in the afternoon
④ to study	④ to practice dancing	④ to do volunteer work
⑤ goes to school	⑤ goes to bed at night	⑤ has lunch on Sundays

---

Grammar: *after/before:* (conj) clause of time with simple pres tense; simple pres tense (habitual); *have/find time* + *to* v; simple pres tense contrasted with pres cont

Expression: describing daily/customary/habitual activities; describing a sequence of events

134 Two Jobs

A: _____   ------ has two jobs now. ①
B: _____   She's working two jobs? What does she do? ②
In the morning she <u>works at a hospital</u>, and in the evening she <u>teaches English</u>. ③
Which job does she like better? ④
<u>Teaching</u>. She doesn't like <u>working at the hospital</u> at all. ⑤

③ does research/repairs cars	③ works at a library/washes dishes	③ does yard work/edits a newspaper
⑤ doing research/repairing cars	⑤ working at the library/washing dishes	⑤ doing yard work/editing the newspaper

---

Grammar: adv: compar *better;* *which* + n: *wh*-ques; simple pres t(habitual); v*(like)* + v-*ing*
Expression: making comparisons; talking about occupations; describing daily activities

Talk to the World

135 Now and Then

A: _____ Do you like <u>to cook</u>? ①
B: _____ No! I hate <u>to cook</u>. ②

Oh. ③

But I didn't use to hate <u>to cook</u>. I used to like it. ④

But you don't like <u>to cook</u> anymore? ⑤

No. Not at all. ⑥

▼**1** ▼**2** ▼**3**

| ① to play tennis | ① jazz | ① to study English

Grammar: *used to* + v customary past; *anymore:* adv
Expression: indicating preferences; reference to a former state or condition

136 Welcome News

A: _____ Aren't you glad that <u>our teacher is coming back</u>? ①
B: _____ Yes, I sure am. ②
I was happy to hear that <u>he's out of the hospital and feeling well again</u>. ③
Me too. ④

▼ 1

① it didn't rain today

③ they forecast nice weather all week

▼ 2

① the buses are in service again

③ the transportation strike is over

▼ 3

① ------ finally found a job

③ he likes the job too

Grammar: adj + *that*-clause; adj + *to* v + *that*-clause
Expression: expressing personal feelings

Talk to the World

137 A Good Story

A: _____ What's it about? ①

B: _____ It's about <u>a young couple</u>. ②

What happens? ③

<u>They fall in love and get married</u>. ④

Sounds interesting. Then what? ⑤

<u>She gets very ill</u>, and . . . ⑥

Don't tell me the ending! I want to see it. ⑦

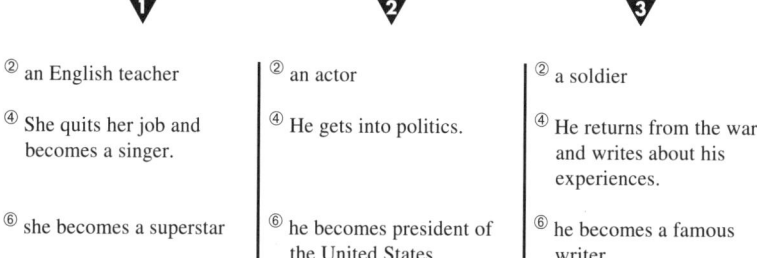

▼1

② an English teacher

④ She quits her job and becomes a singer.

⑥ she becomes a superstar

▼2

② an actor

④ He gets into politics.

⑥ he becomes president of the United States

▼3

② a soldier

④ He returns from the war and writes about his experiences.

⑥ he becomes a famous writer

Grammar: simple pres tense (historical pres)
Expression: relating a story; describing a sequence of events

-137-   Talk to the World

138 No Free Time

A: _____   Are you going to go to ------'s wedding on Saturday? ①
B: _____   No. I can't. I have to go out of town. ②
         You're always busy, aren't you? ③
         I know. I couldn't be at my son's graduation last week either. ④
         Why? ⑤
         Oh, I had to meet a client at the airport. ⑥

▼1

① watch the soccer game on TV tonight

② help my daughter study for her test

④ go to ------'s party yesterday

⑥ work overtime

▼2

① study tonight for the test

② prepare for my seminar

④ go to my English class this morning

⑥ go to the dentist

▼3

① have lunch with your boss today

② go to the bank at lunchtime

④ attend the meeting this morning

⑥ take an express package to the post office

Grammar: *have to, had to, can, could* (past of *can*): modal
Expression: expressing ability/necessity

Talk to the World

139 A Name in the News

A: _____ Didn't you use to know a ------ ------*? ①
B: _____ Yes. <u>She</u> used to <u>be in my class</u>. ②
Did you know <u>her</u> well? ③
Pretty well. We used to <u>play tennis together</u>. Why? ④
<u>Her</u> picture is in the newspaper here. <u>She's running for mayor in the next election.</u> ⑤

* given and family names

② live next door to me	② work with me	② be my boss
④ get together and play golf sometimes	④ share an office together	④ have lunch together sometimes
⑤ She published a mystery novel last week.	⑤ He's the new president of the university.	⑤ He joined the space program yesterday.

Grammar: *used to* + v customary past
Expression: reference to a former state or condition

Talk to the World

140 Might and Might Not

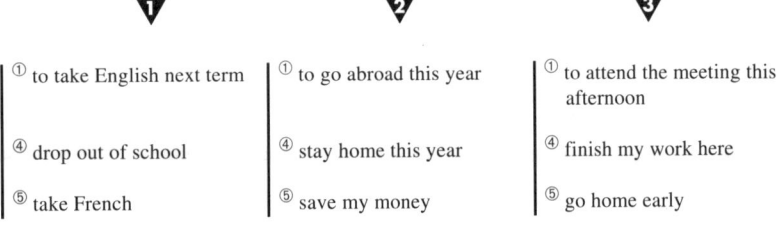

A: _____ Are you going <u>to class this evening</u>? ①

B: _____ I don't know. I might not. ②

Why? ③

I may not be able to. I might have to <u>work overtime</u>.

Do you think you will? ④

I don't know. Maybe I'll <u>go to a movie</u> instead. ⑤

▼❶ ▼❷ ▼❸

① to take English next term | ① to go abroad this year | ① to attend the meeting this afternoon

④ drop out of school | ④ stay home this year | ④ finish my work here

⑤ take French | ⑤ save my money | ⑤ go home early

Grammar: *may, might, be able to, have to* (combinations *may/might + be able to, may/might + have to*): modal; *maybe, instead:* adv
Expression: expressing possibility/ability/necessity

Talk to the World

141 Comparing Hotels

A: _____ Is <u>this</u> <u>an expensive hotel</u>? ①

B: _____ Compared with <u>the Grand Hotel</u> <u>it</u> is. ②

Hmm. ③

But there are <u>more expensive ones</u>. ④

▼1

① ------/an efficient secretary

② your secretary/she

④ more efficient secretaries

▼2

① that/an economical car

② my van/it

④ more economical cars

▼3

① this/a good restaurant

② the university cafeteria/it

④ better restaurants

Grammar: adj: compar adj + -er, more + adj; *compared with:* expression
Expression: making comparisons

142 On a Diet

A: _____ You're losing weight, aren't you? ①
B: _____ Yes, I'm on a diet. ②
Good for you. ③
I'm eating <u>less white bread</u> and <u>fewer potatoes</u>. And I eat more <u>green vegetables</u> now. ④
You look great. ⑤
Thanks. ⑥

| ④ less pie and cake/fewer sweets; more fish | ④ less ice cream/fewer bedtime snacks; more low-fat foods | ④ less spaghetti/fewer snacks between meals; more apples and oranges |

Grammar: quant: compar *more, less, fewer* + n
Expression: making comparisons; talking about food; expressing quantity

Talk to the World

143 Bigger, Not Better

A: _____   Is <u>your new car</u> as <u>roomy</u> as <u>your old car</u>? ①

B: _____   Yes. In fact <u>my new car</u> is a little bit <u>roomier</u> than <u>my old car</u>. ②

           Is <u>it</u>? ③

           Yes, but <u>my new car</u> isn't as <u>economical</u> as <u>my old car</u>. ④

▼1 ▼2 ▼3

| ① English 203/easy/English 180 | ① your daughter/bright/your son | ① the Grand Hotel/expensive/the President Hotel |
| ④ English 203/interesting/English 180 | ④ my daughter/studious/my son | ④ the Grand Hotel/comfortable/the President |

Grammar: adj: compar *as* + adj + *as*; adj + *-er* + *than*, *more* + adj + *than*; *a little bit*: adv of degree
Expression: making comparisons

144 More and Less

A: _____ Is that an interesting novel? ①

B: _____ Well, ... there are more interesting novels. ②

I see. ③

But there are a lot of less interesting ones too. ④

Hmm. ⑤

▼1

① Is your class easy?

② easier classes

④ more difficult classes

▼2

① Is ------ a good student?

② better students

④ worse students

▼3

① Is that restaurant expensive?

② more expensive restaurants

④ less expensive restaurants

Grammar: adj: compar adj + -er + than, more + adj, less + adj
Expression: making comparisons

145 Different Opinions

A: _____ I think <u>Professor --C-- is the most interesting lecturer at this university</u>. ①

B: _____ I think <u>he's the least interesting</u>. ②

Really? <u>Less interesting than Professor --D--</u>? ③

Well, no. <u>More interesting</u> than that. ④

① --C-- is the brightest student in our class	① this is the most beautiful building on campus	① Mr. ------ is the easiest teacher at our school
② the dullest	② the least beautiful	② the most difficult
③ Duller than --D--?	③ Less beautiful than the library?	③ More difficult than Mrs. ------?
④ brighter	④ more beautiful	④ easier

Grammar: adj: compar adj + -er, more/less + adj; super adj + -est, most/least + adj
Expression: making comparisons; ranking things

Talk to the World

146 Products

A: _____ Did <u>the U.S.</u> <u>harvest</u> as <u>much wheat</u> last year as the year before? ①

B: _____ No, it <u>harvested</u> <u>less</u> last year. ②

Did it <u>make</u> as <u>many cars</u> <u>in 1987</u> as <u>in 1986</u>? ③

No, <u>fewer</u>. But they <u>made</u> <u>more cars</u> <u>in 1988</u> than <u>in 1986</u>. ④

▼1 ▼2 ▼3

① Japan/export/many TV sets

② exported/fewer

③ import/much oil/in July/in June

④ less; imported/more oil/in August/in June

① Australia/export/much coal

② exported/less

③ mine/much iron ore/in 1985/in 1984

④ less; mined/more iron/in 1986/in 1984

① Germany/manufacture/many trucks

② manufactured/fewer

③ produce/much lumber/in 1984/in 1983

④ less; produced/more lumber/in 1985/in 1983

Grammar: quant: compar *less, fewer, more* + n + *than, as much/many* + n + *as;* n: noncount
Expression: making comparisons; expressing quantity

Talk to the World

147 Carefully

A: _____   --C-- drives very carefully, doesn't she? ①

B: _____   She doesn't drive as carefully as --D--. ②

She doesn't? ③

No. I agree that --C-- drives carefully, but I think --D-- drives more carefully. ④

① This computer runs very quietly, doesn't it?

② quietly/the other computer

④ this computer runs quietly/the other computer runs more quietly

① --C-- can swim very well, can't he?

② well/--D--

④ --C-- can swim well/ --D-- can swim better

① Your new secretary works very hard, doesn't she?

② hard/my previous secretary

④ my new secretary works hard/my previous secretary worked harder

---

Grammar: adv: compar adv + -er + than, more + adv + than, as + adv + as
Expression: making comparisons

148 World Traveler

A: _____ Have you been to <u>Acapulco</u>? ①
B: _____ Yes, I was there <u>last winter</u>. ②
Have you ever been to <u>Hong Kong</u>? ③
Yes, I've been there too. I was there <u>in April</u>. ④
How about <u>Iceland</u>? ⑤
<u>Iceland</u>? No, I haven't been there. ⑥

▼1 ▼2 ▼3

① Lagos	① Montréal	① Kenya
② last year	② in 1984	② in December
③ Brazil	③ Athens	③ Bangkok
④ in 1985	④ last July	④ in August
⑤ Tokyo	⑤ New Zealand	⑤ New York

Grammar: be: pres pfct with be; ever: adv in yes/no-ques (pfct); pres pfct vs simple past tense
Expression: relating experience; expressing geographic location

Talk to the World

149 The Menu

A: _____ Have you ever had <u>the chicken pie</u> here? ①
B: _____ No, I haven't. Have you? ②
Yes, I have. ③
Is <u>it</u> good? ④
Yes, <u>it</u> is. ⑤
How's <u>the tuna pie</u>? ⑥
I don't know. I haven't had <u>that</u>. ⑦

▼1
① the chow mein
⑥ the fried rice
⑦ that

▼2
① the chili
⑥ the enchiladas
⑦ them

▼3
① the pizza
⑥ the spaghetti
⑦ that

Grammar: *have:* pres pfct with *have; ever:* adv in *yes/no*-ques: pres pfct; short reply: pres pfct; *the:* art
Expression: talking about food; relating experience; soliciting/expressing an opinion

150 A Compliment

A: _____ That's a nice <u>sweater</u>. Is it new? ①

B: _____ Thank you. No, I've had this for some time. ②

How long have you had it? ③

For <u>two months</u>. I <u>got this for a present two months ago</u>. ④

Hmm. It's nice. ⑤

Thank you. ⑥

▼ ❶

① jacket

④ about a year; bought it about a year ago

▼ ❷

① bicycle

④ one month; received that as a gift a month ago

▼ ❸

① teapot

④ several years; got that from ------ for my birthday several years ago

---

Grammar: *have*: pres pfct with *have*; *ago*: adv of time with past tense; *how long* (time); *wh*-ques, pres pfct

Expression: paying a compliment; indicating quantity of time; admiring something

Talk to the World

151 A Little Longer

A: _____ How much longer are you going to <u>be staying here</u>? ①
B: _____ Until <u>I finish typing this letter</u>. ②
How long will it be before <u>you finish typing that letter</u>? ③
<u>Just a little while</u>. Why? ④
Just curious. ⑤

▼ 1

① be watching TV
② this program is over
③ that program is over
④ About ten more minutes.

▼ 2

① be studying here
② they close the library
③ they close the library
④ It closes in an hour.

▼ 3

① be lying in bed
② I feel like getting up
③ you feel like getting up
④ A few minutes.

Grammar: cont: be going to + be + v-ing; v(finish) + v-ing; before, until: conj with time clause; how long, how much longer: wh-ques
Expression: expressing duration of time; indicating quantity of time

152 A Word of Advice

A: _____ What are you going to do <u>this evening</u>? ①
B: _____ <u>I'm going out to eat with ------</u>. ②
        Whatever you do, <u>don't go to that new restaurant across the street</u>. ③
        Why? ④
        <u>I ate there last night and the food was terrible</u>. ⑤

▼1

① this weekend

② I'm going to visit ------.

③ don't tell her about my party

⑤ She's not invited.

▼2

① tonight

② I don't know. I think I'll go to a movie.

③ don't go to see ------

⑤ It got a bad review in the newspaper.

▼3

① after work today

② I'm going to call my brother in Paris.

③ don't call before 8 o'clock

⑤ It's cheaper after 8PM.

Grammar: *whatever:* pron
Expression: offering advice; making recommendations

Talk to the World

153 A Dream

A: _____   I had a <u>strange</u> dream last night. ①
B: _____   What did you dream? ②
          That <u>I climbed to the top of Mt. Everest</u>. ③
          And then what happened? ④
          <u>At the top of the mountain I met several of my friends</u>. ⑤
          Then what? ⑥
          Then my alarm clock went off and I woke up. ⑦

---

① funny

③ I was late for my wedding

⑤ My bride got very angry.

① interesting

③ I gave a speech at the United Nations

⑤ I met many important people.

① scary

③ I was on a sinking ship

⑤ I jumped overboard and started to swim.

Grammar: simple past tense
Expression: describing a sequence of events

154 First Things First

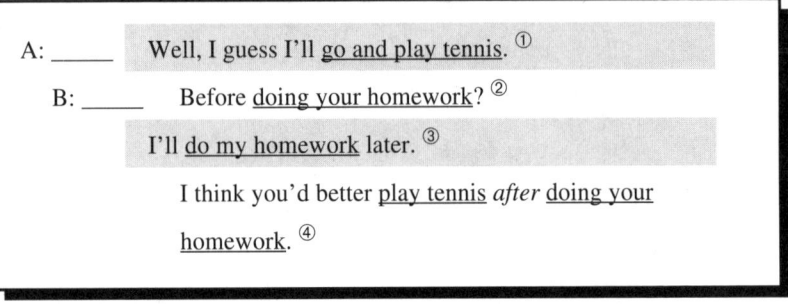

A: _____ Well, I guess I'll <u>go and play tennis</u>. ①
B: _____ Before <u>doing your homework</u>? ②
I'll <u>do my homework</u> later. ③
I think you'd better <u>play tennis</u> *after* <u>doing your homework</u>. ④

▼1

① sit down and watch TV

② washing the dishes

③ wash the dishes

▼2

① go skiing

② cleaning your room

③ clean my room

▼3

① go downtown and do some shopping

② helping your father

③ help my father

Grammar: *before/after* + v-*ing*: adv of time; *will, had better*: modal; v*(guess, think)* + *that*-cl
Expression: describing a sequence of events; offering advice; directing someone to do something

Talk to the World

155 International Trade

A: _____ Which country exported the most steel in 1986? ①

B: _____ Korea. ②

Which country exported the least? ③

The least? France. ④

Which country exported the most cars? ⑤

In 1986? Japan. And Hungary exported the fewest. ⑥

▼1

① made the most ships in 1979

② Japan.

③ made the fewest

④ The fewest? India.

⑤ imported the most rubber

⑥ In 1979? The United States. Malaysia/the least

▼2

① produced the most wheat last year

② Canada.

③ produced the least

④ The least? Japan.

⑤ exported the most apples

⑥ Last year? China. the United States/the fewest

▼3

① had the most rainfall in 1987

② Indonesia.

③ had the least

④ The least? Kuwait.

⑤ had the most earthquakes

⑥ In 1987? China. Great Britain/the fewest

Grammar: quant: compar *the most, the least, the fewest* (+ noun)
Expression: making comparisons

Talk to the World

156 Since When?

A: _____ <u>Are you still practicing the violin every day</u>? ①
B: _____ No, not anymore. ②
Oh, <u>you're not</u>? ③
No, not since <u>I sprained my wrist</u>. ④
Oh, <u>you sprained your wrist</u>? ⑤
Yes, <u>I</u> did. ⑥

▼1

① Do you still like your English class?

③ you don't

④ I failed the first test

▼2

① Are you still planning to quit your job?

③ you aren't

④ I got a raise

▼3

① Does ------ still hope to get married this spring?

③ she doesn't

④ she broke up with her fiancé

Grammar: *since*: conj with clause of time;   *still, anymore*: adv of time
Expression: expressing duration of time; expressing continuity

157 Not Yet

A: _____ You haven't <u>cleaned your room</u> yet, have you? ①
B: _____ No, not yet. ②
When are you going to <u>clean it</u>? ③
I'll <u>clean it</u> after I've <u>watched the news</u>. ④

▼1

① mailed my letters

③ mail them

④ mail them/finished your report

▼2

① washed the kitchen windows

③ wash them

④ wash them/rested awhile

▼3

① called the travel agency

③ call them

④ call them/fixed lunch

Grammar: pres pfct with reg v; *yet:* adv of time; tag ques: pres pfct; *after:* conj with pres pfct
Expression: relating experience

158 Passing Time

A: _____ What time does your flight leave? ①
B: _____ It doesn't leave until 3:30. ②
Not until 3:30? ③
No. ④
Then let's go into that coffee shop until it's time to board the plane. ⑤
OK. ⑥

▼ 1 ▼ 2 ▼ 3

① When does the new semester start?

② it doesn't start/the 21st

⑤ let's go camping/the semester starts

---

① When is this movie going to end?

② it doesn't end/9:30

⑤ I'm going to wait in the lobby/it ends

---

① What time do we have to leave?

② we don't have to leave/ 2:30

⑤ I want to watch TV/we have to go

Grammar: until: prep/conj; adv of time
Expression: discussing scheduled events/activities; indicating the time of activities

Talk to the World

159 Duties

A: ____ Well, ... I'm going to <u>watch TV</u>. ①
B: ____ <u>Make your bed</u> first, will you please! ②
　　　　I've already <u>made my bed</u>. ③
　　　　Have you <u>done your homework</u>? ④
　　　　I've just finished <u>doing it</u>. ⑤
　　　　Oh, ... OK, then. ⑥

▼1

① go outside
② put away your toys
③ put away my toys
④ hung up your clothes
⑤ hanging them up

▼2

① invite some friends over
② do your English assignment
③ done my assignment
④ written your book report
⑤ writing it

▼3

① make a cake
② clean up the mess in your room
③ cleaned up my room
④ washed the dishes
⑤ washing them

Grammar: pres pfct (irreg v); *already:* adv; *just:* adv with pres pfct; v*(finish)* + v-*ing*; imper: strong request
Expression: relating experience; directing someone to do something

Talk to the World

160 Lucky

A: _____ How would you like to have to <u>get up at 5:30 every morning</u> like --C-- does? ①

B: _____ He's lucky he doesn't have to <u>work nights</u> like --D-- does. ②

Oh, really? ③

I wouldn't mind <u>getting up at 5:30 every morning</u>, but I wouldn't want to have to <u>work nights</u>. ④

Me neither. ⑤

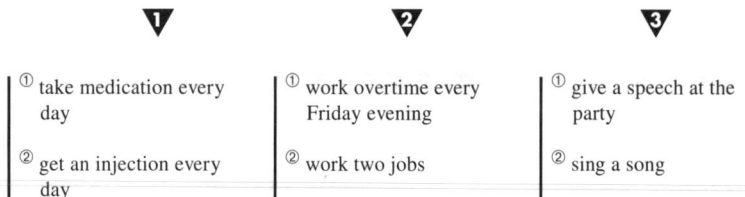

▼1
① take medication every day
② get an injection every day

▼2
① work overtime every Friday evening
② work two jobs

▼3
① give a speech at the party
② sing a song

Grammar: *have to*: modal with *want to*, *would like to*; *how*: *wh-*ques, with *would like to* + v; *like (as)*: conj; *would mind* + v-ing
Expression: making comparisons; expressing necessity/obligation

Talk to the World

161 Experiences

A: _____   What's it like <u>to ride in a helicopter</u>? ①
B: _____   I don't know. I've never <u>ridden in a helicopter</u>.
          Ask ------. ②
          Has she <u>ridden in a helicopter</u>? ③
          I don't know for sure, but I think she has. ④

▼1

① to live in a small town
② lived in a small town

▼2

① to work in a department store
② worked in a department store

▼3

① to drive in New York
② driven in New York

Grammar: pres pfct; *never:* adv of frequency with pfct; *what's it like + to* v: *wh-*ques
Expression: relating experience

Talk to the World

162 A First Time

A: _____ Where did you <u>go for lunch today</u>? ①
B: _____ To ------. That's really <u>a nice restaurant</u>. ②
Yes, it is. Hadn't you been there before? ③
No, I hadn't. Have you? ④
Yes, I've been there several times. And I agree with you. It is <u>a nice restaurant</u>. ⑤

▼1

① spend your vacation

② In Paris; a beautiful city

▼2

① go Saturday night

② To ------ Park; a nice park

▼3

① buy your new coat

② At ------; an incredible store

Grammar: *be:* past pfct; pres pfct contrasted with past pfct; *before:* adv with *yes/no*-ques: past pfct
Expression: relating experience

Talk to the World

163 Ordinary Activities

A: _____ Have you ever <u>taken the bus to work</u>? ①
B: _____ Yes, I have. Why? ②
I <u>took the bus to work this morning</u>. ③
Hadn't you ever <u>taken the bus to work</u> before? ④
Oh, I'd <u>taken the bus to work</u> before, but I hadn't <u>taken it</u> in a long time. ⑤

▼1 ▼2 ▼3

① eaten in the school cafeteria	① used the language lab	① watched the 11PM news
③ ate there this afternoon	③ used it yesterday	③ watched it last night
⑤ eaten there before/eaten there	⑤ used it before/used it	⑤ watched it before/watched it

---

Grammar: past pfct: reg, irreg v; pres pfct vs past pfct; *before:* adv with past pfct; *yes/no-*ques: pfct; *in a long time:* adv of time
Expression: relating experience

164 That's News to Me

A: _____ Did you know that ------ has a new car, and he's going to drive across the country next week? ①

B: _____ I thought he was starting a new job next week. ②

I don't know. ③

Well, I knew he had a new car, but I didn't know he was going to drive across the country. That's news to me. ④

① is graduating from college next week/he's going to get married	① is failing English/she's going to drop out of school	① is selling his house/he's going to move to Germany and live there
② he was going to travel for a year	② she hired an English tutor	② he was studying French
④ he was graduating from college next week/he was going to get married	④ she was failing English/she was going to drop out of school	④ he was selling his house/he was going to move to Germany and live there

Grammar: v(know) + that-clause: simple past tense, past cont; that-clause in yes/no-ques
Expression: indicating intentions; talking about an acquaintance

Talk to the World

165 At the Supermarket

A: _____ My wife <u>said</u> to get some <u>eggs</u>. ①

B: _____ Just <u>eggs</u>? ②

Ah, let's see . . . <u>apples</u> . . . . ③

She <u>told you</u> to get some <u>apples</u>? ④

No. She <u>told me</u> not to get any. We have <u>apples</u>. Let's see . . . . ⑤

▼1

① told me/bread
③ meat
④ said/meat
⑤ told me; meat

▼2

① said/orange juice
③ fish
④ told you/fish
⑤ said; fish

▼3

① told me/mushrooms
③ potatoes
④ told you/potatoes
⑤ said; potatoes

Grammar: *say, tell* in reported speech: imperative; v*(tell)* + obj + *to* + v
Expression: reporting requests/instructions; talking about food

166 Exports and Imports

A: _____ Is coal mined in Japan? ①
B: _____ Yes, but Japan also imports coal. ②
Where is it imported from? ③
From China, Australia, ... ④
What's exported by Japan? ⑤
Cars and high technology products are major exports. ⑥

▼1 ▼2 ▼3

① Is oil found in the United States?	① Is wheat grown in China?	① Are computers manufactured in Germany?
② the United States/oil	② China/wheat	② Germany/computers
④ the Middle East, South America	④ the United States, Canada	④ Japan, the Netherlands
⑤ the United States	⑤ China	⑤ Germany
⑥ agricultural products and chemicals	⑥ minerals and manufactured goods	⑥ machinery and communications equipment

Grammar: passive: pres tense; *by*: prep with adv of agent (passive)
Expression: activities performed

Talk to the World

167 What Am I?

A: _____ Are you <u>larger than a briefcase</u>? ①
B: _____ <u>Yes</u>. ②
Are you <u>used outdoors</u>? ③
<u>No, not usually</u>. ④
Are you <u>used in the home</u>? ⑤
<u>Sometimes</u>. ⑥
Are you <u>a typewriter</u>? ⑦
<u>No, I'm not</u>. ⑧

▼1

① larger than a desk

② No.

③ a CD player

④ No.

⑤ found in offices

⑥ Yes, often.

⑦ a file cabinet

⑧ No.

▼2

① a lamp

② No.

③ square in shape

④ Yes, sort of.

⑤ used by children

⑥ Sometimes.

⑦ heavy

⑧ No, not particularly.

▼3

① used by one person at a time

② Yes.

③ made of wood

④ No.

⑤ plugged in

⑥ Yes.

⑦ a word processor

⑧ Yes.

Grammar: passive: pres tense; by: prep with adv of agent (passive)
Expression: identifying/describing objects; activities performed

168 Putting Things Off

A: _____ You haven't <u>cut the grass</u> yet! ①
B: _____ No, I haven't. ②
        Did you <u>clean your room</u>? ③
        No, not yet. ④
        What have you been doing since <u>breakfast</u>? ⑤
        I've been <u>watching television</u>. ⑥

▼1

① washed the dishes

③ do your homework

⑤ you ate lunch

⑥ reading

▼2

① fixed your bicycle

③ feed the dog

⑤ you got home from school

⑥ listening to the radio

▼3

① gone to the store

③ finish your report

⑤ this morning

⑥ preparing for my trip

Grammar: pres pfct cont; *what:* wh-ques, pres pfct cont; *since:* prep/conj with adv of time; *yet:* adv with pres pfct
Expression: relating experience

169 Teacher and Parent

A: _____ ------ hasn't been <u>doing his homework</u>. ①
B: _____ <u>He</u> hasn't? ②
No, and <u>he</u> hasn't been <u>coming to class on time</u>. ③
Is <u>he</u> <u>paying attention in class</u>? ④
No, <u>he</u> isn't. ⑤

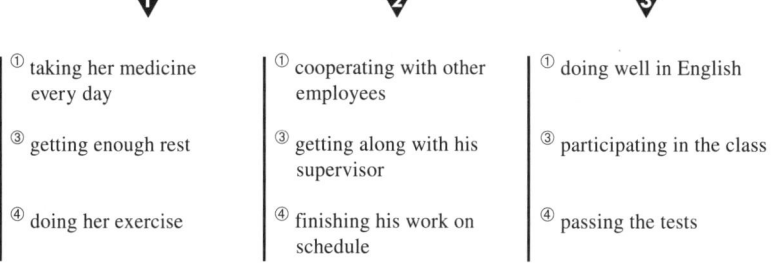

▼1

① taking her medicine every day

③ getting enough rest

④ doing her exercise

▼2

① cooperating with other employees

③ getting along with his supervisor

④ finishing his work on schedule

▼3

① doing well in English

③ participating in the class

④ passing the tests

Grammar: pres pfct cont
Expression: relating experience

170 First Experiences

A: _____ Had you ever <u>had sushi</u> before <u>you went to Japan</u>? ①
B: _____ No, I hadn't. Why? ②
Oh, I was just wondering. ③
No, I'd never <u>had sushi</u> until <u>I went to Japan</u>. Have you ever <u>had sushi</u>? ④
No, I haven't. ⑤

① been hospitalized/you broke your leg

① been to the library/you started high school

① spoken to Mr. ------/he became our teacher

Grammar: past pfct; *before, until:* conj with past perfect
Expression: relating experience

171 Except for One Thing

A: _____ How's your new job? ①

B: _____ I like it, except that I have to get up so early. ②

Otherwise you like it? ③

Yes, except for that I like it. ④

Except for having to get up so early? ⑤

Yes. ⑥

① How's the weather here?	① How was your trip?	① How have you been?
② fine/it rains a lot	② great/I lost my passport	② fine/my eyes have been bothering me
③ it's OK	③ you had a good time	③ you've been OK
④ it's OK	④ I had a good time	④ I've been OK
⑤ the rain	⑤ losing your passport	⑤ the fact that your eyes have been bothering you

Grammar: clause of exception; *except (that)*: conj of exception; *except for*: prep; *otherwise*
Expression: expressing exception

Talk to the World

172 Please Guess

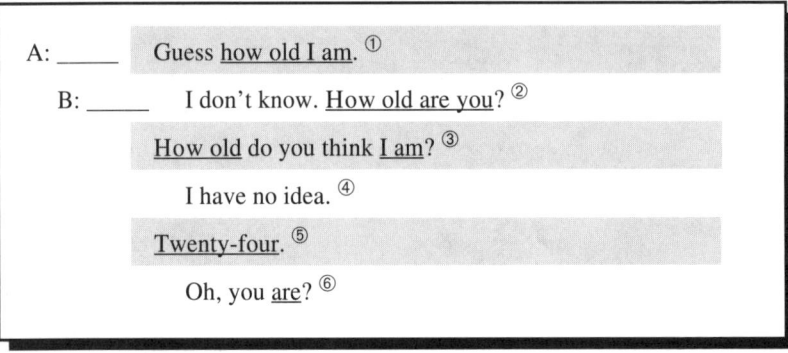

A: _____ Guess <u>how old I am</u>. ①
B: _____ I don't know. <u>How old are you</u>? ②
<u>How old</u> do you think <u>I am</u>? ③
I have no idea. ④
<u>Twenty-four</u>. ⑤
Oh, you <u>are</u>? ⑥

▼1

① where I was last night

② Where were you last night?

③ where/I was

⑤ I was in New York.

▼2

① what I'm going to do this weekend

② What are you going to do this weekend?

③ what/I'm going to do

⑤ I'm going to get married.

▼3

① how many brothers and sisters I have

② How many brothers and sisters do you have?

③ how many brothers and sisters/I have

⑤ Seven.

Grammar: embedded ques: *wh*-ques *(be, have)*; *that*-clause with *wh*-ques *(be, have)*
Expression: requesting information

173 Information, Please

A: _____ Can you tell me <u>what time the flight from Tokyo arrives</u>? ①

B: _____ <u>It arrives at 8:10</u>. ②

Thanks. Do you know if <u>it's on schedule</u>? ③

<u>Yes, it is</u>. ④

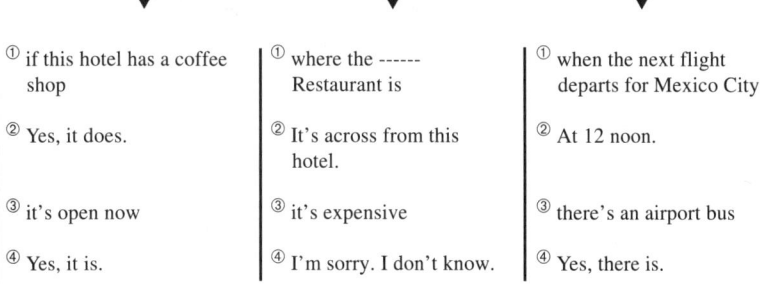

1
① if this hotel has a coffee shop
② Yes, it does.
③ it's open now
④ Yes, it is.

2
① where the ------ Restaurant is
② It's across from this hotel.
③ it's expensive
④ I'm sorry. I don't know.

3
① when the next flight departs for Mexico City
② At 12 noon.
③ there's an airport bus
④ Yes, there is.

Grammar: embedded ques: *wh*-ques, *yes/no*-ques
Expression: requesting/providing information

174 Looking Ahead

A: _____ What are you going to do after you graduate? ①

B: _____ That's pretty far off, but my ambition is <u>to become a doctor</u>. ②

You want to <u>become a doctor</u>? ③

Yes. What about you? ④

My hope is <u>to teach chemistry or work for a pharmaceutical company</u>. ⑤

1
- ② to go on to graduate school
- ⑤ to get a job at a law firm

2
- ② to become a journalist
- ⑤ to go abroad and learn a foreign language

3
- ② to be a teacher
- ⑤ to start my own company

Grammar: noun + *be* + *to* v; *what about* + n: *wh*-ques
Expression: expressing a hope; indicating plans

175 Relating News

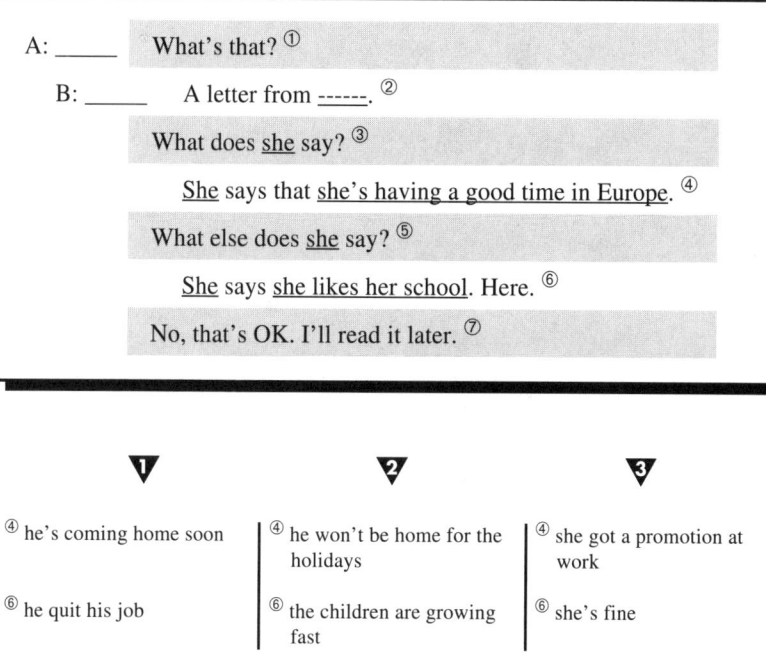

A: ____ What's that? ①
B: ____ A letter from ------. ②
What does <u>she</u> say? ③
<u>She</u> says that <u>she's having a good time in Europe</u>. ④
What else does <u>she</u> say? ⑤
<u>She</u> says <u>she likes her school</u>. Here. ⑥
No, that's OK. I'll read it later. ⑦

▼1

④ he's coming home soon

⑥ he quit his job

▼2

④ he won't be home for the holidays

⑥ the children are growing fast

▼3

④ she got a promotion at work

⑥ she's fine

Grammar: *say*: reported speech; v*(say)* + *that*-clause; *else:* in *wh*-ques, *what else*
Expression: reporting a conversation

Talk to the World

176 Which Person?

A: _____ Do you have a date again tonight? ①

B: _____ Yes. ②

Which one is it tonight? The one <u>with the red sports car</u>? ③

No. ④

The one <u>who has the yacht</u>? ⑤

No. ⑥

The one <u>that's the president of a computer company</u>? ⑦

No, a new one. ⑧

▼1   ▼2   ▼3

③ with the red beard	③ that has the Swiss chalet	③ with eight brothers and sisters
⑤ with the degree in physics	⑤ who has long curly hair	⑤ that has a job in New York
⑦ that's a doctor	⑦ who was here last night	⑦ with the black belt in karate

Grammar: rel clause with *be, have*; *who, that*: rel pron (subj of rel clause with *be, have*); reduced rel clause: *with* in prep phr; *one*: pron
Expression: identifying/describing people

Talk to the World

177 Telling a Friend

A: ____ ------ <u>still hasn't found his passport</u>, you know. ①
B: ____ No, I didn't know. He <u>hasn't</u>? ②
He didn't tell you that he <u>hadn't found it</u>? ③
No. He didn't say anything to me. And I talked to him just a few minutes ago. ④

▼1

① isn't coming to the wedding
② isn't
③ wasn't coming

▼2

① won't be able to join us tonight
② won't
③ wouldn't be able to

▼3

① had to quit his job
② did
③ had to

Grammar: *say, tell*: reported speech; v*(tell)* + obj + *that*-clause; two-word insep v: *talk to*
Expression: reporting a conversation

Talk to the World

178 Someone Intelligent

A: _____ I want a husband <u>who is intelligent</u>. How about you? ①

B: _____ Someone <u>intelligent</u>. And a person <u>from a good family</u>. ②

And someone <u>that has a good job</u>. ③

Right. And I want to marry someone <u>who doesn't smoke</u>. ④

Someone <u>who doesn't smoke</u>. Me too. ⑤

▼1

① who is interested in sports

② interested in sports; with a college degree

③ who is in good health

④ who has a house

▼2

① who is kind

② kind; with a good salary

③ who is from my home town

④ that likes children

▼3

① that is well-off

② well-off; with nice parents

③ who is not selfish

④ who likes to play tennis

Grammar: rel clause with *be, have*; *who, that:* rel pron (subj of rel clause with *be, have*); reduced rel clause with pron *someone* + adj; *with* in prep phr; *someone:* pron

Expression: describing people; making a choice

Talk to the World

179 Getting Used to Things

A: _____ How do you like your new job? ①

B: _____ It's all right. But I'm still not used to the short lunch breaks. ②

You're not used to the short lunch breaks? ③

No. ④

You'll get used to them. ⑤

Oh, I sure hope so. ⑥

▼1
① working here

② getting up at 5 o'clock every morning

⑤ it

▼2
① the weather here

② pushing my car out of the snow in winter

⑤ it

▼3
① having a baby at your house

② waking up with it in the middle of the night

⑤ it

Grammar: be/get used to + v-ing or noun; still: adv of time
Expression: telling what one is accustomed to/used to

Talk to the World

180 Wondering

A: _____ I hear ------ is getting married. ①
B: _____ That's what I heard too. ②
I wonder when the wedding is going to be. ③
I wonder if she's going to marry her boyfriend from California. ④
Do you think she'll invite us to the wedding? ⑤
I wonder. ⑥

▼1

① ------ got a promotion

③ if he got a big raise in salary

④ who his boss will be

⑤ he will have to travel in his new position

▼2

① ------ is going to go to graduate school

③ what he's going to study

④ if he's going to quit his job

⑤ he wants to be a teacher

▼3

① ------ is in the hospital

③ what's wrong

④ if we can visit him

⑤ he was in an accident

Grammar: embedded questions with *I wonder: yes/no-* and *wh-*questions
Expression: expressing interest; wondering about something

Talk to the World

181 See That Man?

A: _____ See that <u>man</u> <u>beside the door</u>? ①
B: _____ What <u>man</u>? ②
The one <u>wearing the blue sweater</u>. ③
The one <u>with the baseball cap</u>? ④
No. The one <u>who's facing us and wearing the blue sweater</u>. ⑤
Oh, . . . that <u>man</u>. What about <u>him</u>? ⑥
<u>He's the new director</u>. ⑦

▼1

① woman/in the corner over there
③ reading the newspaper
④ with the glasses
⑤ that's drinking coffee and reading the newspaper
⑦ She's my teacher.

▼2

① student/up by the teacher
③ holding the books
④ with the red jacket
⑤ who's looking out the window and holding the books
⑦ He's my roommate.

▼3

① girl/near the end of the line
③ talking to the boy in front of her
④ with the camera
⑤ wearing the raincoat and talking to the boy in front of her
⑦ She's pretty.

Grammar: rel clause(reduced); *who, that*: rel pron (subj of rel clause); pres participial phr; *what about* + obj: *wh*-ques
Expression: identifying/describing people

182 Some Time Ago

A: _____ When was the last time that you <u>played tennis</u>? ①
B: _____ Let's see . . . . I haven't <u>played tennis</u> for about <u>two years</u>. How long has it been since you <u>played</u>? ②
I haven't <u>played tennis</u> since <u>I got married</u>. ③
When was that? ④
<u>Ten years</u> ago. ⑤

▼ **1**

① were in New York

② been in New York/three years; were in New York

③ been in New York/I graduated from college

⑤ four years

▼ **2**

① rode a bicycle

② ridden a bicycle/six years; rode a bicycle

③ ridden a bicycle/I was in high school

⑤ a long time

▼ **3**

① bought a present for your wife

② bought a present for my wife/ten months; bought a present for your wife

③ bought a present for my wife/her birthday

⑤ three weeks

Grammar: pres pfct; *how long*: *wh*-ques with pres pfct; *since*: conj; *the last time*, *ago*: adv; *for*: prep with amount of time; cl of time
Expression: relating experience; expressing duration of time; indicating quantity of time

Talk to the World

183 Modern Art

A: _____ What do you think that is? ①
B: _____ I'd say it's <u>a man playing the piano . . . upside down</u>. ②
Ha! <u>A man playing the piano</u>. ③
Well, what would you say it is? ④
I don't know. <u>A woman dancing</u> maybe. I don't understand this modern art. ⑤

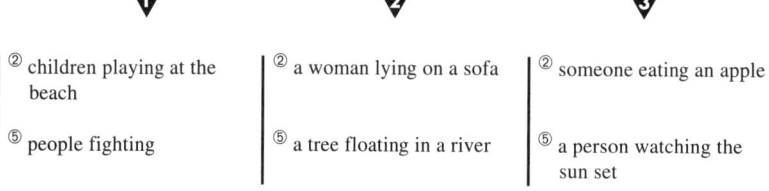

1
② children playing at the beach
⑤ people fighting

2
② a woman lying on a sofa
⑤ a tree floating in a river

3
② someone eating an apple
⑤ a person watching the sun set

Grammar: pres participial phr; *wh*-ques with *that*-clause
Expression: describing people/objects; expressing/soliciting an opinion

Talk to the World

184 Pointing Someone Out

A: _____ Look, ... there's <u>that handsome man</u> who I told you about. ①

B: _____ What <u>man</u>? ②

You know, ... the one <u>who runs that restaurant that I like to go to</u>. ③

Oh, is that <u>him</u>? The one <u>getting off the bus</u>? ④

Yes, that's <u>the man</u>. ⑤

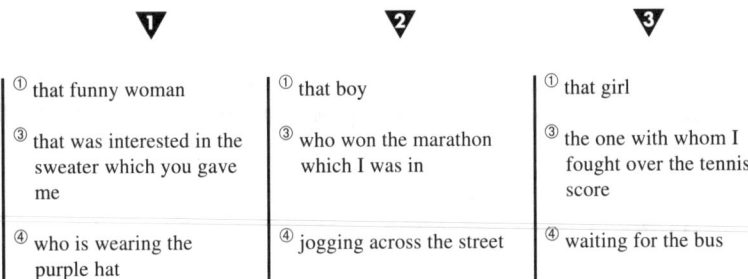

① that funny woman	① that boy	① that girl
③ that was interested in the sweater which you gave me	③ who won the marathon which I was in	③ the one with whom I fought over the tennis score
④ who is wearing the purple hat	④ jogging across the street	④ waiting for the bus

---

Grammar: rel clause; who, (whom), which, that: rel pron as obj of rel clause, preposition; pres participial phr
Expression: identifying people

Talk to the World

185 Good Advice

A: _____ ------ is going to <u>get a part-time job</u>. ①

B: _____ I know. I suggested it. ②

Oh, that was your idea? ③

Yes. I suggested that <u>he get a part-time job</u>, but I also recommended that <u>he not work at ------ Department Store</u>. ④

That's good. ⑤

▼1

① see a doctor about her foot

④ she see a doctor about her foot/she not go to Dr. ------

▼2

① buy a used car

④ he buy a used car/he not buy ------'s car

▼3

① go to a movie

④ she go to a movie/she not see ------

Grammar: *suggest, recommend* (v) + subjunctive
Expression: offering suggestions/advice

186 Interruption

A: _____ Sorry for the interruption. ①
B: _____ That's OK. ②
Now, <u>where did you say you wanted to go</u>? ③
To Mexico. ④
And did you say <u>you wanted to go in January</u>? ⑤
Yes. ⑥
OK. Just a moment, please. ⑦

▼1

③ what did you say your name was

④ ----- -----.

⑤ you lived on 7th Street

▼2

③ what size did you say you wanted

④ Size 10.

⑤ you preferred blue

▼3

③ how old did you say your little boy was

④ Three and a half.

⑤ he was wearing a blue sweater

Grammar: embedded ques: *wh*-ques; reported speech with ques
Expression: reporting a conversation; clarifying/confirming information; apologizing

187 Assistants

A: _____ Are you busy <u>this afternoon</u>? ①
B: _____ Yes. I have to <u>return these books to the library</u>. ②
Have <u>your husband return them</u> for you. ③
Are you serious? ④
I get <u>my husband to return mine</u>. ⑤
You're lucky. ⑥

1

① tonight
② do my homework
③ your sister do it
⑤ my sister to do mine

2

① right now
② prepare dinner
③ your daughter prepare it
⑤ my daughter to prepare ours

3

① on Saturday
② cut the grass
③ your children cut it
⑤ my children to cut ours

Grammar: causatives: *have* + obj + v, *get* + obj + *to* v
Expression: expressing causation; offering advice

188 Hurry!

A: _____ What time is it? ①

B: _____ It's <u>6:45</u>. ②

By the time we get to <u>the airport</u>, it'll <u>be 7:30</u>. ③

And <u>the plane</u> will have <u>left</u>. ④

I know. Let's hurry! ⑤

▼1

② almost 8:20

③ the theater/ten minutes after nine

④ the movie/begun

▼2

② a little after 8:30

③ school/8:50

④ class/already started

▼3

② 7:15

③ the party/10 o'clock

④ all the fun/ended

Grammar: *will*: modal; future pfct; clause of time; *by the time:* conj
Expression: anticipating events; indicating the time of activities; consequences

Talk to the World

189 Tour Guide

A: _____ Excuse me, did you hear our guide? <u>What time did she tell us to be in the hotel lobby?</u> ①

B: _____ <u>9:45.</u> ②
<u>She didn't say what time we were going to have lunch, did she?</u> ③
I don't think so. I didn't hear her say anything about <u>having lunch.</u> ④
Thanks. ⑤

▼1

① Where did she tell us to meet her?

② In front of the museum.

③ She didn't say who designed this building, did she?

④ who designed this building

▼2

① How much farther did she say it was to the hotel?

② About 20 minutes.

③ She didn't say where we were going to have dinner, did she?

④ where we were going to have dinner

▼3

① How often did she say the ferry goes to the island?

② Every 90 minutes.

③ She didn't say what the fare was, did she?

④ the fare

Grammar: embedded ques: *wh*-ques; reported speech with ques; *say, tell*
Expression: reporting a conversation; clarifying/confirming information

190 Choices

A: _____ Which <u>sweater</u> do you prefer: the one <u>which is on sale</u> or the one <u>from Scotland</u>? ①

B: _____ The one <u>that's from Scotland</u>. ②

Oh, you do? ③

I know, . . . you like the one <u>on sale</u>, don't you? ④

Yes, I do. ⑤

① tennis court/on the campus/across the street	① hotel/that has the swimming pool/on the lake	① teacher/who was at the meeting yesterday/over there
② that's across the street	② with the swimming pool	② at the meeting yesterday
④ which is on the campus	④ that's on the lake	④ who's over there

Grammar: rel clause; *which, that*: rel pron (subj of rel cl); reduced rel cl with prep phr; *which* + n: *wh*-ques; *one, ones*: pron

Expression: indicating preferences; describing objects; making/offering a choice

191 Doctor's Advice

A: _____ I feel much better today. ①
B: _____ You look much better. ②
Will I be able to <u>go to work on Monday</u>? ③
You should be able to. ④
Oh, that's good. ⑤
But you'll have to <u>take it easy for a few weeks</u>. ⑥
OK. ⑦

▼1

③ drive again

⑥ wear a neck brace

▼2

③ go back to school soon

⑥ take some medicine every day

▼3

③ practice karate again

⑥ come in and see me again in two weeks

Grammar: *will + have to, will + be able to, should + be able to:* modal combinations
Expression: talking about health; expressing necessity/expectation/ability

192 Regrets

A: _____ I shouldn't have <u>stayed up late last night</u>. ①
B: _____ Why? ②
I'm half asleep now. ③
You should have <u>gone to bed earlier</u>. ④
I know. ⑤

① bought a new car	① gotten married	① quit school
③ I don't have any money now.	③ I hate doing housework.	③ I can't find a decent job.
④ bought a used car	④ stayed single	④ stayed in school

Grammar: *should:* modal (pres perfect t)
Expression: offering advice

Talk to the World

193 Here and There

A: _____ Guess where ------ went on vacation. ①
B: _____ Where? ②
To Tokyo. ③
Isn't Tokyo where his son lives? ④
No. His son lives in Hong Kong. ⑤
That's where I'd like to go on vacation.
Hong Kong. ⑥

▼1

① ------ went last week

③ To Alaska.

④ Alaska/you spent your honeymoon

⑤ We spent our honeymoon in Canada.

⑥ I'd like to go; Canada.

▼2

① ------ is staying

③ At the Ritz Hotel.

④ the Ritz/they had a fire last year

⑤ The fire was at the Grand Hotel.

⑥ my brother stayed in May; At the Grand.

▼3

① ------ had lunch today

③ At the Rainbow Inn.

④ the Rainbow Inn/you took your wife to eat yesterday

⑤ I took her to Jack's Cafe.

⑥ my girlfriend likes to go; To Jack's.

Grammar: *where*: with clause of place; embedded ques
Expression: referring to location; expressing desires

Talk to the World

194 A Short Conversation

A: _____ What did say to you? ①
B: _____ He said that <u>he wasn't inviting me to his party</u>. ②
         <u>He's not inviting you to his party</u>? And what did you tell <u>him</u>? ③
         I told <u>him</u> that <u>I didn't want to go to his party</u>. ④
         And what did <u>he</u> say to that? ⑤
         I didn't hear what <u>he</u> said. <u>He</u> turned away from me. ⑥

▼ ▼② ▼③

② I wasn't doing well in class	② she wanted to play tennis with me on Saturday	② he wouldn't be able to pay me this week
③ You aren't doing well in class?	③ She wants to play tennis with you on Saturday?	③ He won't be able to pay you this week?
④ I was trying hard	④ I was busy on Saturday	④ he should pay me on time

Grammar: *say, tell* in reported speech: past tense, past cont; v + *that*-clause; v*(tell)* + obj + *that*-clause
Expression: reporting a conversation

Talk to the World

195 Most and Least

A: _____ This is <u>the most interesting movie</u> I've ever <u>seen</u>. ①

B: _____ I've <u>seen</u> <u>more interesting ones</u>. ②

I've <u>seen</u> <u>less interesting ones</u> too. ③

Well, I'll grant you that. This isn't <u>the least interesting movie</u> that I've ever <u>seen</u>. ④

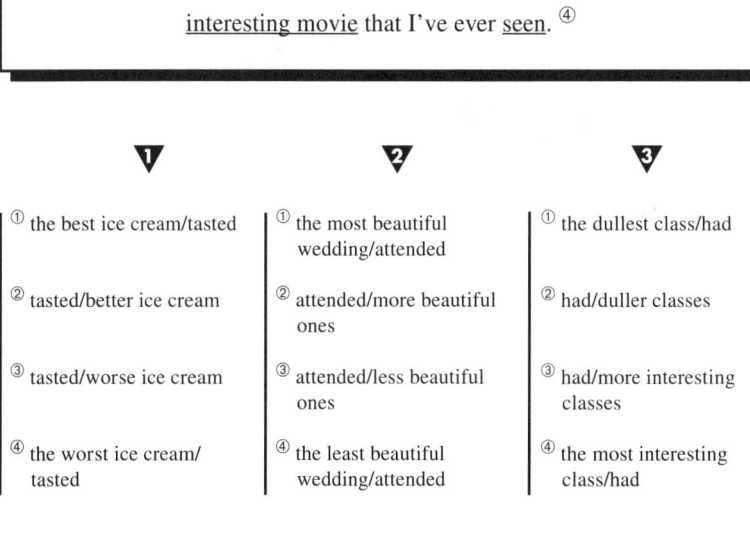

▼1

① the best ice cream/tasted

② tasted/better ice cream

③ tasted/worse ice cream

④ the worst ice cream/tasted

▼2

① the most beautiful wedding/attended

② attended/more beautiful ones

③ attended/less beautiful ones

④ the least beautiful wedding/attended

▼3

① the dullest class/had

② had/duller classes

③ had/more interesting classes

④ the most interesting class/had

Grammar: adj: compar adj + -er, more/less + adj, superlative forms adj + -est, most/least + adj; rel clause; that: rel pron with superlative; pres pfct; ever: adv with pfct

Expression: making comparisons; ranking things

Talk to the World

196 A Good Job

A: _____ What do you like most about your job? ①

B: _____ The thing I like most about my job is <u>that I don't have to come to the office before 9 o'clock</u>. ②

What do you like about your job the least? ③

The part of my job that I like the least is <u>answering the telephone</u>. ④

▼ 1

② not having to commute a long distance

④ dealing with unsatisfied customers

▼ 2

② its good salary and benefits

④ the short lunch break

▼ 3

② that I get to work with such nice people

④ working overtime so often

Grammar: gerund phr: complement of *be*; *that*-clause: complement of *be*; adv: compar super *most, least*

Expression: making comparisons; talking about occupations

197 Maybe

A: _____ ------ didn't <u>come to the party last night</u>. I wonder why. ①

B: _____ He might <u>not have been able to get a ride</u>. ②

Yes, maybe he <u>couldn't get a ride</u>. Or maybe he <u>was studying for a test</u>. ③

That's possible. He might <u>have been studying for a test</u>. ④

▼1

① say hello to me this morning

② not have noticed you

③ didn't notice me; had something important on his mind

④ have had something important on his mind

▼2

① buy ------'s car after all

② not have been able to get a bank loan

③ couldn't get a bank loan; decided he didn't need a car

④ have decided he didn't need a car

▼3

① call me last night

② have forgotten to call you

③ forgot to call me; couldn't get to a phone

④ not have been able to get to a phone

Grammar: *might:* modal with pres pfct, pres pfct cont; *might + be able to* with pres pfct; *maybe:* adv

Expression: expressing possibility/speculation; wondering about something

198 Not Necessarily

A: _____ They must be having a sale at that store. ①

B: _____ Why? What makes you think they're having a sale? ②

It's so crowded. ③

Well, that's true, but that doesn't necessarily mean that they're having a sale. ④

No, I guess not. ⑤

▼1

① ------ must have failed his test.

② he failed his test

③ He looks depressed.

④ he failed his test

▼2

① ------ must not like her class.

② she doesn't like her class

③ She skips class so often.

④ she doesn't like her class

▼3

① ------ must have finished his work already.

② he finished his work already

③ He's leaving his office early today.

④ he finished his work already

Grammar: *must*: modal with simple pres tense, pres cont, pres pfct
Expression: making an assumption; expressing deduction; acknowledging something

Talk to the World

199 What's This For?

A: _____ What's this for? ①

B: _____ It's used for <u>washing clothes</u>. <u>It's a washing machine</u>. ②

I know it's used for <u>washing clothes</u>! I mean, where did it come from? What's it doing here? Of course I know it's used for <u>washing clothes</u>! ③

Oh, ------ brought that here. She's going to use it. ④

| ② ironing clothes; It's an ironing board. | ② wrapping packages; It's wrapping paper. | ② diving under water; It's a wet suit. |

Grammar: prep phr: *for* + *v-ing*; passive (pres tense): *It's used for . . .*; *what...for*: *wh*-ques
Expression: indicating purpose; activities performed

Talk to the World

200 Snapshots

A: _____ When was this picture taken? ①
B: _____ That was taken when <u>I was a student</u>. ②
Where was this taken? ③
In Paris when I was traveling in Europe. ④
This is nice. Who took this picture? ⑤
That was taken by <u>a friend</u>. ⑥

② I was learning to drive	② I was in the hospital	② I first came to this school
④ At home when I had my graduation party.	④ In the hospital when my teacher visited me.	④ At a golf course when I was playing golf for the first time.
⑥ me	⑥ my teacher	⑥ my girlfriend

Grammar: *when:* with clause of time; passive: past tense
Expression: activities performed

Talk to the World

201 Changes

A: _____ Did they tear down that old hotel across from the subway station? ①

B: _____ I don't know. ②

That's what I heard. I heard that old hotel across from the subway station was torn down. ③

I don't know. It's hard to keep up with all the changes around here. ④

▼❶

① Have they closed down the shopping mall?

③ the shopping mall has been closed down

▼❷

① Have they completed the repair work on the bridge?

③ the repair work on the bridge has been completed

▼❸

① Are they going to lay off a hundred employees here this summer?

③ a hundred employees here are going to be laid off this summer

Grammar: *they* (impersonal pron) passive; passive: pres pfct, past, pres cont
Expression: activities performed; reporting past events/activities

Talk to the World

202 Something to Say

A: _____ It couldn't be a more beautiful day, could it? ①
B: _____ No, it couldn't. ②
          No, it certainly couldn't. ③
          The weather was terrible yesterday. ④
          Yes, it was, wasn't it? ⑤

▼ 1

① It's a perfect day for fishing, isn't it?

② Yes, it is.

③ Yes, it certainly is.

④ It's been nice all week.

⑤ Yes, it has, hasn't it?

▼ 2

① That building was really put up fast, wasn't it?

② Yes, it was.

③ Yes, it certainly was.

④ It's not a very interesting building though.

⑤ No, it isn't, is it?

▼ 3

① Number 9 can really run fast, can't he?

② Yes, he can.

③ Yes, he certainly can.

④ He did well last year too.

⑤ Yes, he did, didn't he?

Grammar: tag questions
Expression: opening a conversation

Talk to the World

203 Everything's Ready

A: _____ Have those reports been typed? ①
B: _____ Yes, they were typed this morning. ②
Have the mailing lists been made? ③
They're being made now. ④
That's good, because the boss is on his way here now. ⑤

① Has the conference room been cleaned?

② it was cleaned last week

③ Have the tables been set up?

④ They're being set up now.

⑤ the delegates are arriving

① Have the beds in room 203 been made?

② they were made this morning

③ Has the bathroom been cleaned?

④ It's being cleaned now.

⑤ the guest is waiting to use the room

① Have the dishes been washed?

② they were washed after breakfast

③ Has the living room been vacuumed?

④ It's being vacuumed now.

⑤ mother is coming home early today

Grammar: passive: past tense, pres pfct, pres cont
Expression: activities performed

204 The Work Is Done

A: _____ I hope <u>you put the car in the garage</u>. ①

B: _____ <u>It's been put in the garage</u>. ②

Oh, good. ③

<u>I didn't put the car in the garage, but it's been put there</u>. ④

① you're going to paint the kitchen tomorrow	① you've washed your dishes	① you'll do your homework before you go out
② It'll be painted.	② They've been washed.	② It'll be done.
④ I'm not going to paint it, but it'll be painted.	④ I didn't wash them, but they've been washed.	④ I'm not going to do it, but it'll be done.

Grammar: v(hope) + that-clause; passive: with will and perfect forms
Expression: expressing a hope; activities performed

Talk to the World

205 Finishing Up

A: _____   Do you think <u>they</u>'ll be finished <u>painting the room today</u>? ①

B: _____   Well, <u>the ceiling</u> can't be <u>painted today</u>, because <u>they</u> don't have <u>a ladder</u>. ②

When will <u>they</u> get <u>a ladder</u>? ③

<u>Tomorrow</u>, probably. ④

Then, <u>the ceiling</u> will be <u>painted tomorrow</u>? ⑤

Yes, I think so. <u>They</u> should be finished with everything <u>tomorrow</u>. ⑥

▼ 1

① he/installing the computer today

② printer/installed today/ he/the proper cable

③ he/the proper cable

④ on Monday

⑤ printer/installed on Monday

⑥ he/on Monday

▼ 2

① she/making everything by noon

② cake frosting/made by noon/she/any powdered sugar

③ she/some powdered sugar

④ after lunch

⑤ the cake frosting/made after lunch

⑥ she/after lunch

▼ 3

① you/repairing the engine before I get out of work

② carburetor/repaired before you get out of work/I/any help

③ you/some help

④ this evening

⑤ the carburetor/repaired this evening

⑥ I/this evening

Grammar: passive: with modals *will, should, can*; *be finished + v-ing/be finished with*
Expression: expressing assurance, ability; activities performed

Talk to the World

206 A Reminder

A: _____   Please remind me <u>to turn left when we get to the school</u>. ①

B: _____   Yes! Don't forget <u>to turn left when we get to the school</u>. ②

I know. Just don't forget to remind me. ③

I won't. I mean I won't forget to remind you. ④

▼   ▼   ▼

 to thank ------ for the present when I see her

 to make the flight reservations when we get back to the hotel

 to take my umbrella when I leave

Grammar: *when:* with clause of time; v + obj + *to* v
Expression: making requests

207 Things That Annoy

A: _____ Do you like <u>to play tennis</u>? ①

B: _____ Yes, but I don't like <u>to play when it's windy</u>. ②

I don't either. I like <u>to play when I have a weak partner</u>. ③

Oh, . . . when <u>you have a weak partner</u>. Hmm. ④

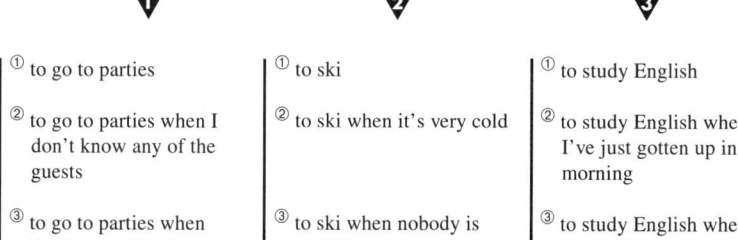

▼1	▼2	▼3
① to go to parties	① to ski	① to study English
② to go to parties when I don't know any of the guests	② to ski when it's very cold	② to study English when I've just gotten up in the morning
③ to go to parties when they're small and informal	③ to ski when nobody is watching me	③ to study English when the teacher is a woman

Grammar: clause of time: *when*-clause with simple pres tense, pres cont, pres pfct
Expression: indicating preferences

Talk to the World

208 This One or That One?

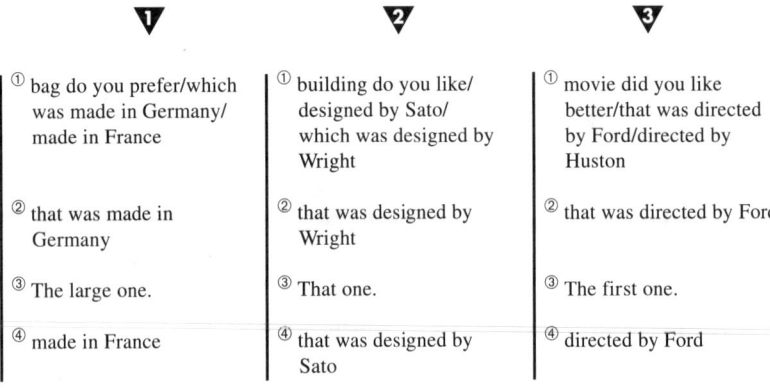

A: _____ Which <u>picture do you like</u>: the one <u>that was painted by Picasso</u>, or the one <u>painted by Miro</u>? ①

B: _____ Which one is it <u>that was painted by Picasso</u>? ②

<u>This one</u>. ③

Hmm . . . then I like the one <u>painted by Miro</u>. ④

▼1 ▼2 ▼3

① bag do you prefer/which was made in Germany/made in France	① building do you like/designed by Sato/which was designed by Wright	① movie did you like better/that was directed by Ford/directed by Huston
② that was made in Germany	② that was designed by Wright	② that was directed by Ford
③ The large one.	③ That one.	③ The first one.
④ made in France	④ that was designed by Sato	④ directed by Ford

---

Grammar: passive: past tense; *by:* prep with adv of agent; rel clause with passive; *that, which:* rel pron (subj of rel cl); past part phr

Expression: indicating preferences; making/offering a choice; expressing alternatives; identifying objects

Talk to the World

209 Complainers

A: _____ I didn't like that when the teacher gave us a test and he didn't tell us about it in advance. ①

B: _____ You know what I don't like? ②

What? ③

I don't like it when he calls on me in class when I'm looking out the window. ④

I know what you mean. ⑤

▼1

① I didn't like that when ------ dominated the conversation at the party.

④ she talks about her rich uncle

▼2

① I don't like it when holidays fall on a Tuesday.

④ we have to work overtime on Fridays

▼3

① I don't like this when the bus is late.

④ there aren't any seats left on the bus

Grammar: *when, what:* with clauses
Expression: complaining

210 A Few Favors

A: _____ Are you by any chance <u>on your way to the store</u>? ①
B: _____ <u>Yes, I am</u>. ②
Do you suppose <u>you could do me a favor and get me some fruit juice</u>? ③
Sure. ④
And I don't suppose <u>you could drop this off at the post office for me on your way to the store</u>. ⑤
<u>Drop that off at the post office</u>? I suppose so. ⑥

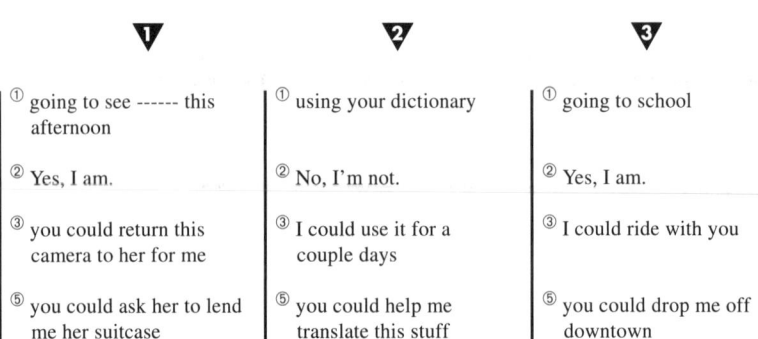

① going to see ------ this afternoon	① using your dictionary	① going to school
② Yes, I am.	② No, I'm not.	② Yes, I am.
③ you could return this camera to her for me	③ I could use it for a couple days	③ I could ride with you
⑤ you could ask her to lend me her suitcase	⑤ you could help me translate this stuff	⑤ you could drop me off downtown

Grammar: *suppose*: in requests; *do someone a favor*; *suppose so* (pro-clause with *so*)
Expression: asking favors; making requests

Talk to the World

211 Supposing

A: _____ Aren't we supposed to clean this mess up before class begins? ①

B: _____ Who said so? ②

_____. ③

He said it was supposed to be cleaned up before class began, but he didn't say we were supposed to clean it up. ④

Yes, but don't you suppose he meant us? ⑤

Hmm. I suppose so. ⑥

① you/erase the boards after class

③ the teacher

④ she/they/erased after class/she/I/erase them

⑤ she/you

① we/fix dinner before mother comes home

③ mother

④ she/it/fixed before she came home/she/we/fix it

⑤ she/us

① --C--/enter that stuff in the computer by lunchtime

③ Mr. --D--

④ he/it/entered by lunchtime/he/--C--/enter it

⑤ he/him

Grammar: suppose + that-cl, pro-cl with so; suppose + to v; passive: supposed to be + pp
Expression: expressing obligation/expectation; supposition

Talk to the World

212 Shortcomings

A: _____ What do you think of <u>our new library</u>? ①

B: _____ I like <u>it</u>. ②

Really? Even though <u>it's so difficult to find anything there</u>? ③

That's true; <u>it *is* difficult to find anything there</u>, but I like <u>it</u> anyway. ④

▼1

① that new shopping center

③ it closes so early

④ it *does* close early

▼2

① our new English teacher

③ she's so strict

④ she *is* strict

▼3

① this job

③ we have to work overtime so often

④ we *do* have to work overtime often

Grammar: *even though, but . . . anyway* conj in clause of concession; emphatic *do*
Expression: expressing an opinion; indicating preferences; making a concession

Talk to the World

213 Really?

A: _____ Is it true that ------ and ------ were married by a justice of the peace yesterday, and that they are going to France on their honeymoon? ①

B: _____ Oh, really? I heard they got married, but that's all I know. ②

That's great. ③

Yes, it is. ④

▼1

① ------ was arrested by the police yesterday/he's in jail now

② he got arrested

③ too bad

▼2

① ------ was invited by the ambassador to a party at the embassy/he didn't attend it

② he got invited to the embassy

③ strange

▼3

① ------ was promoted by her company/she is going to be the new vice-president

② she got promoted

③ great

Grammar: passive: past tense; *get* passive; *by:* prep with adv of agent
Expression: clarifying/confirming information; activities performed

214 How Not to Get Along

A: _____ Those two don't get along very well, do they? ①

B: _____ I know. First they didn't agree on <u>what to have for dinner</u>, ... ②

Really? ③

And now he doesn't go along with her idea on <u>how they should cook the main dish</u>. ④

That's too bad. They're both really very nice people. ⑤

| ② what time to have the meeting | ② what color to paint the kitchen | ② what movie to see |
| ④ where they should hold the meeting | ④ how they should arrange the furniture in the living room | ④ what they should do after the movie |

Grammar: *should*: modal; *what, how, where*: ques word with infin phr; infin replacement of *should*
Expression: expressing disagreement

Talk to the World

215 When and While

A: _____ Did you <u>do your homework</u>? ①

B: _____ Yes, <u>I did it</u> while <u>you were on the telephone</u>. ②

Did you <u>clean your room</u>? ③

No, not yet. ④

When are you going to <u>clean it</u>? ⑤

<u>I'll clean it</u> when <u>I finish reading this article in the newspaper</u>. ⑥

▼ ❶

① take a shower

② I took a shower/you were outside working in the garden

③ put away the tools in the garage

⑤ put them away

⑥ I'll put them away/I get up in the morning

▼ ❷

① read the contract

② I read it/you were talking to ------

③ sign it

⑤ sign it

⑥ I'll sign it/I get to my office

▼ ❸

① go shopping for food

② I went shopping/you were playing golf

③ tell ------ about the party

⑤ tell him about it

⑥ I'll tell him about it/he comes home

Grammar: *when, while:* with clause of time
Expression: indicating the time of activities; reporting past events/activities

Talk to the World

216 Smooth Talker

A: _____ --C-- is really a smooth talker. ①

B: _____ You can say that again! He convinced me that I should <u>drive him to the ski grounds tomorrow</u>. ②

Ha! He persuaded me to <u>lend him my skis</u>! ③

Really? ④

And he talked --D-- into <u>doing his homework for him</u>. ⑤

--C-- would make a good salesman. ⑥

Yes, he would. ⑦

▼1

② take this English class with him

③ help him study for the test in this class

⑤ writing his term paper for him

▼2

② buy his old typewriter

③ let him use my word processor

⑤ taking him to lunch today

▼3

② help him clean up his garage

③ let him keep his car in my garage

⑤ rotating the tires on his car for him

Grammar: v(convince) + obj + that-clause; v + obj to verb; should, would: modal; talk someone into doing something; persuade someone to do something

Expression: persuading

Talk to the World

217 How Come?

A: _____ My wife doesn't like this restaurant. ①
B: _____ Why? Because it's so expensive? ②
No, that's not why she doesn't like it. ③
How come she doesn't like it? ④
The reason why she doesn't like it is that a waiter here spilled coffee on her once. ⑤

▼1

① I didn't take the test in this class last week.

② you didn't study for it

③ I didn't take it

④ you didn't take it

⑤ I didn't take it/I had a sore throat and a headache

▼2

① I haven't applied for a passport yet.

② you've been too busy

③ I haven't applied for one

④ you haven't applied for one

⑤ I haven't applied for a passport yet/I don't have a passport-size photo

▼3

① My husband doesn't like to go to movies.

② they cost so much these days

③ he doesn't like to go

④ he doesn't like to go

⑤ he doesn't like to go to movies/he always falls asleep in movie theaters

Grammar: *why, the reason (why) . . . is that:* with clause of reason
Expression: requesting/stating reasons

218 Conditions

A: _____ Are you going <u>to the party tonight</u>? ①

B: _____ Yes, unless <u>I have to work overtime</u>. If <u>I have to work overtime</u>, I'm not going <u>to the party tonight</u>. ②

Hmm. ③

Are you? ④

Yes, if <u>you're going</u>. ⑤

▼1

① to play tennis this Saturday

② it rains/to play tennis

⑤ it's a nice day

▼2

① to get up early tomorrow

② I get to bed late tonight/ to get up early tomorrow

⑤ my alarm clock goes off

▼3

① to go to the meeting this afternoon

② I'm busy/to go to the meeting

⑤ I have nothing else to do

Grammar: fut cond; *if, unless:* conj; clause of cond
Expression: expressing conditions

Talk to the World

219 Dreamers

A: _____ If you could <u>meet any movie star</u> you wanted, <u>who</u> would you like to <u>meet</u>? ①

B: _____ If I could <u>meet any movie star</u> I wanted? ②

Yes. ③

Well, I guess I'd like to <u>meet --C--</u>. ④

I'd like to <u>meet --D--</u>. ⑤

Oh, me too. ⑥

① go anywhere in the world/where/go

④ go to Rome

⑤ go to Peru

① talk to any world leader/who/talk to

④ talk to --C--

⑤ talk to --D--

① eat at any restaurant/which restaurant/eat at

④ eat at the Rainbow Inn

⑤ eat at the Ming Garden

Grammar: pres cond (unreal cond); clause of condition; *could*: modal in pres cond; *if*: conj
Expression: expressing conditions; hypothetical situation

220 Giving Permission

A: _____ Are you going to <u>let ------ use your car</u>? ①

B: _____ Yes, provided that <u>he promises to drive carefully</u>. ②

You are? ③

Yes. Well, if <u>he doesn't promise to drive carefully</u>, I'm not going to <u>let him use it</u>. Why? ④

Oh, nothing. I was just wondering. ⑤

▼1 ▼2 ▼3

① go on the company picnic

② it doesn't rain

④ it rains/go on the company picnic

---

① study for the test

② there's nothing good on TV tonight

④ there's something good on TV/study for the test

---

① use ------'s word processor

② he says it's OK

④ he doesn't say it's OK/ use his word processor

Grammar: *provided that (providing), if:* conj; fut cond; clause of cond
Expression: expressing conditions; granting permission; indicating provisions

Talk to the World

221 An Excuse

A: _____ You weren't in class today! ①

B: _____ No, I wasn't. ②

Why? ③

I missed the bus. If I hadn't missed the bus, I would have been in class. ④

① You didn't call me last night!	① You weren't at the meeting this afternoon!	① You didn't come to my party Saturday!
② I didn't	② I wasn't	② I didn't
④ I lost your telephone number. If I hadn't lost your telephone number, I would have called you.	④ I was busy. If I hadn't been busy, I would have been at the meeting.	④ I wasn't feeling well. If I had been feeling well, I would have gone to your party.

Grammar: clause of condition; *if*: conj; past cond
Expression: expressing conditions; requesting/stating reasons

222 Wouldn't You?

A: _____ ------ is really excited. ①
B: _____ Oh, really? Why? ②
He's leaving for Europe tomorrow. ③
Oh, well, I'd be excited too if I were leaving for Europe tomorrow. Wouldn't you be? ④
Oh, sure. Of course. ⑤

▼1 ▼2 ▼3

▼1	▼2	▼3
① disappointed	① worried	① happy
③ He won't be able to attend his graduation ceremony.	③ He can't find his passport.	③ She received a ring from her boyfriend for her birthday.
④ disappointed/if I couldn't attend my graduation ceremony	④ worried/if I couldn't find my passport	④ happy/if I had received a ring from my boyfriend for my birthday

Grammar: clause of condition; *if*: conj; pres cond; past cond; subjunctive with cond
Expression: expressing conditions; hypothetical situation

Talk to the World

223 Unbelievable

A: _____ I heard that you have to <u>take four years of Chinese</u> in order to <u>graduate from that university</u>. Do you think that's true? ①

B: _____ Do you believe that? ②
Well, that's what --C-- said. If you want to <u>graduate from that university</u>, you have to <u>take four years of Chinese</u>. ③
I think --C-- was pulling your leg. ④

① pay a fee to the teacher/ get permission to take a make-up test | ① have a PhD/teach at that kindergarten | ① be a millionaire/live in this neighborhood

Grammar: *if, in order to:* conj; clause of cond; fut cond
Expression: expressing conditions; confirming information

Talk to the World

224 Reasons

A: _____ Did you study for the big test today? ①

B: _____ No. I would have, but I wasn't feeling well last night. ②

I would have too, only I fell asleep after dinner. ③

Oh, you didn't study either? ④

No, I didn't. ⑤

▼1 ▼2 ▼3

① Are you going to class today?

② I would/I haven't done my homework

③ I would/I'm too tired

④ aren't going

① Have you paid your taxes yet?

② I would have/I haven't had time

③ I would have/I spent all my money

④ haven't paid your taxes yet

① Do you intend to go to the meeting?

② I would/I have to meet a friend at the airport

③ I would/I want to watch the game on TV

④ don't intend to go to the meeting

Grammar: but, only: conj; clause of condition; past cond
Expression: expressing conditions; stating reasons

Talk to the World

225 Just in Case

A: _____ I brought my swimming suit in case the water at the lake is warm. ①

B: _____ Do you think the water will be warm? ②

I don't know. It might. ③

I doubt it. ④

Well, I brought my swimming suit anyway—just in case it is. ⑤

▼ ❷ ❸

① made a lunch for you/you get hungry on the golf course

② I'll get hungry on the golf course

③ You might.

⑤ made a lunch for you/ you do

① brought my credit card/ we don't have enough money

② we won't have enough money

③ We might not.

⑤ brought my credit card/ we don't

① am giving a house key to ------/he gets home before we do

② he'll get home before we do

③ He might.

⑤ am giving a house key to him/he does

Grammar: *in case:* conj; clause of cond; *anyway:* adv
Expression: expressing conditions

226 Would You?

A: _____ Would you <u>sell your house without consulting your wife first</u>? ①

B: _____ No, I wouldn't <u>sell my house</u> if I <u>didn't consult my wife first</u>. Why? ②

 did. ③

Well, I wouldn't. ④

Neither would I. ⑤

▼ ▼ ▼

① take home an office computer without getting permission before hand

② take home an office computer/didn't get permission before hand

① go to a wedding party without an invitation

② go to a wedding party/ didn't have an invitation

① interview for a job without being interested in the position

② interview for a job/ wasn't interested in the position

Grammar: clause of condition; *if*: conj; pres cond with subjunctive; reduced cond clause: prep phr *without* + v-*ing*
Expression: expressing conditions; hypothetical situation

Talk to the World

227 A Good Thing

A: _____ It's a good thing <u>I have a cold</u>. ①

B: _____ You're *glad* <u>you have a cold</u>? ②

Yes. If <u>I didn't have a cold</u>, <u>I would have to go to school today</u>. ③

Uh-huh. ④

And if <u>I went to school today</u>, <u>I would have to take the English test</u>. ⑤

Oh, I see. ⑥

▼ 1

① I missed the bus this morning

③ I hadn't missed the bus/I would have been on time for work

⑤ I had been on time for work/I would have had to attend a boring sales meeting

▼ 2

① I broke my arm

③ I hadn't broken my arm/I wouldn't have come to this hospital

⑤ I hadn't come to this hospital/I wouldn't have run into you here

▼ 3

① I can't find my car keys

③ I could find my car keys/I would have to let my son use the car

⑤ I let my son use the car/he wouldn't bring it back until late

---

Grammar: *if:* conj; clause of condition; pres/past cond; pres cond with subjunctive
Expression: expressing conditions; stating reasons; hypothetical situation; consequences

228 Free Advice

A: _____   Are you going to the party? ①
B: _____   Yes. ②
           You'd better call a taxi if you want to get there on time. ③
           Do you think so? ④
           I would if I were you. The buses don't run very often at this time of day. ⑤

① Do you have a history test tomorrow?	① Are you going for a job interview tomorrow?	① Aren't you going to visit ------ in the hospital?
③ memorize the important dates if you want to get a good grade	③ get a haircut if you want to make a good impression	③ visit her soon if you want to see her
⑤ Prof. ------ always asks for important dates on his tests.	⑤ Employers don't want people with long hair like yours.	⑤ She's going to be released from the hospital tomorrow.

Grammar: had better: modal; if: conj; pres/fut cond; clause of condition
Expression: offering advice; consequences

229 Thanks

A: _____   Thanks for <u>introducing me to Mr. --C--</u>. ①
B: _____   That's OK. You're welcome. ②

If it hadn't been for you, <u>I wouldn't have gotten the job</u>. ③

Oh, it was nothing. ④

Really! If <u>you hadn't introduced me to Mr. --C--, I wouldn't have gotten the job</u>. ⑤

Well, I'm glad I could help. ⑥

1

① lending me your car yesterday

③ I would have been late for my appointment

⑤ you hadn't lent me your car/I would have been late for my appointment

2

① meeting me at the airport

③ I would probably still be looking for my hotel

⑤ you hadn't met me at the airport/I would probably still be looking for my hotel

3

① helping me with my English

③ I know I would have failed the test

⑤ you hadn't helped me with my English/I know I would have failed the test

---

Grammar: cl of cond; past cond with *if it hadn't been for . . .*; *if*: conj; *thanks for* + *v-ing*
Expression: expressing gratitude; expressing conditions

Talk to the World

230 Unaware

A: _____   The store was closed. ①

B: _____   I know. You didn't know that? ②

No. If I had known that <u>it was closed</u>, <u>I wouldn't have gone there</u>. ③

Sorry. If I had known you didn't know <u>it was closed</u>, I would have told you. ④

▼ 1

① --C-- is driving us to the airport.

③ --C-- was driving us to the airport/I would have brought my large suitcase

▼ 2

① --C-- got married last week.

③ --C-- had gotten married last week/I would have sent her a wedding card

▼ 3

① Bus drivers are on strike today.

③ bus drivers were on strike today/I would have gotten up earlier

---

Grammar: clause of condition with *if I had known*; past conditional; *if*: conj
Expression: expressing conditions

Talk to the World   -230-

231 Afterthought

A: _____ Sometimes I think I shouldn't have <u>bought this car</u>. ①

B: _____ Why? ②

Because if I hadn't <u>bought this car</u>, I could have <u>invested in the stock market</u>. ③

Oh, you never know. You might have <u>invested in the stock market</u> and <u>lost all your money</u>. ④

Yes, that's possible. ⑤

① taken this class	① gotten married	① spent my money on this trip
③ taken this class/gotten a part-time job	③ gotten married/taken a trip this summer	③ spent my money on this trip/bought a car
④ gotten a part-time job/ found it very boring	④ taken a trip this summer/ been very lonely	④ bought a car/had an accident

Grammar: past cond; *because if*: conj; clause of cond
Expression: expressing conditions; requesting/stating reasons; hypothetical situation

232 Do You Mind?

A: _____ Do you mind if I use your bicycle as long as you're not using it? ①

B: _____ Use my bicycle? ②

Yes, since you're not using it. ③

Hmm... well, I guess so. As long as you bring it back by 3 o'clock. ④

I'll bring it back by 3 o'clock. ⑤

OK. Then you can use it. ⑥

▼1 ▼2 ▼3

① Could I take your umbrella as long as you aren't going out?

① Is it OK if I watch TV as long as I've finished my homework?

① I was wondering if I could borrow your car as long as you're not using it.

④ you don't lose it

④ you don't watch it more than one hour

④ you put some gas in the tank

⑤ I won't lose it.

⑤ I won't watch it more than one hour.

⑤ I'll put some gas in the tank.

⑥ take it

⑥ watch it

⑥ borrow it

Grammar: *as long as*: conj of condition; *as long as, since*: conj of reason; cl of cond/reason
Expression: making requests; expressing conditions; imposing on someone

Talk to the World

233 Working Together

A: _____ Could you see if <u>you can close this suitcase</u>? ①
B: _____ Oh, sure. ②
Do you know <u>what time the bus leaves for the airport</u>? ③
No. Shall I <u>call the front desk</u> and see? ④
Yes, would you please. <u>Call the front desk</u> and see <u>what time the bus leaves for the airport</u>. ⑤

① you have time to get a get-well card for ------	① you can find the umbrellas	① you can help me with my math
③ if she's still in the hospital	③ if the rain is going to let up	③ when the next test is
④ call the hospital	④ listen to the weather report	④ check the bulletin board

Grammar: clauses with *see if;* *see* + embedded ques
Expression: making requests

234 It Depends

A: _____ Do you like <u>to travel</u>? ①
B: _____ It depends. ②
On what? ③
It depends on <u>who I'm traveling with</u> for one thing. ④
What do you mean? ⑤
Well, <u>I don't like to travel with people who are in a hurry</u>. ⑥

▼ 1   ▼ 2   ▼ 3

① movies
④ the kind of movie
⑥ I don't like horror films

① to go to wedding parties
④ on what kind of wedding party it is
⑥ I don't like to go to very formal wedding parties

① sports
④ the sport
⑥ I like individual sports but I don't like team sports

Grammar: *depend on*
Expression: requesting an explanation; indicating preferences

235 Nagging

A: _____ I wish <u>you had done your homework before you went to the movie</u>. ①

B: _____ I know. ②

And I wish <u>you wouldn't leave your jacket on the chair</u>. ③

OK. ④

And I hope <u>you're not going to watch television now</u>. ⑤

I wish you would stop nagging. ⑥

▼1   ▼2   ▼3

① you would turn down the radio	① you had gotten a haircut yesterday	① you would make your bed once in a while
③ you wouldn't slouch	③ you wouldn't wear those dirty old jeans	③ you would help me in the yard for a while now
⑤ you'll clean up your room before your friend comes	⑤ you won't be late for school again today	⑤ you aren't going to leave that newspaper on the floor

Grammar: *wish*: with subjunctive; v(*hope, wish*) + *that*-clause
Expression: expressing a wish, a hope

236 The Truth of the Matter

A: _____ I've decided not to go back to school next fall because then I'd have to give up my job. ①

B: _____ Oh, really? ②

Yes, and besides, I really don't feel like going back to school. ③

I see. So you wouldn't go back to school next fall even if you didn't have to give up your job. ④

No, probably not. ⑤

① move to an apartment/I wouldn't be able to keep my dog	① go to Europe this July/I would have to use up all my savings	① have a large wedding/I couldn't afford a nice honeymoon
③ I guess I really like this house	③ I'm more interested in Asia	③ I don't want all my relatives there
④ move to an apartment/ you could keep your dog	④ go to Europe/you wouldn't have to use up all your savings	④ have a large wedding/ you could afford a nice honeymoon too

Grammar: pres cond; *even if:* conj; clause of cond; *so:* conj with reason; *because then:* conj with clause of reason; *besides:* adv; v*(decide)* + *to* v

Expression: indicating intentions; expressing conditions; stating reasons; making decisions

237 Decision Making

A: _____ Have you decided whether or not <u>you're going to take a trip this summer</u>? ①

B: _____ Yes. I've decided <u>to take a trip</u>. ②

Oh, you have? Have you decided <u>where you're going to go</u>? ③

No. I've decided that <u>I'm going to take a trip this summer</u>, but I haven't decided <u>where I'm going to go</u>. ④

▼1

① you're going to go to the party tonight

② not to go

③ what you're going to do

④ I'm not going to go to the party tonight/what I'm going to do

▼2

① you're going to retire next year

② not to retire

③ when you're going to retire

④ I'm not going to retire next year/when I'm going to retire

▼3

① you're going to work overtime this evening

② to work overtime

③ how long you're going to work

④ I'm going to work overtime/how long I'm going to work

Grammar: v(decide) + to v, that-clause, embedded ques with whether or not, if (conj), wh-ques
Expression: indicating intentions; making decisions

238 Hope for the Best

A: _____ I hope <u>the teacher isn't going to give us a test today</u>. ①
B: _____ <u>She's going to</u>. ②
       Well, I wish <u>she weren't</u>. ③
       Yes, it would be nice if <u>she weren't going to give us a test today</u>, but <u>she is</u>. ④

▼1   ▼2   ▼3

① they haven't raised the tuition	① the teacher will let us go home early	① ------ bought some ice cream
② They have.	② She won't.	② He didn't.
③ they hadn't	③ she would	③ he had
④ they hadn't raised the tuition/they have	④ she would let us go home early/she won't	④ he had bought some ice cream/he didn't

Grammar: v(wish, hope) + that-clause; subjunctive with wish/condition; pres, past cond with if-clause: it would be nice if; wish vs hope; clause of condition; if: conj
Expression: expressing a wish/a hope

Talk to the World

239 Wishes

A: ____ I wish <u>I owned a house</u>. ①

B: ____ Why? ②

If <u>I owned a house, I could play my stereo as loudly as I wanted</u>. ③

If <u>you owned a house, you would have to spend a lot of time keeping it up</u>. ④

That's true. I didn't think of that. ⑤

That's why I don't wish <u>I owned a house</u>. ⑥

① I had a lot of money	① I were two meters tall	① I had more children
③ I had a lot of money/I could take a cruise around the world	③ I were two meters tall/I could get on the basketball team for sure	③ I had more children/it would be more fun
④ If you had a lot of money, everyone would be trying to borrow some of it.	④ If you were two meters tall, you would always be ducking your head when you went through doorways.	④ If you had more children, you would have to work much harder to save money for their future.

Grammar: subjunctive with *wish*/cond; *if*: conj; cl of cond; pres cond
Expression: expressing a wish/conditions

Talk to the World

240 Exceptions

A: _____ How was your trip? ①

B: _____ Fine, except for <u>the long wait we had at the airport</u>. ②

Oh, really? ③

Yeah, aside from that it was fine. Yes, I'd go again next summer except that <u>my wife wants to go to summer school instead</u>. ④

Sounds like you had a good time. ⑤

Yes, I did. ⑥

▼1

② the fact that I couldn't communicate with anyone because I don't speak Chinese

④ I won't have enough money

▼2

② when I fell into the River Thames

④ I have to work on a new project for my company

▼3

② the weather

④ I'm saving my money for a new car

Grammar: *except for:* prep; *except (that), except for the fact that:* conj; clause of exception
Expression: expressing exception

241 Hardly Ever

A: _____ ------ has a nice car. ①

B: _____ I know. And she hardly ever uses it. ②

She doesn't? ③

No, except when she has to go out of town. ④

Oh, really? ⑤

And except to pick up her husband at the airport once a month. ⑥

▼1

① ------ has a brand new leather jacket.

② wears it

④ if I wear mine

⑥ when his wife tells him to wear it

▼2

① ------ has got a very nice cabin on the lake.

② goes there

④ in July for a few days

⑥ to clean up the place in the spring

▼3

① ------'s house has a lot of room.

② invites people over

④ on her birthday

⑥ if there is some very special occasion

Grammar: except: conj; except to (in, on, at): prep phr; clause of exception
Expression: expressing exception

Talk to the World

242 In a Hurry

A: _____ ------ would like <u>the windows cleaned in the lounge</u>. ①
B: _____ I know. He also wants <u>the chairs rearranged</u>. ②
<u>The chairs</u> don't have to be <u>rearranged</u> until later, but he is in a hurry to have <u>the windows cleaned</u>. ③
Oh, OK. ④
Yeah, <u>the windows</u> had better be <u>cleaned</u> right away. ⑤

▼1
① the shrubs trimmed
② the grass cut
⑤ the shrubs/trimmed

▼2
① the dishes put away
② the living room vacuumed
⑤ the dishes/put away

▼3
① those flowers delivered
② these orders filled
⑤ the flowers/delivered

Grammar: wo: s + vt + obj + compl; modals *have to, had better; be in a hurry to have* + obj + pp: passive; *want/would like* + obj + pp: causative in passive
Expression: expressing causation; activities performed

Talk to the World

243 Tennis or Swimming?

A: _____ Would you rather <u>go to the pool or play tennis</u>? ①
B: _____ I don't know. <u>What would you rather do</u>? ②
<u>What would *you* rather do</u>? ③
Well, I'd rather <u>go to the pool</u> than <u>play tennis</u>. ④
OK. ⑤
But I'd really rather not <u>go to the pool</u> either. I guess I'd prefer to <u>stay home and watch TV</u>. ⑥

▼ 1

① go to Europe in July or in August

② When would you rather go?

④ go in July/in August

⑥ go in July; go in December

▼ 2

① ride with --C-- or with --D--

② Who would you rather ride with?

④ ride with --D--/with --C--

⑥ ride with --D--; walk

▼ 3

① watch the news or listen to music

② Which would you rather do?

④ watch the news/listen to music

⑥ watch the news; go outside and get some exercise

Grammar: would rather (. . . than); prefer to
Expression: indicating preferences; expressing alternatives

Talk to the World

244 Instructions

A: _____ Weren't you told <u>to enter that data in the computer</u>? ①
B: _____ No. ②
<u>What did ------ say for you to do</u>? ③
He said <u>I should make graphs with the statistics</u>. ④
He told me that he told you <u>to enter that data in the computer</u>. ⑤
No, I was told <u>to make graphs with the statistics</u>. ⑥
I think you misunderstood him. ⑦

▼1

① to take this stuff to the conference room

③ Where did --C-- say for you to take it?

④ I should take it to Mr. --D--'s office

⑤ to take it to the conference room

⑥ to take it to Mr. --D--'s office

▼2

① to throw these old journals away

③ What did ------ say for you to do with them?

④ I should put them in the file cabinet

⑤ to throw them away

⑥ to put them in the file cabinet

▼3

① to be here at 8:30

③ What time did ------ say for you to be here?

④ I should be here at 9:30

⑤ to be here at 8:30

⑥ to be here at 9:30

Grammar: reported speech: embedded imperative; *say, tell* with reported speech; infinitive replacement of *should*; passive with reported speech and imperative
Expression: reporting a conversation/requests/instructions; directing someone to do something; activities performed

Talk to the World

245 Getting Things Done

A: _____ Are you in a hurry to have <u>your car overhauled</u>? ①

B: _____ Well, I'd like to have <u>it overhauled</u> before <u>I go on my ski trip</u>. ②

When are you going on your ski trip? ③

On the tenth of the month. ④

Do you think you can get <u>it overhauled</u> by then? ⑤

I hope so. ⑥

1

① the tape recorder repaired

② it repaired/my classes begin

③ When do your classes begin?

④ Next Tuesday.

⑤ it repaired

2

① the work done on your house

② it done/I retire

③ When are you going to retire?

④ In July.

⑤ it done

3

① your film developed

② it developed/my vacation is over

③ When is your vacation over?

④ At the end of next week.

⑤ it developed

Grammar: *have, get something done:* causatives in passive
Expression: expressing causation

Talk to the World

246 Whether or Not

A: _____ Are you going to <u>read the new novel by ------</u>? ①

B: _____ I don't know. First I want to find out whether or not <u>it got good reviews</u>. ②

I see. ③

After I find out whether or not <u>it got good reviews</u>, then I'll decide whether or not to <u>read it</u>. ④

▼1

① buy a new car

② the local car dealer is going to have a sale

④ buy one

▼2

① apply for a job after you graduate

② I can get into graduate school

④ apply for a job

▼3

① go to the dance on Friday

② my wife is interested in going

④ go

Grammar: *decide whether or not to; whether or not:* conj
Expression: making decisions

247 Determination

A: _____ Is ------ going to <u>buy that TV</u>? ①
B: _____ Yes. ②
Even though <u>it's not on sale</u>? ③
Yes, <u>she</u>'s going to <u>buy it</u> whether <u>it's on sale</u> or not.
Don't you think <u>she</u> should? ④
No, not if <u>it's not on sale</u>. ⑤

▼1 ▼2 ▼3

| ① go camping this weekend | ① walk to school in the rain | ① play tennis |
| ③ she has a final exam on Monday | ③ she has a bad cold | ③ he has just had surgery on his back |

Grammar: *even though:* conj; clause of concession; *whether . . . or not:* conj
Expression: indicating preferences; expressing determination

248 Because

A: _____ ------ is leaving work early so she can get good seats at the theater. ①

B: _____ I'm leaving work early too. ②

You are? ③

Yes, but not so that I can get good seats at the theater. ④

How come you're leaving early? ⑤

Because I have to pick my wife up at the hospital. ⑥

▼1

① ------ is going to walk to school today/she doesn't meet Mr. ------ on the bus

② I'm going to walk too.

④ I don't meet Mr. ------

⑥ I want to get some exercise

▼2

① ------ is going to skip class this afternoon/he can watch the World Cup on TV

② I'm going to skip class too.

④ I can watch the World Cup

⑥ I'm going to go for a job interview

▼3

① I'm getting up early tomorrow/I'm not late for class

② I'm getting up early tomorrow too.

④ I'm not late for class

⑥ I want to watch the six o'clock news

Grammar: *so that, because:* conj; clause of reason; clause of purpose
Expression: stating/requesting reasons

249 Trying to Recall

A: _____ <u>When was it that we went camping last summer?</u> ①

B: _____ The last week of July. ②

And <u>who was it that we borrowed that tent from?</u> ③

My cousin. ④

Oh, yes. <u>That's who I thought it was.</u> ⑤

① What day was it that you went to the doctor last week?	① Why was it that they cancelled the conference last month?	① How was it that you met Mrs. ------?
② Tuesday.	② Because it was raining.	② Through my wife.
③ what was the name of the doctor you saw	③ where was it that they had planned to meet	③ what was it that she did for a living
④ Dr. ------	④ At the university.	④ She's a nurse.
⑤ That's what I thought it was.	⑤ That's where I thought they had planned to meet.	⑤ That's what I thought she was.

Grammar: emphasis on question words
Expression: clarifying/confirming information; emphasizing questions

250 Mysteries

A: _____ Did you know that ------ is going to <u>buy a yacht</u>? ①

B: _____ No, really? What would he want to <u>buy a yacht</u> for when <u>he doesn't even have a car</u>? ②

That's a good question. ③

You might think he would want to <u>buy a car so that he could take his family out</u>. ④

Yes, you would think so. ⑤

I wonder why he wants to <u>buy a yacht</u>. ⑥

▼1

① move to Hawaii

② move to Hawaii/he has such a good job here

④ stay here so he could be with his grandchildren

▼2

① study law

② study law/there are so many lawyers these days

④ study engineering so that he could get a good job

▼3

① drop his English class

② drop his English class/he did so well on the tests

④ finish the class so that he could graduate on time

Grammar: *when*: with cl of time; *so that*: conj; clause of reason; *would* (expectation): modal; *even*; *you*: impersonal pron

Expression: questioning judgement; wondering about something

Talk to the World

Teaching/Study Notes

Teaching/Study Notes

1 What is it? Guess!

① Statement word order: <u>It's a necklace</u>. *Yes/no*-ques word order: <u>Is it a necklace</u>?
   ❖ Note that only the singular forms of nouns and *be* are used in this dialogue. ❖ The definite articles *a/an* are used with reference to nonspecific things. Use *a* before a consonant sound, and *an* before a vowel sound.

② Contractions: *It is* may be contracted to *it's*, but not when the two words constitute an entire sentence. The negative *it is not* may be contracted to *it isn't*, or *it's not*. Use the contracted form whenever possible in spoken English.

④ **B** repeats part of **A**'s question — <u>A watch?</u> — in order to confirm the question.
   ❖ Compare the two contracted forms with *not* in lines two and four.

⑤ <u>Uhm</u> is an utterance with no lexical meaning here. It is used to signal an interruption or pause in speech.

⑦ <u>Oh</u>! expresses surprise here. ❖ <u>Thank you very much</u>. **OR** <u>Thanks a lot</u> — a less formal expression.

Practice Use indefinite articles. ♦ T: <u>ring</u> S: <u>a ring</u> ❖ Practice the negative. ♦ T: <u>It's a ring</u>. S: <u>It isn't a ring</u>. **OR** <u>It's not a ring</u>. ❖ Make *yes/no*-ques from statements. ♦ T: <u>It's a ring</u>. S: <u>Is it a ring</u>?

Communication Cover an object on a desk with a cloth. Students guess what the object is from its shape and size. ♦ S: <u>Is it a pen</u>? T: <u>No, it isn't a pen</u>. S: <u>Is it a pencil</u>? T: <u>Yes, it is</u>.

2 Downtown

① Demonstrative pronouns: *this* refers to a relatively near animate or inanimate thing, and *that* to one more distant in time or space. Point to objects to demonstrate the meanings of *this* and *that*. ❖ The definite article *the* is used with reference to specific nouns, and is generally used with nouns that are identified by name: **the** *World Trade Center*, **the** *Canadian Embassy*. Exceptions: *General Hospital, North High School*.

② Short reply: *it* is used in a short reply to the question in line one, not *this*. Also, the contracted *be* is not used in an affirmative short reply. ❖ The negative short reply is <u>No, it isn't</u>. **OR** <u>Not, it's not</u>.

③ *And* here is used to indicate that the speaker has not finished asking questions.

④ <u>No</u>. **OR** <u>No, that's not the post office</u>. **OR** <u>No, it isn't</u>. ❖ <u>Over there</u> indicates a point distant from both the speaker and the listener.

⑤ <u>Oh</u> here indicates that an utterance has been heard or understood.

⑧ <u>That's all right</u> always includes the contracted form of *be*. This expression is less formal than <u>You're welcome</u>.

Practice Make *yes/no*-ques. ♦ T: <u>That's the library</u>. S: <u>Is that the library</u>? ❖ Practice *this* and *that*. ♦ T: <u>Is this a ring</u>? S: <u>No. That's (It's) a bracelet</u>.

Communication Use a city or campus map or objects to elicit short replies.
♦ T: <u>Is this a post office</u>? S: <u>Yes, it is</u>. **OR** <u>No, it isn't</u>. Students should have opportunities to ask questions too.

Teaching/Study Notes

3 At Airport Customs

① Statement word order: <u>This is a sweater</u>. *Wh*-ques (with *be*) word order: <u>What's this</u>? Note that *what* replaces *sweater*. Use the contracted form *what's* in spoken English. ❖ The appropriate question here is <u>What's this</u>? not <u>What is it</u>?
② <u>It's a sweater.</u> OR <u>A sweater.</u>
③ Note the use of *this* rather than *the* here. ❖ The preposition of place, *in*, is introduced here. T can demonstrate its meaning by placing objects *in* a container.
④ The short reply, <u>A doll</u>, is also possible here.
⑥ See **Appendix 2** for the pronunciation of the noun plural -*s* suffix. ❖ Important: no article is used with the plural nouns when the reference is not to specific objects. There is no plural form of the indefinite articles *a/an*. ❖ *And* is introduced here as a connective.

Practice Form noun plurals. ♦ T: <u>a book</u> S: <u>books</u> ❖ Practice listing words using rising intonation. See the intonation guide in **Appendix 1**. ♦ T: <u>What's in your desk (pocket, purse, etc.)</u>? S: <u>A pen, an eraser, and a notebook.</u>
Communication Try the game "What am I thinking of?" ♦ T: <u>I'm thinking of an object in this room. What is it</u>? S1: <u>Is it the blackboard</u>? T: <u>No</u>. S2: <u>Is it that eraser</u>? T: <u>Yes</u>. ❖ To learn vocabulary, students bring pictures of objects to class. They hold the pictures up in front of the class and ask <u>What's this</u>? If no one in the class can identify the object in English, the teacher writes the English name of the object on the blackboard.

4 Window Shopping

① The <u>be + adj</u> pattern is used here for the first time.
③ <u>That dress</u> is short for <u>That dress is nice</u>. The short reply is appropriate here.
④ Note the intonation pattern. Additional stress is given to *is* to indicate that speaker **B** agrees emphatically with **A**. Because of the stress on *is*, the verb is not contracted. An unstressed *is* would suggest less enthusiasm in the agreement.
Practice Additional adjectives that may be used in the substitutions include *expensive* and *attractive*. Other items of clothing include *a sweater, a jacket,* and *a hat*. Only singular nouns may be used in the substitutions, because the plural demonstratives have not been introduced yet.
Communication Express a compliment or admiration. ♦ S1: <u>That's a pretty scarf.</u> S2: <u>Thank you.</u>

5 From China

① The following are the subject pronouns and their corresponding *be* forms, uncontracted and contracted: I am → *I'm*; you are → *you're*; he is → *he's*; she is → *she's*; it is → *it's*; we are → *we're*; they are → *they're*
② The contracted form of *be* is not used in an affirmative short reply, but it may be used in the negative short reply: <u>No, we aren't</u>. OR <u>No, we're not</u>.
④ <u>No. We're from Harbin.</u> OR <u>No, we're not. We're from Harbin.</u>

Teaching/Study Notes

Practice Note the need in the substitutions to change the verb *be* in the dialogue to agree with the singular or plural subject pronouns. ❖ Use contracted forms.
▶ T: <u>She is not from Tokyo</u>. S: <u>She isn't from Tokyo</u>. **OR** <u>She's not from Tokyo</u>. ❖ Play "Guess Where I'm From." Students decide where they are "from" by selecting a city or country from a list on the blackboard. Students ask their classmates where they are "from." ▶ S1: <u>Are you from Paris</u>? S2: <u>No, I'm not</u>. S3: <u>Are you from Tokyo</u>? S2: <u>Yes, I am</u>.

6 Hello!

① <u>Hello</u>. **OR** <u>Hi</u>. *Hi* is less formal than *Hello*, and *Hi* is more common in American than in British English. Some people regard *Hi!* as a familiar greeting.
② In spoken English <u>How are you</u>? is often contracted to <u>How're you</u>? Stress on *you* suggests familiarity and communicates warmth and friendship.
③ The shorter, one-word reply <u>fine</u> is suitable here too. Other replies that might be used in place of *fine* include *good, great, OK,* and *not bad*.

7 Austrian

② <u>No</u> here does not answer a question. It is used to express disagreement, and it adds emphasis to the negative *he isn't*. If *no* were not used here, **B** would have to make the long reply: <u>He's not from Germany</u>.
③ <u>Yes</u> is not a response to a question. It stresses the affirmative opinion held by **A**.
⑤ A *yes/no*-ques can be formed from a declarative sentence with *yes/no*-ques rising intonation. This kind of question usually suggests that confirmation is desired.
Practice Learn the adjectives of nationality. One student gives the name of a country, and the teacher gives the adjective. ▶ S: <u>He's from Canada</u>. T: <u>He's Canadian</u>. Students then exchange roles with the teacher. ❖ Practice making questions using rising intonation with declarative sentences. ▶ T: <u>He's German</u>. S: <u>He's German?</u> T: <u>Yes, he is</u>. ❖ Other kinds of personal information can be substituted for country and nationality in this dialogue. ▶ Age: ① <u>He's 18</u>. ⑥ <u>He's 19</u>. Occupation: ① <u>She's a teacher</u>. ⑥ <u>She's an artist</u>.
Communication Try the dialogue with true information using the names of students in class. ▶ T: <u>------ is from Thailand</u>. S: <u>No, she isn't</u>. <u>She's Malaysian</u>.

8 These Things

① Note that *these* and *those* are the plural forms of *this* and *that*. ❖ See **Appendix 2** for the pronunciation of the possessive *'s*. The *s* is omitted when the name or noun is in its plural form. ▶ <u>the *teachers'* books, the *Smiths'* house</u>
② <u>No</u>. **OR** <u>No, they aren't</u>.
③ <u>Are these things --D--'s too</u>? **OR** <u>Are these --D--'s things too</u>?
④ The conjunction *but* introduces contrasting information in this dialogue.
Practice Make sentences with *but*. ▶ T: <u>The camera is the student's</u>. <u>The bag isn't the student's</u>. S: <u>The camera is the student's, but the bag isn't</u>. **OR** T: <u>The camera</u>

-255-

Teaching/Study Notes

is the student's. The bag is the teacher's. S: The camera is the student's, but the bag is the teacher's.
Communication Holding objects belonging to three or four students, the teacher asks the rest of the class questions about ownership. ♦ T: Is this --C--'s? S: No, it isn't. It's --D--'s. OR Yes, it is. ❖ The teacher holds up an object belonging to one student. The other students guess who the owner of the object is. ♦ S: Is it --C--'s? T: No, it isn't. S: Is it --D--'s? T: Yes, it is.

9 Where's the Hotel?

① Excuse me. OR Pardon me. ❖ The *where*-ques (with *be*) is introduced here. *Where* replaces the adverb of place. Statement word order: The Grand Hotel is across from the city hall. *Where*-ques word order: Where is the Grand Hotel?
② Across from OR opposite. These and the following prepositions should be illustrated on the blackboard, or on a simple map of a familiar area: *behind, beside, between, in back of, in front of, kitty-corner from, near, next to.*
③ Uhm has no lexical meaning here. It is a sound of hesitation.
④ Behind OR in back of ❖ Note that *up* and *down* in *right down/up this street* often have no literal meaning and are used to suggest *in this/that direction.*
Communication Use a city or campus map, or draw a familiar neighborhood on the blackboard. Students ask one another about locations of buildings or landmarks using *where*.

10 That's My Bag

① The following possessive adjectives are introduced in this dialogue: *my, your, his, her, our, their.* The possessive adjective *its* does not occur in this dialogue.
③ Note the position of the adverb *there. Here* could replace *there* in this position. The following word order is not acceptable in the context of this dialogue: A blue bag is there. ❖ Note the adverb *there* gets additional stress in line three.
④ Yes is a response to the implied question in line three: Is that your bag?
Practice Note that only singular nouns are used in the dialogue and in the substitutions. ❖ Practice the dialogue with the possessive adjective *her*, as it has not been included in the dialogue or in the substitutions.
Communication Use possessive adjectives. The teacher takes several objects from some students and asks about ownership. ♦ T: Is this your jacket? S1: No, it isn't. My jacket is brown. T: Is this your jacket? S2: Yes, it is.

11 In Your Shirtpocket

② The following prepositions of place are used in this dialogue and/or in the substitutions: *by, in, next to, on, on top of, under.* Their meanings can be illustrated using classroom objects.
③ On the suitcase is a shortened form of It's on the suitcase.
④ How about + noun or noun phrase is introduced here. This question is used to

Teaching/Study Notes

request additional information, and it suggests repetition of a previous question. How about the tickets? could be restated as Where are the tickets?
Practice Be sure to use the proper subject pronoun in line two in the substitutions.
❖ Note the combination of two expressions of location in substitution three, line three: *on the floor + by the chair*. Students should practice similar combinations.
▶ T: *in, on* S: in the box on the table (or other combination using *in* and *on*). Make additional combinations using the following pairs of prepositions: *in* and *on top of; on* and *under; in* and *next to; on* and *by*.
Communication Talk about the locations of objects in the classroom. Use combinations of two adverbs of place. ▶ T: Where's the dictionary? S: On the shelf next to the door.

12 Yours or Hers?

① See **Appendix 1** for *or*-ques intonation. ❖ The following possessive pronouns are introduced in this dialogue: *mine, yours, his, hers, ours, theirs*. The possessive pronoun *its* does not occur here, and though students should be familiar with it, *its* is relatively infrequently used in spoken English.
② It's --C--'s. **OR** --C--'s.
④ The magazines? This questions seeks confirmation, but speaker **B** has anticipated an affirmative response and answered yes.
Practice Try the dialogue using singular demonstrative pronouns in line three, and plural demonstrative pronouns in line one. Note that changes will be necessary in lines two and four. ❖ Using objects belonging to the students, practice the dialogue in class. Students should have ample opportunity to practice the *or*-question.

13 Everybody's Things

② **B** seeks confirmation of **A**'s question, but then **B** answers the question without waiting for the response. ❖ **B** could also reply with a negative No, they aren't.
③ Note the use of How about . . .? with the possessive. *How about* + noun was introduced in dialogue 11.
④ Caution: if the answer in line two is *no, too* cannot be used in line four.
Practice Note that the proper pronoun must be supplied by students for use in line two in the substitutions. ❖ For more practice with demonstratives and possessives, try the following variation of the dialogue, using objects belonging to the students.

A: Are those --C--'s gloves?
B: No, they aren't. They're mine.
A: Is this your book?
B: No, it's not. That's (It's) --D--'s.

14 Suggestions

① The present forms of *have* and *do* are introduced in this dialogue: I, you, we,

Teaching/Study Notes

they: *have, do*; he, she, it: *has, does*. Note the use of *do* in forming a *yes/no*-ques with *have*. Statement word order: She has a tennis racket. *Yes/no*-ques word order: Does she have a tennis racket? The question Has she a tennis racket? may also be heard, but it is not common in American English.

② Yes, she does is the short reply. Note the use of the pro-verb *do*. The long reply is Yes, she has a tennis racket.

④ Introduce cardinal numbers. ❖ Note *two* gets additional stress.

⑧ Note that the negative of *have* is usually formed with *do + not*. ♦ She doesn't have a photo album. I don't have a watch. Note also the contracted forms: *do not* becomes *don't; does not* becomes *doesn't*. ❖ Idiom: *Thanks for* + noun phrase.
Practice Use *thanks/thank you + for* + noun phrase. ♦ T: the birthday present S: Thanks for the birthday present. T: the bracelet S: Thanks for the bracelet. ❖ Make *yes/no*-ques with *have*. ♦ T: She has a watch. S: Does she have a watch?
Communication Talk about possessions. Answer *yes/no*-questions with *have*. ♦ T: Do you have a CD player? S: No, I don't. OR Yes, I do. Students ask questions too.

15 Fruit and Vegetables

① Note the use of the plural *tomatoes*. The plural form of count nouns is used when referring to a category of things.

③ Noncount nouns are introduced here. A noncount noun requires a singular verb form and is used without a definite article when it refers to a nonspecific thing.
Practice In the substitutions, students should remember that noncount nouns require a singular verb and pronoun, and plural count nouns require plural verb and pronoun forms. ❖ Students bring to class pictures of food cut from magazines. The English name for any unfamiliar food item is written on the blackboard, and then the pictures are used for additional substitutions in the dialogue.

16 Take Ten Guesses

① This dialogue demonstrates a popular game that offers opportunities to make *yes/no*-questions and short replies. Students should be allowed no more than ten questions in order to identify the classmate whom the teacher is thinking of. If the students cannot identify the person in ten or fewer guesses, the teacher is the winner. ❖ Note the use of *it* in lines one and seven and eight to refer to a person. Note the use of the pronoun *she* in line six.

③ Hair is a noncount noun and requires no article here.

⑤ Note the use of the indefinite article here: a yellow sweater

⑧ Yes, it is. OR No, it isn't.
Practice The game may be used at more advanced levels too. ♦ Is she wearing a yellow sweater? OR Is she the student who comes from China?

17 In the Refrigerator

② The *there + be* pattern is very common in English, and here it is used for the first

Teaching/Study Notes

time. Do not confuse *there + be* with the adverb of place, *there*. ❖ Note the use of *some* in an affirmative sentence.
③ *Any* is used in place of *some* in a *yes/no*-question; in fact, however, though *any* is the correct form in this position, *some* is sometimes heard.
④ *Any* is used in place of *some* in a negative sentence. ❖ Short reply: No, there isn't. OR No, there isn't any. OR No, we don't have any.
Practice Students are reminded to use the singular form of *be* with noncount nouns and the plural form of the verb with the plural count nouns in the substitutions.

18 Flour and Eggs
① Note the use of the definite article with *flour* in reference to a specific thing. ❖ Compare the following sentences: Where is the flour? Do we have any flour? Note the difference between *the* and *any*.
② Since noncount nouns are regarded grammatically as singular, *it* is used here as the pronoun for the flour.
④ We don't have any. OR There aren't any.
⑥ There's some could be replaced by it's in this line. In the substitutions, students are reminded that the form of *be* in line six depends upon whether the substitution in line five is a count or noncount noun.
Practice Tape pictures of food cut from magazines in a "refrigerator" or "cupboard" drawn on the blackboard. Students ask one another questions about the contents of the refrigerator. ♦ S1: Is there any cream? S2: Yes, there is. S1: Do we have any chicken? S2: No, we don't.

19 Photographs
① Note the use of *this* with reference to a person. The demonstrative pronoun here is more natural than the subject pronouns *he* or *she*.
② *That* is the natural demonstrative here, not *this*, even though the speakers are not distant from the photograph. *It* would not be a natural substitute for *that*, either.
③ Note the use of *yes/no*-question intonation with a declarative sentence; the speaker expresses surprise, and seeks confirmation.
④ The object pronouns *me, you, him, her, us, them* are introduced here. The object pronoun *it* does not occur in this dialogue.
Communication Introduce the names of relatives: *father, mother, sister, brother, cousin, aunt, uncle, grandmother, grandfather, son, daughter*. ❖ Students bring photographs of their families to class and ask each other questions about the identities of the persons in the pictures. ♦ S1: Is this your brother? S2: No. That's my cousin. S3: Is this your sister? S4: No, that's me.

20 For Me?
① The object pronouns in this dialogue are objects of the prepositions *for* and *from*.
⑦ From --F--? OR Is it from --F--? Note that in casual conversational style, the

Teaching/Study Notes

subject and verb *(it's)* have been dropped from the question in line seven.
Practice Students give the object pronoun forms with *for* and *from*. ▶ T: he/from S: from him. T: I/for S: for me

21 Photo Album
① Note the use of *this* with reference to a person.
③ The *who*-question (with *be*) is introduced here. Statement word order: He's my friend. *Who*-question word order: Who is he? ❖ *He* is appropriate in this line, not *that*, though the demonstrative pronoun may be used with a *who*-question (see line five). The name of an unfamiliar person has been given in line two, and the Who's he? question requests additional information about the person.
⑥ Note the use of the indefinite article in *a friend*. The indefinite article here implies one of several unspecified friends. *My friend* would suggest a specific friend, or it might suggest that **B** has only one friend.
Communication Continue the communication activity from dialogue 19. Use *who*-questions in asking about identities.

22 Who Has It?
① Note the use of *who* as the subject of the question with *have*. Statement word order: ------ has the tennis racket. *Who*-question (with *have*) word order: Who has the tennis racket?
② *I* is stressed in this sentence. The object pronoun *it* is used here for the first time. *It* is used to refer to a specific thing.
③ *Also* may replace *too* here, but *too* is more commonly heard.
④ No. OR No, I don't.
Practice *Dad* is also a subject substitution that could be used in line two. *Mom* in the substitutions could be replaced with *mother*.

23 Spinach
① This is the first use of the simple present tense with verbs other than *be, have,* and *do*. ❖ The transitive verb *like* must always have an object. Present forms of the verb are: I, you, we, they: *like*; he, she, it: *likes*.
② Yes, I do. OR Yes.
③ Do you like eggs? not Do you like an egg? The plural form of count nouns is used when referring to a category of countable things.
⑤ The implied question in How about mushrooms? is Do you like mushrooms?
⑥ Yes, I like mushrooms. OR No, I don't like mushrooms. *Yes* and *no* are not necessary here, but they are commonly a part of this kind of reply. The short replies Yes, I do and No, I don't are not appropriate responses to How about mushrooms?
Practice One or two pairs of students produce their variation of the dialogue for the class. Other students are asked questions about the preferences of the students who

Teaching/Study Notes

performed the dialogue. ♦ T: <u>Does ------ like fruit</u>? S: <u>No, he/she doesn't.</u> OR <u>Yes, he/she does.</u>

Communication Students ask each other about their preferences regarding familiar TV programs, sports, cities, and other topics. They may also tell what they do not like.

24 Belongings

③ *Belong to* is the first two-word verb to be introduced. It is transitive and inseparable, and as with *like* in the previous dialogue, it refers to a state rather than an activity. As a stative verb, *belong to* does not normally occur in the continuous verb form. ❖ Note the use of object pronouns with *belong to*. See dialogue 19 and 20 to review object pronouns.

Practice Ask questions and make responses with <u>*belong to* + object pronoun</u>. The teacher picks up objects from students' desks and asks questions about ownership.
♦ T: <u>Does this (Do these/those) belong to you</u>? S: <u>No, it doesn't (they don't). It belongs (They belong) to him/her.</u> Students should have opportunities to ask questions too. Note that plural nouns with *these* and *those* can be used as well as singular nouns with *this* and *that*.

25 Do You Know Him?

① Two adverbs of place are used in this sentence—*there* and *over there*—a redundancy common in spoken language. In conversation, the singular form of <u>*there* + *be*</u> is often used with plural nouns. ♦ <u>There's Mr. and Mrs. ------.</u>

② *Know, hear, remember,* and *see,* as well as *like* and *belong to,* are stative verbs; they indicate a state or condition rather than an observable activity. These verbs are transitive as they have been used here, and they must take an object.

③ After answering **B**'s question, **A** calls out to Mr. --C--.

⑦ *No* in line seven does not answer a question. It expresses agreement with **B** in line six.

26 Occupations

① Compare the simple present tense in <u>He sells cars</u> with the use of the simple present tense in dialogues 22, 23, and 24.

② *No* in line two does not answer a question. It expresses disagreement with **A**'s assertion in line one. Compare the use of *no* here with the use of *no* in line seven of dialogue 25, where it signifies agreement.

③ Note that *yes* is used to express disagreement with **B** in line two.

④ *Trucks* receives additional stress, because the speaker wants to contrast it with *cars* in line one. The additional stress signifies a correction or contradiction.

⑤ He does? OR Does he?

Practice The verb in line four may be changed to contrast it with *sell* in line one. Try *assemble, buy, fix, paint, rent, repair.* ♦ He <u>repairs</u> cars.

Teaching/Study Notes

27 Where Are You From?

② I'm from Japan. **OR** I come from Japan. Use the present form *come*, not the past tense.
③ Where in Japan? **OR** Where in Japan are you from? **OR** Where are you from in Japan?
④ I'm from Oita. **OR** I'm from Oita in the southern part of the country.
⑤ Near Nagasaki? **OR** Is that near Nagasaki?
⑦ I see is an informal expression which indicates that the listener has heard, not that he necessarily understands or agrees with the speaker.

Practice Introduce additional vocabulary: *eastern, western, northern, southern, northeast, northeastern; northwest, northwestern; southeast, southeastern; central, north central, south central; middle*. ❖ Use a map and ask for locations.
♦ S1: Where's Munich? S2: It's in the southern part of Germany. ❖ Use a map and ask questions about locations. ♦ T: Is Los Angeles north of San Francisco? S: No, it's south of San Francisco.
Communication Students talk about where they are from. S1: Where are you from? S2: I'm from Chiengmai. S1: Where's that? S2: It's in northern Thailand.

28 Looking for Things

① Note the use of *the* in line one and *a* in line three. **A** assumes that **B** knows which tape recorder **A** is referring to. *The* singles out and makes a choice.
② The pronoun *it* is used to refer to a specific thing: the tape recorder.
③ **OR** Now, where's there a cassette? ❖ A cassette here means *any one* cassette—not a particular cassette. **A** assumes there is a cassette somewhere; if **A** were not certain, the question might have been: Is there a cassette here? **OR** Do you have a cassette? ❖ *Now* in this line is not an adverb of time.
④ *One* is an indefinite pronoun that replaces *a cassette*. *One* replaces the indefinite article *a/an* + noun. ❖ *There* occurs in line four twice—once as part of the expression *there + be*, and again as the adverb of place *there*.

Practice Using a map of a familiar city or neighborhood, students make questions using *a/an*, or *the*. ♦ S1: Where's a bank? **OR** Where is there a bank? S2: There's one next to the post office. S1: Where's the high school? S2: It's in the middle of the town.
Communication Answer questions with the pronouns *it* or *one:* T: Do you have a bicycle? S: Yes, I have one. T: Do you like English? S: Yes, I like it. T: Do you have my pencil? S: No, I don't have it.

29 At a Bookstore

① Note the use of the relational *of:* a guidebook *of* France, **OR** a book *on* France, **OR** a book *about* France—not a France's guidebook. Also, a guide *to* France, a guidebook *on* France, but not a book *of* France ❖ Note the use of *you* in line one to refer to the bookstore.

-262-

Teaching/Study Notes

② Note the use of *we* to refer to the bookstore. **B** might have said <u>No, but I have a book about France right here</u>. **OR** <u>Yes, there's one right here</u>.
③ **OR** <u>Is there a map of France in it</u>?
④ Note: <u>in *the* front of . . .</u>, not <u>in front of . . .</u>; <u>at</u> or <u>in the back/middle/front of the book</u>; <u>at the end of the book</u>; <u>at the top of page 10</u>, <u>on page 10</u>, <u>on the last page of chapter 2</u>.
Practice Additional expressions for substitutions: *a calendar of events, a list of restaurants, the title of the book, the name of the author, a chapter on museums.*
Communication Assume a situation at a travel agency and ask for information using the relational *of* with expressions. ♦ S1: <u>Do you have a list of hotels near here</u>? S2: <u>Yes, we do</u>. S1: <u>Do you know the name of a good restaurant</u>? S2: <u>Yes, there's a good restaurant in front of this hotel</u>.

30 Whose?

① **OR** <u>Is this pen yours</u>? Possessive adjectives and possessive pronouns have been used in dialogues 10, 12, 13, and others.
② **OR** <u>No, that's not mine</u>.
Practice Listen for the differences: <u>Whose is it</u>? *vs* <u>Who is it</u>? Also: <u>Whose is in the room</u>? *vs* <u>Who's in the room</u>? ❖ Ask questions about objects belonging to students in the class. ♦ S1: <u>Whose hat is this</u>? S2: <u>Is it --S3--'s</u>? S3: <u>No, it's not mine. Maybe it's --S4--'s</u>. S4: <u>Yes, it's mine</u>. ❖ T: <u>Whose is this</u>? S1: <u>I don't know. It's not mine. Maybe it's --S2--'s</u>. T: <u>Is it yours, --S2--</u>? S2: <u>Yes, it is</u>.

31 Is This Yours?

② The modified pronouns *one/ones* are new. Note that in contrast to *one* in line four of dialogue 28, *one* refers here to a specific noun, because it is modified by *the*— <u>the blue one</u>. ❖ Note also: <u>red book,</u> or <u>red one</u>; but <u>history book</u>, not <u>history one</u>.
Practice Holding up two or more similar objects, the teacher or a student asks about one of them. T: <u>Is this (one) yours</u>? S: <u>No, the blue one is mine</u>.

32 Which One?

③ <u>Which ones are yours</u>? **OR** <u>Which are yours</u>?
④ **OR** <u>That one (there) is mine</u>. ❖ Note the order of the adjectives: *big brown*, not *brown big*; other common adjective combinations are *black and white, old red, large old, small green, big new.*
Practice Try the conversation replacing *yours* in line three with other possessives.
♦ <u>Which ones are his wife's</u>? ❖ Use questions from dialogues 30, 31, and 32.
♦ T: <u>Which pen is yours</u>? S1: <u>That new red one</u>. T: <u>Whose pencil case is this</u>? S1: <u>Maybe it's --S2--'s</u>. S2: <u>No, the blue one's mine</u>. ❖ Use *which* in questions. T: <u>Which bag do you like</u>? S: <u>I like the small one</u>. <u>Which one do you like</u>? T: <u>This one</u>.

Teaching/Study Notes

33 What's It Like?

① *Like* is an adverb here, not a verb. The question here elicits a physical description, but What's . . . like? may also be used to elicit a more subjective descriptions—descriptions of a person's personality, or feelings about a thing or person.
♦ S1: What's Mrs. ------ like? S2: Oh, she's nice. She's also a good teacher.
② OR blue leather. OR blue corduroy.
④ OR It's brown with fur trim.
Practice Learn the names of colors. (The question What color . . .? is introduced in lesson 71.) ❖ Learn basic parts, patterns, styles of clothing: *pocket, collar, cuff, stripes, polka dots, zipper, pleats, button, buckle, cotton, wool, blend, wool blend, cotton blend.* Use *with* in describing clothing. ♦ T: My shoes are brown and they have black shoe laces. S: My shoes are brown with black shoe laces. T: My shirt is blue and it has brown stripes. S: It's blue with brown stripes.

34 Two Places for Rent

① Note the use of *and* here to introduce contrasting information. *And* in line one could be replaced by *but*.
② *But* is used to introduce a point to convince or to persuade.
③ So does the apartment. As a conjunction *so* may be used to join two sentences: The house has a patio and *so* does the apartment. The pro-verb *do* replaces *have* in the second clause. This replacement is optional with have. Also acceptable: The house has a patio and so has the apartment. With verbs other than *have*, however, the pro-verb *do* is required. ♦ He likes school and so *do* I.
⑤ Note that *be* is used in line five with the conjunction *so*.
⑥ *Too* and *so* are both used to express positive agreement. *But* is used to contrast information: The house as a large kitchen *but* the apartment doesn't.
Practice Use a picture of two objects or persons and make comparisons.
♦ T: A is tall. S: So is B. OR B is too. Similar comparisons might be made of cities, schools, or classmates. ♦ S1: New York is large. S2: So is Tokyo. S1: I like ice cream. S2: So do I. OR I don't. ❖ Practice using *but*. ♦ He likes English but I don't.

35 Small Talk

① The verb *like* also appears in dialogue 23. *Like* here is transitive and must have an object. ❖ No article is required with *school* here. This is because *school* is being used in a general sense, or as a concept. Nor is an article used with *history class* in the substitutions, though *our* could be used as a determiner here. ❖ See **Appendix 22** for a list of noncount nouns.
③ OR I don't like sports either. *Either* is used as a rejoinder to show negative agreement. ♦ He doesn't like school, and I don't either.
④ *Sports* — not *a sport* or *the sport*. Individual sports may be used here in singular form: *swimming, baseball,* etc.

Teaching/Study Notes

⑥ I do too. OR Me too. ❖ Here *too* is used for positive concurrence. The You do? question is used for confirmation.
Practice Compare feelings about a variety of things. ♦ S1: Do you like English? S2: No, I don't. S1: I do. OR S2: Do you like phy-ed? S1: Yes. S2: I do too. ❖ Classmates ask questions with *have*. ♦ S1: Do you have a car? S2: No, I don't. S1: I don't either. OR S1: Do you have a car? S2: Yes, I do. S1: I do too. ❖ Try the practice using other familiar verbs. ♦ S1: Do you play tennis? S2: No, I don't. S1: I don't either.

36 A New Restaurant

① A *wh*-question with *do* occurs here for the first time. Note that *what* is the object of the sentence. They have what? becomes the normal question What do they have? *They* refers to a restaurant or company.
② Note the use of count and noncount nouns here. See **Appendix 22** for a list of count and noncount nouns.
⑤ How are their desserts? The question with *how* to elicit descriptive adjectives is used here for the first time since dialogue 6. The word *delicious* is not generally used in the question, though it is often the reply. ♦ Is it good? Yes, it's delicious.
⑥ Answer with an adjective or an adjective + noun. ♦ They're good. OR They're delicious. OR They have great desserts.
Practice Note that in previous dialogues the *wh*-question word has been the subject with *be* and *have*. Practice the *wh*-word as an object. ♦ T: Do you like baseball? S: No, I don't. T: What do you like? S: I like soccer. S1: Do you like spaghetti? S2: Yes, I do. What do you like? S1: I like pizza. ❖ Students make menus listing various dishes representing different nationalities or cultures. Classmates take the roles of customers in a restaurant and ask about the menus. ♦ S1: What do you have? S2: We have *sushi*. S1: Do you have onion soup? S2: No, we don't.

37 What Kind?

③ What kind (of) is used just like any other *wh*-question word. Note that *of* is omitted when the question word is not followed by a noun.
④ Use a name brand. ♦ *a Honda motorcycle, an IBM computer, a Grundig radio.*
⑥ *Car* is singular, so the singular form of *kind* is used. The plural form What kinds of cars do you like? solicits more than one name.
Practice Use *a kind of* in replies. ♦ T: What's a Honda? S: It's a kind of car. T: What's an apple? S: It's a kind of fruit.
Communication Ask *what kind of*-questions with *like*. ♦ S1: What kind of food do you like? OR What kinds of foods do you like? S2: I like Italian food. And I like salads. ❖ Ask also about *music, fruit, movies,* and other topics. Note that What kinds of movies do you like? is not the same as What movies do you like? Also, the question What sports do you like? is more likely than What kinds of sports do you like? (*What* + noun question is introduced in dialogue 41.)

Teaching/Study Notes

38 That Goes Here

① Note the idiomatic use of *go* here. *Go* and *belong* are intransitive verbs in this conversation, and they do not take objects. An alternative question is <u>Where do you want this</u>? The reply with *want* however, is very strong: <u>I want that over there</u> expresses a degree of authority. Also possible: <u>Where do you keep this</u>? A good reply to both of these questions is <u>That goes over there</u>.

② Note that the use of *belong* here is different from its use in dialogue 24, where the two-word verb *belong to* was introduced. ❖ In addition to *in the corner* and *on the TV*, the following expressions of place are included in the dialogue and substitutions: *above, beside, between, in, next to, on, on the right side of, on top of, under*. ❖ Note that two expressions of place or location are used together in this dialogue. Use them in the order suggested here, though the position of two expressions of location is often flexible. Dialogue 11 and others provide additional practice with expressions of place.

Practice Review dialogue 11, including **Practice** in the **T/S Notes**.

Communication The teacher hides an object while students have their eyes closed. Students ask *yes/no*-questions to locate the object. ▶ S1: <u>Is it in the bag on the desk</u>? T: <u>No</u>. S2: <u>Is it on the shelf in the cabinet in the corner</u>? T: <u>No</u>.

39 Lost and Found

② The simple past tense of *be* is introduced in dialogue 15.
③ The following prepositions are included in this dialogue: *behind, in, on, under*.
Practice Students are given a set time to observe a table on which several objects have been arranged. Cover the objects and ask questions about location. Prepositions and adverbs of place from previous dialogues should also be reviewed. ▶ T: <u>Where was the dictionary</u>? S: <u>It was under the eraser</u>.

40 What Time Is It?

④ 1:01 through 1:09 should be read *one-oh-one; one-oh-two, . . . one-oh-nine*. Other time expressions are read as follows: 1:10 = *one-ten;* 1:30 = *one-thirty* or *half past one;* 1:45 = *one-forty-five* or *a quarter-to*(or *of*)*-two;* 1:15 = *one-fifteen* or *a quarter after one.* ❖ <u>What time is your class</u>? means <u>What time does your class start</u>? See dialogue 42 for additional practice with <u>What time . . . ?</u> with verbs other than *be*. ❖ In addition to *almost*, other common adverbs with time include: *about, approximately,* and *exactly*.

⑤ The preposition *at* is used with time expressions to refer to a point in time.
Practice Talk about a school or company schedule that has been written on the blackboard. ▶ S1: <u>What time is the math class on Wednesday</u>? S2: <u>It's at 2:15</u>. S1: <u>What time is the meeting on Friday</u>? S2: <u>It's at 9:30</u>.

41 Wednesday the 19th

② The preposition *on* is used with days and dates; <u>on the 19th of July</u>, **OR** <u>on</u>

Teaching/Study Notes

January the 19th, **OR** on January 19th. ❖ It's on may be omitted in colloquial speech.

④ Note the use of the indefinite article with *Wednesday* to indicate an unspecified Wednesday. Omission of the article would imply the coming Wednesday, or a specific Wednesday.

Practice Review days of the week. ♦ T: Today is Wednesday. S: Tomorrow is Thursday. T: Today is Sunday. S: Tomorrow is Monday. ❖ Practice dates: T: Today is the 31st. S: Tomorrow is the first. T: Today is the second. S: Tomorrow is the third. ❖ Refer to a calendar and ask about days and dates. ♦ T: What day is the second? S: That's (It's) a Wednesday. T: Is the 14th a Wednesday? S: No, it's a Monday. The past tense of *be* may also be used.

Communication Students give their dates of birth. Do any fall on the same date? Students give the dates of some national holidays or other events in the their home countries.

42 Schedules

① The simple pres tense is used here to express a fact or a truth. He likes tennis is also an example of the simple present tense used to express a fact or a truth.

Practice Use *at* with a point in time and *in* to express an amount of time.
♦ T: ten o'clock S: *At* ten o'clock. T: ten minutes S: *In* ten minutes. ❖ Make a chronological list of activities for one day. Each student contributes one activity: ♦ S1: I get up at 7 o'clock. S2: I wash my face. S3: I eat breakfast. S4: I brush my teeth. S5: At 8:30 I go to school, etc.

Communication Make questions with what time . . .? using *get up, wake up, eat breakfast, arrive at school*, etc. Students ask each other questions about their daily schedules. ♦ S1: What time do you get up? S2: I get up at 7:30. S3: What time does class begin? S4: It begins at 1 o'clock.

43 Two Tours

② Do both of them go to Japan? **OR** Do both Tour A and Tour B go to Japan? **OR** Do they both go to Japan?

③ **OR** And both of them go to Hong Kong. ❖ The preposition of direction *to* with a place occurs here for the first time.

Practice Compare objects using *both*. Note the word order with *both* and *be* and with v other than *be*. They both study English. **OR** Both (of them) study English. **OR** Both students study English. **Also**, They are both red. Both of the pencils are red. **OR** Both the pencils are red. **OR** Both pencils are red. **OR** Both are red.

Communication Talk about classmates or about people whom all the students are familiar with. ♦ S: --C-- is from France and --D-- is from France. Both of them are from France. Both of them have short hair. They both like tennis. But --C-- is a graduate student and --D-- is an undergraduate student. Compare two cars, two schools, or two people, or pairs of other things.

Teaching/Study Notes

44 Travel Information
① **OR** Are there any departures . . . . ❖ Note the idioms: *a departure for* + a place and *to depart for* + a place
③ *On* is needed only once with a day and date together: *on Monday the 19th*
④ Note the use of the preposition *in* with time expressions: *in the afternoon, in the morning, in the evening.*
⑤ **OR** I see. OK. Thank you.
Practice See also dialogue 17 and **T/S Notes** 17 for review of *some* and *any*.
Communication Refer to an airline timetable or other transportation schedule and ask about departures. ▶ Do you have any departures for Paris on Saturday? What time is the flight?

45 How About Jam?
① **OR** Do we have any milk in the refrigerator?
② Use *a little* with noncount nouns and *a few* with count nouns. ❖ Note that *some* can be used with both plural count nouns and with noncount nouns, as in line six.
④ **OR** Yes, there are a few apples, but there aren't any oranges.
Practice Students ask about the contents of a large grocery bag. ▶ S1: Is there any coffee in the bag? T: No, there isn't. S2: Are there any oranges in the bag? T: Yes, there are. ❖ If necessary, review *some* and *any* in dialogue 17 and others.
Communication Students ask each other what they have at home. ▶ S1: Do you have any orange juice at home? S2: No, I don't. **OR** No, we don't.

46 Delicious Cake
① delicious **OR** really good
② The tag question in line two is a comment and does not seek confirmation or information. See **Appendix 1** for tag question intonation.
Practice Using the dialogue as a model, make conversation openers for the following situations: • you are in a new class at school; • you are a new employee at a company; • you see a new neighbor on the street; • you are at a party.

47 Her Car
① This is a confirmation question. See **Appendix 1** for tag question intonation.
④ **OR** You're right. She does have a 1990 Mercedes Benz, but that's not her car.
Practice Guessing game: use confirmation intonation with tag questions. ▶ S1: You have three brothers and sisters, don't you? S2: No, and you don't either. **OR** No, but you do. S1: You're right. I don't. **OR** You're right. I do. S1: You have a driver's licence, don't you? S2: Yes, and you do too. S1: You're right. I do. **OR** You're wrong. I don't.

48 Is It Expensive?
④ Other intensifiers include *fairly, reasonably,* and *sort of.* Use *not very* in this

Teaching/Study Notes

way: It's *not* in *very* good condition. It's *not very* cheap. Use *sort of* and *kind of* like this: It's *sort of* in good condition. Isn't that car *kind of* expensive? Also possible: *not so*. ♦ That's *not so* expensive.
Practice Use intensifiers or adverbs of degree. ♦ T: Is this class easy? S1: No, It's very difficult. S2: It's sort of easy.

49 Korea, Not Japan

② **B** corrects **A**, and gives additional stress to *Korea* and *Japan*. Note that the subject pronouns in the dialogue may have to be changed in the substitutions.
⑤ *No* in line five, and *yes* in line six get additional stress because they offer contrasting positions.
Practice Use additional stress on corrected information. ♦ T: He lives in New York. S: No, he lives in Paris (stress on *Paris*). T: He lives in New York. S: No, he *works* in New York (stress on *works*). ❖ Students are assigned various nationalities for this exercise, and they guess where their classmates are from. Answer questions with additional stress if it is necessary to make a correction.
♦ S1: Are you from France? S2: No, I'm from *Canada*. **OR** Yes, I am.

50 Once in a While

① **OR** What do you like to do in your free time? **OR** How do you spend your free time?
② See **Appendix 1** for the intonation pattern used with lists.
④ Common adverbs of frequency include (in order of descending frequency): *always, usually, very often, quite often, sometimes, once in a while, seldom, rarely, hardly ever, never*. Note the adverbs of degree *very* and *quite*. Note also: No, almost never, and No, rarely—the adverbs are qualifications of *no*. *But* may be used to introduce a qualified reply with *yes*: Yes, but almost never, and Yes, but rarely.
Practice Students talk about what they do *on weekends, evenings, after school* in place of *in your free time* in line one. ❖ Make sentences with adverbs of frequency. ♦ T: never S: I never get up at 6 o'clock. T: sometimes S: Sometimes I don't eat breakfast. ❖ Common activities with *go* include: *go fishing, go bowling, go hiking, go on a hike, go swimming, go driving*.
Communication Students ask each other about their daily activities. Use *ever*.
♦ Do you ever take the bus to school? Do you ever shop at the store across from the library? Do you ever come late to class? Do you ever go to bed at 9 o'clock? Use adverbs of frequency in replies to the questions.

51 How Often?

① Note that *to* is not required with *go abroad*. Other expressions that do not take the preposition include: *go overseas, go downtown, go there, go home, come here, go away*.

Teaching/Study Notes

② OR No, rarely. OR Yes, but very seldom.
③ OR How often? Note: if a transitive verb is used in line one, an object is usually required when the verb is used in line three. ♦ ① Do you ever skip class? ③ How often do you skip class? The verb *play* is an exception. ♦ A: Do you ever play tennis? B: Yes. A: How often to you play?
④ OR about once a year. OR around once a year. ❖ *Or so* means *approximately* or *about*.
Communication Students get information from classmates using *how often*. ♦ S1: How often do you use the language lab? S2: I never use the language lab. S3: How often do you go to a movie (or to movies)? S4: I go about twice a month.

52 Gift Suggestions
② *She* in the dialogue can be replaced with *he* and *they* for additional practice.
⑥ *Thanks for* + noun. Introduce other common expressions with *thanks:* thanks for dinner, ~ the good time, ~ the birthday present, ~ your help, etc.
Practice Provide a list of sports and other leisure activities to expand vocabulary in this area. What activities or sports do the students like? ♦ Do you like to play golf?
❖ See also expressions with *go* in **T/S Notes** 50 and in **Appendix 25**. Additional vocabulary for substitutions: *play chess, play baseball, play cards, play with dolls, play with model airplanes.*
Communication Students tell the class what they like to do, and what they don't like to do. ♦ S1: I like to go to movies. S2: I don't like to study English. ❖ Students ask classmates what they like to do. ♦ Do you like to ski? ❖ Students find classmates with similar interests and report to the class. ♦ S1: --A-- and I both like to play chess. S2: Both --B-- and I like to watch television.

53 Wants and Desires
① Note the use of *want* + noun phrase in line one and *want + to* v in line three.
Communication Tell what you want. ♦ S1: I want a new bicycle. S2: I want a good part-time job. S3: I want an A in English. S4: I want some free time. ❖ Tell what you want or don't want to do. ♦ S1: I want to go fishing. S2: I want to go for a drive. S3: I don't want to study for a test.

54 Smile!
Practice Other expressions for substitution: *move to the left/right, come forward, hold still, stand together, hold hands.*

55 Picnic Plans
① The present continuous is used for the first time in this dialogue. Here the present continuous expresses future intention. The present continuous is used to express present activity in dialogue 56.
② --C-- is. OR --C-- is bringing the salad.

Teaching/Study Notes

③ The quantifier *some* may be omitted here.
Practice Additional food items for substitutions include: *barbecue sauce, butter, charcoal, cooking oil, fire wood, ice, margarine, onions, pickles, plastic spoons and forks, sausages, soda pop, a table cloth, watermelon,* and other dishes representing different nationalities in the classroom. The following verbs may also be used in conversations about preparing food: *make, fix, prepare.*
Communication Ask about intentions using *wh-*ques. ♦ S1: Where are you having lunch today? S2: I'm having lunch in the cafeteria. S3: What time are you going home? S4: I'm going home at noon.

56 Who Am I Thinking Of?

③ Note *have on* is a two-word separable verb. ♦ I *have* my heavy coat *on*. Do you *have on* your expensive hat?
⑦ *Think of* is a two-word inseparable verb.
Practice This guessing game begins "I'm thinking of someone in this room." Students should be permitted to ask no more than about ten questions to guess the name of the person the teacher is thinking of.

57 To the Kitchen

② **OR** I'm going to the kitchen. *To* in line two indicates direction to a place.
③ **OR** Are you going to the kitchen to wash the dishes? ❖ Clause of purpose: *to + v*. To wash the dishes expresses the purpose or reason for going to the kitchen.
④ **OR** I'm not going to the kitchen to wash the dishes.
Practice Use *to + v* in clauses of purpose. ♦ T: You're going to the library. S: I'm going to the library to study. T: You're going downtown. S: I'm going downtown to go shopping.

58 Gossip

① Guess what! is imperative in form, but the expression does not, in fact, usually anticipate a guess. The response is often *What?*
Practice Use *be going to + v* in *yes/no-*questions. ♦ S1: Are you going to study in the library tonight? S2: Yes, I am. S3: Are you going to come to school tomorrow? S4: No, I'm not.
Communication Students tell the class what they are going to do or not going to do on the coming weekend. Encourage humorous responses. ♦ S1: I'm not going to climb Mt. Everest. S2: I'm going to teach English.

59 At a Sale

① Note that *look at* is an inseparable two-word verb, and *try on* is a separable two-word verb.
② not my size **OR** not my style **OR** not my taste
③ Try it on, not Try on it. A separable verb must be separated by the object when

Teaching/Study Notes

the object is a pronoun.
④ **OR** <u>I want to try on this leather jacket.</u>
⑤ Note that *look for* is an inseparable two-word verb.
Practice Two useful separable verbs are *put on* and *take off*. Note that *put on* is different from *wear*. See **Appendix 21** for additional two-word verbs. ❖ Introduce additional items of clothing, and the quantifier *a pair of: blouse, skirt, cap, coat, dress shirt, sweater, tie, hat, underwear(noncount n), undershirt;* the quantifier *a pair of* may be used with: *pants, shorts, slacks, underpants, stockings, glasses.*

60 Doing Things

① *Everyone* appears here for the first time.
② **OR** <u>She's changing her clothes.</u> *In her room* may be omitted if it does not precede *changing clothes,* because the nature of the activity suggests it is taking place in her room. <u>She's changing her clothes in her room</u> is also possible, however that word order gives unnecessary attention to the activity in response a *where*-question. If the location is more important than the activity, the adverb of place should precede the activity. ▶ <u>She's in the kitchen eating.</u>
Practice Make *wh*-questions. ▶ S1: <u>I'm going home.</u> S2: <u>Where are you going?</u>
S3: <u>I'm looking for my dictionary.</u> S4: <u>What are you looking for?</u>
S5: <u>I'm going home at 3 o'clock.</u> S6: <u>When (What time) are you going home?</u>
Communication Talk about the present activities of friends or relatives using *probably*. ▶ S1: <u>What is your husband doing now?</u> S2: <u>He's probably having lunch.</u>
S3: <u>What is your mother doing now?</u> S4: <u>She's probably cleaning the house.</u>

61 Plans

① **OR** <u>Are you studying this afternoon?</u> Although the present continuous may be used, intention is more commonly expressed with <u>*be going to* + v</u>.
Communication Ask about intentions. ▶ S1: <u>Are you going to take the bus home today?</u> S2: <u>No, I'm going to walk home.</u> S3: <u>Are you going to invite me to your party?</u> S4: <u>Yes, of course.</u> ❖ Students tell what their plans are for after school. Use *first* and *then*. ▶ S1: <u>First I'm going to go home, and then I'm going to go to a basketball game.</u> S2: <u>First I'm going to go to the barber shop, and then I'm going to my friend's house.</u>

62 Right Now

① Note that *be going to* + v expresses intention in line one. Contrast this with the present continuous in line two, which expresses an activity happening now.
④ Note how the adverb of place comes after *be* and before the present participle. This is the most logical position for the adverb of place in this line.
Practice The expressions *get ready for* and *complain about* are introduced in the substitutions. ❖ Practice the present continuous with adverbs of place. Usually the adverb of place goes between *be* and the present participle. See the **T/S Notes** for

Teaching/Study Notes

dialogue 60. Put the adv of place after the present participle if the location is unusual for the activity. ♦ T: <u>She's washing her hair</u>. S1: <u>She's *in the bathroom* washing her hair</u>. S2: <u>She's washing her hair *in living room*</u>.

63 Late for Work
② Note the short confirmation question. Also possible: <u>Really</u>? <u>Is that so</u>?
④ **OR** <u>He doesn't</u>?
⑤ *No* is also a possible response here. <u>No</u> means <u>No, he doesn't finish his work</u>. <u>Yes</u> means <u>Yes, really</u>. <u>It's true</u>.
⑥ <u>He doesn't deserve a promotion</u>. **OR** <u>He doesn't deserve to have</u> (or *get*) <u>a promotion</u>.
Practice Note that in the substitutions, the verb in line two may have to be changed to agree with the verb in line one. Practice short questions as replies. ♦ T: <u>They come to class late every day</u>. S: <u>Do they</u>? T: <u>He's studying in his room</u>. S: <u>Is he</u>? T: <u>I don't like to drive</u>. S: <u>You don't</u>? ❖ Try the dialogue again with positive attributes of the employee and change lines six and seven to: B: <u>He really deserves a promotion</u>. A: <u>Yes, he does</u>.
Communication Talk about a good student. What does he or she do? ♦ <u>He studies three hours every day</u>. <u>She always does her homework</u>. Talk about a good worker or employee. What does he or she do? ♦ <u>She is very polite to customers</u>. <u>He is never late for work</u>.

64 By Yourself?
② Reflexive pronouns are introduced in this dialogue: *myself, yourself, himself, herself, (itself), ourselves, yourselves, themselves*. *Itself* is not used in the dialogue.
③ **OR** <u>No, I'm not going to play tennis by myself</u>.
Practice Use reflexive pronouns. ♦ S: <u>Is ------ going downtown by himself</u>? T: <u>No, he isn't</u>. **OR** <u>Yes, he is</u>.

65 Newer Than That
① The negative question suggests certainty here—that **A** is quite confident that he or she knows whom the dictionary belongs to.
Practice The following adjectives form the comparative with the *-er* suffix: *big, cheap, clean, dirty, easy, far (farther), fast, fat, funny, good (better), heavy, high, large, low, long, narrow* (or *more narrow*), *new, old, poor, pretty, rich, safe, shiny, short, slow, small, thick, thin, wide, young*. Use *-er* to form the comparative of adjectives. ♦ T: <u>clean</u> S: <u>cleaner</u> ❖ Ask *yes/no*-questions with comparatives in this guessing game. ♦ T: <u>I'm thinking of something in this room</u>. S: <u>Is it smaller than an eraser</u>? T: <u>No</u>. S1: <u>Is it an eraser</u>? T: <u>No</u>. S2: <u>Is it larger than that bag</u>? T: <u>Yes</u>. S3: <u>Is it that chair</u>? T: <u>Yes</u>. ❖ Compare pictures of two things, or pairs of objects, using the adjectives listed above. ♦ T: <u>this book and that book</u> S: <u>That</u>

Teaching/Study Notes

book is thicker than this book. ❖ Make questions with <u>which</u>. Review *which* in dialogue 32 if necessary. ♦ S1: <u>Which book is newer, this one or that one</u>? S2: <u>This one is newer than that one</u>. S3: <u>Which class is easier, the morning class or the afternoon class</u>? S4: <u>The morning class is easier than the afternoon class</u>.

66 A Difficult Language

① Adjectives of more than one syllable usually form the comparative with *more*.
Practice The following adjectives form the comparative with *more: ambitious, beautiful, comfortable, convenient, crowded, dangerous, difficult, expensive, famous, honest, important, interesting, modern, useful*. Replace the final *-y* with *-ier* in some two-syllable adjectives to form the comparative. See also **Appendix 26** for a list of some adjectives with two or more syllables. ❖ Use both *-er* and *more* comparative forms: ♦ T: <u>important</u> S: <u>more important</u> T: <u>funny</u> S: <u>funnier</u>
Communication Compare cities, countries, people, cars, or other things of interest to the class. Use as many adjectives as possible. ♦ S1: <u>Who is taller, --C-- or --D--</u>?
S2: <u>--D--- is taller than --C--</u>. S3: <u>Is your brother older than you or younger than you</u>? S4: <u>He's younger than I</u>.

67 The World's Longest

① The *-est* superlative suffix for adjectives is introduced here.
Practice Use the *-est* superlative suffix with one-syllable adj. Replace the final *-y* in some two-syllable adj with *-iest* to form the superlative: *big, cheap, clean, dirty, easy, far (farthest), fast, fat, funny, good (best), heavy, high, large, long, low, narrow* (or *most narrow*), *new, old, poor, pretty, rich, safe, shiny, short, slow, small, thick, thin, wide, young*. ♦ T: <u>clean</u> S: <u>cleanest</u>

68 The Most Expensive

② Adjectives of more than one syllable usually form the superlative with <u>*most* + adj</u>. The definite article *the* is usually used along with superlative forms of adjectives.
④ The intensifier or adverb of degree *much* is introduced here. Another adverb of degree is *a little*. ♦ <u>This restaurant is *a little* more expensive than that one</u>.
Practice Use *the most* superlative form with the following adjectives: *ambitious, beautiful, comfortable, convenient, crowded, dangerous, difficult, expensive, famous, honest, important, interesting, modern, useful*. See also **Appendix 26** for a list of adjectives of two or more syllables. ❖ Form superlatives with *-est* and *most*.
♦ T: <u>important</u> S: <u>most important</u> T: <u>low</u> S: <u>lowest</u> ❖ Compare three things: ♦ T: <u>Tokyo - New York - Mexico City</u> S1: <u>Tokyo is larger than New York</u>. S2: <u>Mexico City is the largest of the three</u>. ❖ Students choose three cities, countries, people, movies, etc. to compare. ❖ Practice adverbs of degree. Use *much, a lot, a little, a little bit*. ♦ T: <u>Is --C-- taller than --D--</u>? S: <u>Yes, --C-- is much taller than --D--</u>. T: <u>Is English more difficult than French</u>? S: <u>It's a little more difficult than French</u>.

Teaching/Study Notes

Communication Students report to the class on some world records using superlative forms. ♦ The oldest person in the world lives in France.

69 Busy People

④ Plural forms of days of the week and some other time expressions may be used to express habitualness. ♦ I teach English *Wednesday afternoons*. I spend *weekends* in the countryside. The same meaning may be expressed with *every*. ♦ I teach English *every* Wednesday afternoon. I spend *every* weekend in the countryside.
Practice Note: I'm meeting a friend and I have a meeting with a friend are not the same. ❖ *Have a date* is an idiom. Some other idioms with *have* include: *have a class, have an appointment, have a lecture, have an engagement, have a lesson.* Also, *date* and *appointment* should not be used interchangeably; they are not necessarily synonymous.
Communication Talk about weekly activities. Use the plural forms of time expressions if possible. ♦ I have a piano lesson on Monday afternoons. I work weekdays from 5 to 7.

70 Good Movies

① The pattern *as* + adj + *a* noun + *as* is used with count nouns. Comparisons of noncount nouns can be made using the following pattern: *as* + adj + *as* ♦ Is this coffee as good as that coffee?
Practice Ask questions using the patterns in lines one and three. ♦ S1: Is Montréal as large as New York? **OR** Is Montréal as large a city as New York? S2: No, New York is larger.
Communication Make comparisons of topics or things of interest. ♦ S1: Is the air here as clean as the air in your town? S2: No, the air here is cleaner. S3: Is the morning class as large as the afternoon class? S4: The morning class is larger than the afternoon class.

71 Size and Shape

① **OR** What are the dimensions of the desk?
⑤ The question What color...? is used here for the first time.
⑦ **OR** What condition is it in? (answer: It's in good condition. **OR** It's not in good condition.)
⑧ **OR** Yes, it is.
Practice Make questions with *how* + adj. Use *big, cold, expensive, heavy, high, hot, tall.* ♦ How cold (or warm) is it outside today? How tall is this building? How expensive was that restaurant?

72 A Shopping List

④ Is that all? **OR** Anything else?
⑤ No. **OR** No, that's not all. ❖ some ice cream, **OR** a carton of ice cream, **OR** a

Teaching/Study Notes

liter (or gallon) of ice cream.
⑥ Anything else? **OR** Is that all?
Practice Study the list of quantifiers in **Appendix 23**. Use quantifiers with noncount nouns. ♦ S1: milk S2: a bottle of milk, or a carton of milk ❖ Plan a party. Students think of the things they would need to buy for the party. The class makes a list. Be sure to take into account the number of people in the class. ♦ We need four watermelons. We need five kilograms of chicken.

73 Quantities
① **OR** There isn't enough juice. *Enough* and *more* can be used with both count and noncount nouns.
② Use *much* with noncount nouns and *many* with count nouns. How much is there? **OR** How much do we have?
⑤ Note that *enough + of* must be used here, while in line one, *of* cannot be used with *enough*. The preposition *of* must be used with a determiner. Thus, *enough of the music, enough of this weather, enough of the speech,* but *enough music, enough money, enough time, enough rain.*
Practice Review: use *much* with noncount and *many* with count nouns. ♦ T: apples S: How many apples? T: rice S: How much rice? ❖ Practice how much and how many and quantifiers. S1: How much butter do you have at home? S2: We have one package (500 grams) of butter. S3: How many cartons of milk do you have? S4: We have two cartons of milk.

74 Let's Go to a Movie
① *Let's* is a contraction for *let us*. Do not confuse it with the third person singular form *lets*, which means *allow*.
② Let's not go to a movie again. **OR** Not again.
④ Let's go out to eat. **OR** Do you want to go out to eat? **OR** How about going out to eat?
⑤ Go out to eat? is a rhetorical confirmation question that communicates indifference to the suggestion.
Practice Make rhetorical confirmation questions. ♦ T: Let's study. S: Study? T: Do you want to go to a movie? S: Go to a movie?

75 Pastimes
① . . . knits *a lot*. **OR** . . . knits *often*. **OR** . . . ------ certainly does a lot of knitting. Also possible in substitution one: She does a lot of piano practicing. **OR** . . . practicing on the piano.
④ **OR** Knitting is her hobby. A pastime, however, may not necessarily be a hobby. A hobby is usually a creative or educational activity. A pastime is broader in meaning, and includes regular, free-time activities.
Communication Ask classmates about their hobbies and pastimes. ♦ S1: What is

Teaching/Study Notes

your favorite pastime? S2: <u>Playing chess</u>. S1: <u>Do you have a hobby</u>? S2: <u>Yes</u>. S1: <u>What is it</u>? S2: <u>Studying the moon through my telescope</u>.

76 Doing Well

① *How + be + s + doing*? can be used to inquire about the physical health of a person, or about something which is of concern to the person. ♦ <u>How are you doing with your new job</u>? <u>How is ------ doing with her project</u>? *Coming* and *going* are also used in similar idioms: <u>How are you coming in your English class</u>? <u>How is ------ coming with his driving lessons</u>? <u>How is ------ coming in the hospital</u>? <u>How's your new job going</u>?
② Although it is not strictly correct, *good* is often heard in place of *well* in conversational English. ❖ *Quite* is an adverb of degree. Other intensifiers include *extremely, really, very, rather, pretty, fairly, not very, terribly.*
③ *Well* is optional here.
Practice Talk about classes or other activities ♦ <u>Are you doing well in your history class</u>? <u>How're your swimming lessons going</u>?

77 Getting Better

① **OR** <u>How are you feeling today</u>? ❖ <u>How are you today</u>? is generally not a request for information about one's physical condition, however, in the context of a hospital or other health or medical environment, for example, it can be.
③ **OR** <u>How does your leg feel</u>? Other vocabulary items that might be used in substitutions include: *arm, eye, finger, foot, hand, head, heel, knee, stomach, toe.*
④ *Much* is used with the comparative form only: *much better*, but *very good*.

78 A Self-Introduction

① **OR** Hello. <u>I'm --C-- --D--</u>. **OR** <u>Excuse me. I don't think we've met. My name is --C-- --D--</u> (given name and family name).
② **OR** <u>I'm --E-- --F--</u>. ❖ <u>How do you do</u>? is an expression for making introductions and does not express interest in another's physical condition.
④ The *wh*-question is usually characterized by falling intonation. Note the rising intonation in this *wh*-ques with *again:* <u>What's your last name again</u>? Rising intonation in a *wh*-ques is usually used to seek a repetition of some information.
Practice Use rising intonation in *wh*-questions to seek a repetition of information.
♦ T: <u>I'm from India</u>. S: <u>Where are you from</u>? **OR** <u>You're from where</u>? T: <u>It's 3:30</u>. S: <u>What time is it</u>? T: <u>Dr. Braun has a new car</u>. S: <u>Who has a new car</u>? **OR** <u>What does Dr. Braun have</u>?
Communication Introduce yourself to one or more classmates.

79 Tourist Attractions

① **OR** <u>What does Honolulu have to see</u>? **OR** <u>What are some tourist attractions in Honolulu</u>?

Teaching/Study Notes

③ **OR** Does Honolulu have a zoo?
⑦ **OR** That sounds interesting. *That* is frequently omitted in this situation.
Communication Students tell the class about their hometowns or countries or other familiar places. What are some tourist attractions in those places?

80 At Dinner
① **OR** Would you please . . .. **OR** Could you please pass the salad to me.
③ Note that all the food items in the substitutions take the definite article.
④ **B** might also make an offer here. ♦ How about some more bread too?
Practice Try dialogue 54 using the polite expressions *could* and *would* with *please*. In requests, *would* is slightly more direct than *could*. ❖ Note how the negative request is formed with *would*. ♦ Would you please not open the window. *Would* is preferred to *could* in negative requests.

81 A Request
① **OR** Please show the new contract to --C-- and --D--.
② *Right now* expresses more immediacy than *now*.
④ **OR** OK. **OR** All right. **OR** Of course.
Practice Other verbs for substitutions include: *fax, lend, loan, pass, send, take.* See **Appendix 11** for additional verbs. ❖ Make requests in the classroom. ♦ S: --C--, please give your pen to --D--. **OR** S: --C--, please give --D-- your pen.

82 Why?
③ The *why*-question occurs here for the first time. ❖ **OR** Why aren't you going to class?
④ How come you're not going? **OR** Why aren't you going? ❖ The question with *how come* is more informal than the question with *why*. *How come* should usually not be used in formal or written English.
⑤ Other reasons may be given here too, including those not beginning with the personal pronoun *I*. ♦ Because my car is not running. **OR** Because it's going to rain this afternoon.
⑥ **OR** That's a good reason for not going to class. **OR** That's a good reason not to go to class.
Practice Use *why* in questions with *be* and *do*. ♦ T: The class wasn't difficult. S: Why wasn't the class difficult? T: They didn't come to class. S: Why didn't they come to class? ❖ Make questions with *why* and *home come*. ♦ T: Why were you late for class? S: How come you were late for class? T: How come you didn't do your homework? S: Why didn't you do your homework?

83 Getting Around
① **OR** How are you *getting* to the party tonight? **OR** How are you *going* to the party tonight?

-278-

Teaching/Study Notes

② *By* is also used with other modes of transportation: *by car, by train, by subway, by plane, by ship;* exception: *on foot.* Perhaps more likely to be heard, however, are: I'm walking home. I'm flying to London. I'm driving to the party. I'm taking the subway. I'm taking the ferry. I'm taking my bicycle to school. I'm going in -- A--'s car. I'm going with my friend in his car.
④ The word *cab* is sometimes heard for *taxi,* or *taxicab.*
Communication How do you come to school? Take a survey in your classroom. How do the students in the class come to school? What is the most popular means of transportation?

84 I Think So Too
① *That* is optional in line one.
⑤ Note: *that* is not used with the pro-clause with *so.* ❖ I think so, too. **OR** Me too.
Practice Do you agree? Use *think so* to agree or disagree with the affirmative opinions of others. T: I think this lesson is interesting. S: I think so too. **OR** I don't think so. T: I think the weather here is wonderful. Don't you think so too? S: Yes, I do. **OR** No, I don't think so.

85 Predictions
① *Will* is used here to make a prediction, but in discussing future activities or plans and intentions *going to* + verb is preferable. *Will* is also used to state something very emphatically, or to make a promise or to offer assurance: ♦ I won't be there next Tuesday. I'll help you. I won't tell anyone. ❖ In the *yes/no*-question, *be going to* + v is preferable to *will* when asking about intentions, because the question with *will* sometimes sounds like a request. Compare: Will you play tennis this weekend? and Are you going to play tennis this weekend?
② **OR** That's nice. **OR** I see. **OR** Oh, really?
⑤ **OR** Perhaps. **OR** Yes, you will.
Communication What do you predict? Make predictions about people or events.
♦ I predict that I won't be here next year. I predict that I'll be a doctor some day. I predict that it won't rain tomorrow.

86 Offering Help
① *Would like* can replace *want* here, and *would like* sounds gentler. Would you like me to mail this letter? ❖ *Wh*-ques: What would you like me to do? ❖ Note that *want* + obj + *to* v is very strong as a request: I want you to mail that letter. The boss wants us to finish this work by noon.
② **OR** Will you please mail that. ❖ *Would* sounds a little gentler than *will* and can replace *will* in lines two and four. ♦ Yes, mail that, would you please. Would you buy some stamps too.
Practice Make requests with *would* and *will.* ♦ Would you please lend me your pen? Will you please help me for a minute? ❖ See also requests in dialogue 80.

Teaching/Study Notes

87 Dining Out
① *Be going to + v* indicates intention in this line; *will* is not likely in this context.
❖ *the trout* or *trout;* the definite article can be used because *the trout* refers to an item on the menu.
② *That* is optional after *think,* and is commonly dropped. ❖ **OR** I think I'm going to... ❖ *Going to* can replace *will* here, but *will* is more typical after *I think*....
④ I think I will too. **OR** I think I'll get some potato salad too.
⑥ Why? means Why do you ask?
Practice Make a menu and set up restaurant situations in the classroom. See **Appendix 22** for additional food vocabulary. Students work in pairs and talk about what they would like to have for dinner. ♦ S1: What would you like to have for lunch (or dinner or supper) today? What are you going to have? S2: I think I'll have soup. ❖ Talk about plans for the weekend using the patterns in lines one and two in replies to questions. ♦ S1: What are you going to do this weekend? S2: I'm going to clean up my apartment. **OR** I think I'll clean up my apartment.

88 Hopeful
① **OR** I hope the weather will be nice tomorrow. *Hope* expresses what is both desirable and possible.
② *So* replaces the *that*-clause. ❖ *Be* (with *will be*) is necessary in line two, but the verb *rain* (with *will rain*) is not necessary in line four.
④ **OR** I don't think that it will rain.
⑤ **OR** I hope it doesn't (rain).
Practice Elicit responses with *hope* from classmates. Ask questions with *do you think*...? ♦ S: Do you think the test will be easy? S2: I hope so. S3: Do you think it will rain tomorrow? S4: I hope not.

89 The Weekend
② *Will* is often used with *probably* when talking about oneself.
⑤ When it describes one's own intentions, *I think* is usually followed by *will*, rather than by *be + going to.*
Practice Talk about plans. Use *be going to* for definite plans, and *will probably* for plans that are not definite. ♦ I'm going to go home after this class. I'll probably go for a bicycle ride on Sunday. **OR** I think I'll go for a bicycle ride on Sunday.

90 Keeping Busy
① **OR** What do you plan on doing...?
② **OR** I plan to take a nap. **OR** I'm planning to take a nap. **OR** I'm planning on taking a nap.
④ Here the present continuous is used to express future intention. **OR** I'm going to have dinner.... **OR** I'm planning on having dinner.... **OR** I'm planning to have dinner....

Teaching/Study Notes

⑥ **OR** I don't have any definite plans for tomorrow though. ❖ *Though* is used to express a concession.
Practice Use the following expressions: *plan to* + v; *plan on* + v-*ing*. Make short replies to questions. ♦ T: Do you plan to study tonight? S1: No, I don't. T: Are you planning on staying home on Saturday? S2: Yes, I am. ❖ Make *wh*-ques and ask about intentions. S1: What do you plan to do this weekend? S2: I'm going shopping. S1: What are you planning on buying? S2: I'm planning to buy a belt. S1: What store are you going to go to? S2: I don't know.
Communication Reply to the questions truthfully. Do you have any plans for the weekend? What do you plan to do after class? Are you doing anything tomorrow? Are you planning on doing anything tonight?

91 Starting Tomorrow

① Note that *stop* + v-*ing* is very different from *stop* + *to* v. Compare I'm going to stop smoking with I'm going to stop to smoke.
② **OR** Are you?
④ **OR** Beginning when?
Practice *start/stop* + v-*ing* may be used to admonish someone. ♦ When are you going to start coming to class on time! When are you going to stop teasing your brother! ❖ Note: When does the class start? The opposite is: When is the class over? not When does the class stop?

92 Another Roll?

① The quantifier *more* is used with noncount nouns and plural count nouns, and *another* is used with singular count nouns in this conversation.
② If the food item in line one is a count noun, be sure to use the plural pronoun *they* here: They are delicious though. If a quantifier is used — a bowl of soup — use the singular *it* in line two. Note: *delicious* is not normally used in questions. ♦ Is it delicious? is not heard in colloquial English. Instead, ask Is it good? **OR** How is it?
③ Offers may be made with *will* or *won't* or *would* with little or no change in meaning. ♦ Won't you have another roll? **OR** Would you care for another roll?
④ *I'd* is a contraction of *I would*; other contracted forms with would: *she'd, he'd, it'd, you'd, we'd, they'd*.
Practice Make a list of food items, including the national dishes of various countries. Practice making offers using *more, another* and items of food with quantifiers. See **Appendix 23** for a list of quantifiers. See also dialogues 72 and 73 for additional practice with count and noncount nouns.

93 More Salad?

① *Care for* is used in question patterns with polite offers, and in the negative as in line four, but generally not in affirmative statements. *Would care* is also used

Teaching/Study Notes

with _to + v_, and it may be used with _for + v-ing_.
Practice Make offers. ♦ S1: Would you care to have lunch with me this evening. S2: Yes, thank you. ❖ Indicate personal preferences using _care to + v_ or _care for + v-ing_: ♦ S1: I don't care to go to horror movies. S2: I don't care for skiing.

94 Some of Them
① Use a given name here, or a family name with an honorific: Mr., Mrs., Miss, Ms.
② **OR** Yes? a more formal response.
③ _Some_ is occasionally heard where _any_ is used in line three, but that usage is not strictly correct.
④ Use _them_ to replace a plural count noun and _it_ in place of a noncount noun.
⑥ **OR** Yes, and one is --D--'s, and the rest are --E--'s.
Practice It is also possible to ask specifically about quantity with _how many of_ (with count nouns)/_how much of_ (with noncount nouns) + noun or pronoun: ♦ How many of them are yours? How much of it is yours? See also dialogue 73 for practice with _how many_ and _how much_ questions. ❖ Note that _part of_ (in substitution one) is used with noncount nouns only: part of the cake. It is not used correctly with plural count nouns. _Half of_, on the other hand, can be used with both count and noncount nouns. ♦ Half of the chairs belong here and half in the other room. _The other_ (see _other_ in dialogue 95) _half_, _the other part_, etc., might also be introduced. _A piece of_ may also be introduced for use with some noncount nouns.
Communication Students do a survey in the class. How many of the students walk to school? Get information from classmates, such as which countries the students represent, favorite sports of the students, etc. Make reports about the class. ♦ Three of the students are from Switzerland. Six students like tennis.

95 Helping Others
④ Note that the singular form of _there + be_ is often heard with the plural noun: There's six of them.
⑥ There's another. . .. **OR** There's another one. ❖ _Another_ means literally _one other;_ the plural form is _two others, three others_, etc. ❖ the other one, **OR** the other.
Practice See also dialogue 104 for additional practice with _another, the other, the others, other, others_.

96 Feeling Ill
② **OR** I've got a fever. I feel dizzy. I feel sick. I don't feel well.
④ Note the difference between I've got (or I have) in line two and I've got to (or I have to) in line four.
⑤ Note that _have got to_ is generally not used in a _yes/no_-question. Use _have to_ in _yes/no_-questions. Do you really _have to_ go to the store?
Practice Tell something _you've got to do_ today. ♦ I've got to go shopping.

Teaching/Study Notes

97 A Dining Experience
③ Use *have*, not *eat* for good idiomatic usage. ❖ **OR** What did you have to eat?
④ I had chicken . . . . *not* I ate chicken . . . .
⑤ <u>*Have + to* v</u> in this line is not the modal of necessity. The limited use of *have* with certain infinitives *(eat, drink, play with, read)* usually suggests availability.
▶ <u>What did the children *have to play* with?</u> (**OR** <u>What was there for the children to play with?</u>) <u>We don't *have* anything *to eat* in the refrigerator.</u> <u>Does he *have* anything *to read?*</u> ❖ Note that this use of *have + to* v is pronounced differently from the modal of necessity *have to*.
⑦ Note: *have for dessert* (or *have to eat for dessert*). Also, *have for dinner, have for breakfast*.
Practice What did your classmates have to eat for breakfast today? What are they going to have for lunch? Make a survey of students in the class.

98 A Great Trip
② The past tense of regular verbs is introduced here. See **Appendix 2** for pronunciation of the *-ed* suffix of *arrived, liked, stayed, visited*. See **Appendix 19** for a list of high-frequency regular verbs.
⑤ **OR** <u>Did your husband have a good time?</u>
Practice Give the past tense form of regular verbs. ▶ T: <u>follow</u> S: <u>followed</u>

99 Travel Experiences
① **OR** <u>We had a lot of fun in England.</u> <u>We enjoyed England.</u>
④ See **Appendix 20** for a list of high-frequency irregular verbs.
Practice Use an *or*-ques to elicit past tense forms. ▶ T: <u>Did you buy a jacket or a sweater?</u> S: <u>I bought a sweater.</u> T: <u>Did you lose your passport or your purse?</u> S: <u>I lost my passport.</u> T: <u>Did you take the train or the bus?</u> S: <u>I took the bus.</u>
Communication Introduce regular and irregular verbs and expressions to use in a discussion of a trip: *buy, leave, lose, make reservations, see, take a train*. First the teacher, and then the students talk about trips that they have made, or would like to make. Where did you go? What did you do? Where did you stay? What did you buy? **OR** Where would you like to go? What would you like to do there?

100 The Baby
② **OR** <u>What happened?</u>
Practice Students should be encouraged to make humorous dialogues using two-word verbs when possible. See **Appendixes 19** and **20** for past forms of high-frequency verbs, and **Appendix 21** for a list of two-word verbs.

101 Who Did It?
① Use a person's first name here.
② **OR** <u>Yes?</u> ❖ *What?* in reply is less formal than *Yes?*

Teaching/Study Notes

③ A tag question is used here to make the question seem less abrupt or confrontational. The *yes/no*-question: <u>Did you take the last piece of chocolate cake</u>? may seem very abrupt. ❖ Tag question intonation here can be rising or falling, but rising intonation suggests more suspicion on the part of the speaker. ❖ A tag question could also be used to gently solicit help in locating a lost item. ▶ <u>You didn't see my purse, did you</u>?
④ <u>Why</u>? here means <u>Why do you ask me</u>?
⑤ <u>Somebody did</u> means <u>Somebody took it</u>.
⑥ The response here is said somewhat indignantly with stress on *I*.
⑦ The response here is said reassuringly with stress on *think:* <u>I didn't *think* you took it</u>. OR <u>I didn't *think* you did</u>.
Practice Review tag questions in previous lessons. ❖ Additional substitutions for line three: <u>You didn't put the sugar in the freezer, did you</u>? <u>You didn't borrow my pen, did you</u>? <u>You didn't put salt in the sugar bowl, did you</u>?

102 The What to Whom?
② The article may be omitted with the object *what*.
④ Use the indirect object with *to* here. When the direct object is a pronoun, use the pattern <u>v + ind obj + *to* obj</u>
⑤ OR <u>Whom did you give it to</u>?
Practice See **Appendix 11** for a list of verbs that may be used in the following pattern: **v + ind obj + d obj or v + d obj + *to* ind obj**.

103 Correcting Someone
① OR <u>I can't wait until this summer</u>.
④ OR <u>Didn't you go to Europe just recently</u>?
⑤ See also dialogue 49 for practice with the pro-form *not*.
Practice Use <u>look forward to + noun</u>, or <u>look forward to v-ing</u>. Try to use true information. ▶ S1: <u>I'm looking forward to the World Cup tennis match on TV tonight</u>. S2: <u>I'm looking forward to playing volleyball this Saturday</u>.
Communication A student relates a past activity. Classmates decide if the speaker is telling the truth. ▶ S1: <u>Yesterday I bought a new car</u>. S2: <u>False</u>. S1: <u>No, it's true</u>. S3: <u>Last year I broke my leg</u>. S4: <u>True</u>. S3: <u>No, it's false</u>. S5: <u>Yesterday I didn't come to school</u>. S6: <u>True</u>. S7: <u>Yes, it's true</u>.

104 What Do They Do?
② *Daughter* may be used in place of *son* in line two, and *in the city* may also be changed. ❖ <u>. . . another one in New York</u>. OR <u>. . . another in New York</u>.
Practice Using the conversation as a model, ask about brothers or sisters. Try to use *another, the other, the others, other,* or *others*. ▶ T: <u>How many brothers do you have</u>? S1: <u>I have three brothers in Mexico</u>. OR <u>I have one brother in Canada and another two</u> (or *two others*) <u>in Mexico</u>.

Teaching/Study Notes

105 Weight Watcher
③ *Much* is used with noncount nouns and *many* with count nouns in this dialogue.
❖ **OR** . . . as much rice as you had. ❖ See the list of count and noncount food items in **Appendix 22**, and quantifiers in **Appendix 23**.
④ Note that the quantifier in line four *(much* or *many)* must be the same as the quantifier used in line three.
⑤ I'm watching my weight. **OR** I'm on a diet. I'm dieting. I'm trying to lose weight.
Practice For additional practice with count and noncount food items see dialogues 72, 73, 92 and others. ❖ Try *as much as* and *as many as* using count and noncount nouns. ♦ S1: I don't have as many books as ------ has. S2: I don't have as much free time as my brother has. S3: I don't have as many brothers and sisters as you.

106 Well, I Can!
② The rising question intonation suggests doubt about the speaker's plans.
③ **OR** Why? What's wrong with that?
④ Note that although the past form of the verb *can* is used, the meaning is present.
⑤ **OR** Well, I *can* cook!
Practice Make comments using *know* or *think* + *that*-clause with appropriate tenses. ♦ T: think S: I think he has a new car. T: thought S: I thought he was a student. T: know S: I didn't know tomorrow was a holiday.

107 Things to Do
① **OR** What do you want to do tonight? **OR** What do you feel like doing tonight?
❖ *Should* in line one solicits suggestions.
③ *Could* is used here to express a possibility or an option. Also possible: Do you want to visit --C--?
⑧ **OR** That'd be fun.
Practice Try the following dialogue. Notice the two uses of *could*. A: Could (polite request) you take this to the library for me? B: Can't you take it? A: I have to go to work. B: Couldn't (suggestion) you take it after work? ❖ Make suggestions with *could*. ♦ T: My car won't start, and I have to go to work. S1: You could take a bus to work. S2: Couldn't you ask a friend for a ride?

108 Me Neither
① **OR** . . . today's English homework.
② **OR** I didn't either. **OR** Me neither.
⑤ **OR** Neither did I. **OR** Me neither.
Practice Use *either, neither,* or *too*. Make true sentences if possible. ♦ S1: I'm not coming to school tomorrow. S2: I'm not either. **OR** Neither am I. **OR** Me neither. **OR** I am (stress *I*). S3: I'm tired. S4: I am too. See also dialogues 34 and 35 for practice with *too* and *either*.

Teaching/Study Notes

109 Similar People
② **OR** <u>How</u>?
⑤ **OR** <u>Neither ------ nor his father likes team sports</u>. Use the singular verb with *neither*.
Practice Talk about a friend or a family member who shares some similarities with you. Use <u>*both*</u> and <u>*neither . . . nor*</u>. ♦ <u>My brother and I both love to play basketball. Neither my best friend nor my teacher likes ice cream.</u>

110 Saturday and Sunday
① **OR** <u>What did you do on the weekend? **OR** . . . *over* the weekend</u>?
② The preposition *on* is occasionally omitted with certain time expressions in conversation, as it has been in line two: <u>Saturday evening **OR** on Saturday evening</u>.
④ See the sentence intonation for listing items in **Appendix 1**. ❖ <u>I read a book.</u> **OR** <u>I did some reading.</u>
Practice What did you do last night? Tell the class. How did you spend the weekend or a recent holiday?
Communication Play "Scavenger Hunt." Make a list of about ten past activities: <u>watched the news on TV last night, studied for an hour after class yesterday</u>, etc. Students ask classmates questions to find persons who match the activities in the list. ♦ S1: <u>Did you watch the news on TV last night</u>? S2: <u>No, I didn't</u>. S1: <u>Did you watch the news on TV last night</u>? S3: <u>Yes, I did</u>. Each student makes a list of the persons who match the activities. The first person who finds students to match all the activities is the winner. Only one student's name should be used with each activity. ❖ Scavenger Hunt can be use to practice other verb forms as well. For example, students can match classmates with activities in the simple present tense.
♦ Find someone who *has a birthday in July*.

111 For You
① The verb *paint* must be followed by the preposition <u>*for* + ind obj</u> in this sentence. It is not possible to ask <u>Who painted you your room</u>? However, it is possible to use the <u>ind obj + d obj</u> pattern when talking about a picture. ♦ <u>He's going to paint me a picture of the mountains.</u>
③ **OR** <u>It was nice of him to do that for you</u>. *For* must be used with the indirect object when the verb is *do*. <u>It was nice of him to do you that</u> is not correct. Also, try line three with the negative: <u>That wasn't nice of him to do that.</u>
Practice <u>*For* + indirect object</u> in line one can be used with other verbs to indicate that an action was done for someone. ♦ He <u>*moved* the furniture *for us*</u>. He <u>*lifted* the heavy box *for me*</u>. Make similar examples. ❖ See **Appendix 12** for a list of verbs that may be used in substitutions for lines five and six. Note that most of the verbs incorporate the notion of *make*, *create*, or *do* (though *do* is not one of the verbs on the list). Make sentences using both patterns <u>ind obj + d obj</u> and <u>d obj + *for* + indo</u>

Teaching/Study Notes

obj. ♦ T: <u>Who wants to get me my coat</u>? S: <u>I'll get your coat for you</u>. T: <u>Who wants to fix me a sandwich</u>? S: <u>I'll fix a sandwich for you</u>.

112 Travel Time
① **OR** <u>How long does it take you to get to school</u>?
② **OR** <u>Driving</u>?
Practice There are many ways to ask about time: <u>How long does it take . . .</u>? **OR** <u>How much time does it take . . .</u>? **OR** <u>How many minutes (days) does it take . . .</u>?
Communication Look at a transportation schedule and ask about travel times.
♦ <u>How long does it take to get from Chicago to New York by plane</u>? **OR** <u>How many hours does it take</u>? <u>How long does it take to drive to Berlin from</u> <u>Paris</u>? Also, <u>What's the travel time between Los Angeles and San Francisco by car</u>? ❖ Make questions in the past tense with *how long*. ♦ <u>How long did it take you to do your homework last night</u>? <u>How long did you watch TV yesterday</u>?

113 Last Night
① **OR** <u>Where did you go last night</u>?
③ **OR** <u>Which movie did you go to</u>? though, *what* movie is more strictly correct.
⑤ **OR** <u>Then what did you do</u>? **OR** <u>What did you do after that</u>? **OR** <u>What did you do next</u>?
Practice Try the conversation using *be going to* + v. ♦ <u>What are you going to do tonight</u>? Change lines seven and eight to: ⑦ <u>Have a good time</u>! ⑧ <u>Thank you</u>.
Communication Ask classmates about their weekends. Use *what* + noun-ques.
♦ S1: <u>What did you do on Saturday</u>? S2: <u>I went fishing</u>. S1: <u>What lake did you go to</u>?

114 Housework
③ **OR** <u>What did you do to help her</u>?
④ **OR** <u>. . . took out the garbage</u>.
Practice Try to use two-word separable verbs in line four or line seven in the substitution practice. Some common verbs that might be used include: *put--away, pick--up, rinse--off, pack--up*. See **Appendix 21** for a list of two-word verbs.
Communication Refer to the list of separable two-word verbs in **Appendix 21**. Tell the class one of the household chores that you have or haven't done during the past week. Try to use a two-word verb.

115 Guess My Occupation
⑤ **OR** <u>Did you attend college</u>? **OR** <u>Did you go to college</u>?
⑧ **OR** <u>. . . kind of</u>.
Communication Play "Scavenger Hunt." (See **T/S Notes** 110.) Use the simple present tense. Students look for a classmate <u>who lives more than an hour from school</u>, <u>. . .almost never chews gum</u>, <u>. . .doesn't like pizza</u>, etc.

Teaching/Study Notes

116 By Coincidence
③ **OR** <u>We are too</u>! ❖ The verb in <u>So are we</u> may have to be changed in the substitutions, depending on the verb used in line one.
⑤ <u>So do we</u>! may have to be changed, depending on the verb used in line four.
Practice Do you have anything in common with anyone in the class? Try to use <u>the same</u>. ♦ S: <u>--A-- and I take the same bus to school</u>.

117 The Same or Different
② <u>almost</u> **OR** <u>just about</u>
④ **OR** <u>The engine is different, but it has the same interior</u>.
⑤ <u>similar</u> **OR** <u>almost the same</u> **OR** <u>a lot alike</u>
Practice Bring similar things to class, and talk about how they are different and how they are the same. ♦ S: <u>These books are the same color, but they are different sizes</u>.

118 Causes
⑤ **OR** (more informally) <u>How come</u>?
⑥ Note there is no need to repeat *to class* here. ❖ **OR** <u>Because I didn't do my homework</u>.
Practice Use the conjunctions *so* and *because*. ♦ T: <u>He was tired, so he stayed home</u>. S: <u>He stayed home, because he was tired</u>. T: <u>I failed the test, because I didn't study</u>. S: <u>I didn't study, so I failed the test</u>. ❖ Additional practice with *why* is provided in dialogue 82.

119 Too Tired
① *Let's* is a contraction of *let us*. The uncontracted form is too formal for conversation. See also *let's* in dialogues 74 and 124.
② The pattern <u>too</u> + adj + <u>to</u> is introduce here.
Practice Use <u>too</u> + adj + <u>for me</u> (+ <u>to</u> v) in questions or statements. ♦ T: <u>This book is difficult</u>. S: <u>Is it too difficult for you (to understand)</u>. T: <u>That mountain is high</u>. S: <u>It's too high (for us) to climb in one day</u>. **OR** (with the negative) <u>But it's not too high for us to climb</u>.

120 Where Were You?
① **OR** <u>Where were you yesterday morning at about 10:30</u>? ❖ The time expressions in lines one and three may also be changed in the substitution practice.
② Note the position of the adverb of place: <u>I was at the library studying</u>. **OR** <u>I was studying at the library</u>. ❖ See also dialogue 60 for additional examples of word order with the continuous verb form and adverbs of place.
④ *Let's see . . .* is not a suggestion here, but an utterance to fill a pause in speech.
Practice In line four of the first substitution, the idiom *on one's way* is used. This replaces the present continuous with *go* or other verb that expresses movement to a

Teaching/Study Notes

destination. ♦ I was going home from school. OR I was driving home from school. Also, I was on a plane *on my way* to London. ❖ Talk about recent activities. Use true information. ♦ S1: Where were you last night at about 7:00. S2: I was in my car on my way home from a movie.

121 A Telephone Conversation
① The modal *will* in this dialogue is used to give assurance or to state something positively. This is in contrast to the use of *will* in dialogue 85, where it is used to make a prediction.
② Substitutions for *arrival lounge: in the first floor lobby*, or *in front of the building*.
④ I wear glasses does not require the continuous tense, because it is a condition, or a general state; I have brown hair is a similar state. But one would say I'll be wearing sunglasses, because sunglasses are not normally worn all the time.
Practice Also possible in substitutions: I'll have my wife with me. OR My wife will be with me. ❖ Try the future continuous with the negative. Students tell what they won't be wearing, or carrying, or holding at the next class. ♦ I won't be wearing sunglasses to class tomorrow.

122 Tomorrow
② OR We'll be sipping cool drinks on the beach. Be careful of the pronunciation of *we'll* and *will*; they are not the same. ❖ Note the difference in meaning between the future continuous in dialogue 121 where *will* expresses assurance, and in 122 where it expresses speculation or a prediction.
⑤ Not me. OR I won't be playing tennis.
Communication Ask questions using the the future continuous. ♦ S1: What will you be doing at 9 o'clock tonight. S2: I'll be at home watching TV. ❖ Make comments about what you think you will be doing in the future. ♦ At this time next month I'll probably be visiting my parents.

123 Fond Memories
② *Ago* is introduced as a time expression in dialogue 150.
④ *Complain about* is an inseparable two-word verb.
Practice See also dialogue 120 for additional practice with the past continuous. ❖ Use *complain (to someone) about something*. What do you sometimes complain about? ♦ I sometimes complain about the weather.
Communication Ask about past activities. ♦ What were you doing yesterday at this time? What were you doing Saturday evening at around 7?

124 Tomorrow's Activities
① *Should* is also heard in the position of *shall*. ♦ What should we do tomorrow? *Want to* may also be used: What do you want to do tomorrow? ❖ Additional

Teaching/Study Notes

examples of *should* and *shall* with *wh*-questions: What *should/shall* I do about this? What time *shall/should* we leave?
② **OR** What do you want to do?
③ *Shall* is the tag in suggestions with *let's* . . . .
④ **OR** That sounds fine to me. **OR** That's a good idea.
Practice Note that *shall* can sometimes sound very formal when it is used frequently in *wh*-questions; also, the use of *shall* is more typical of British than American English.

125 Permission

① **OR** *Can (or Could)* I ride to school with you? *May* is more strictly correct, because *can* suggests ability; but *can* and *could* are often used to express or request permission.
③ **OR** *Could* my friend . . .?
④ The adj + *(that)* clause appears here for the first time with . . .*afraid that* . . . . See dialogue 136 for additional practice with adj + *that*-clause. ❖ *Let* (allow or permit) is used in the pattern: *let* + obj + v.
Practice Use I'm afraid . . . to introduce news which may be unpleasant to the listener. ♦ T: I can't come to your party tomorrow night. S: I'm sorry, but I'm afraid I can't come to your party tomorrow night. T: I had an accident with your car. S: I'm afraid I had an accident with your car.

126 Happy to Help

① *Could* may replace *can* here. ❖ Can I help you with the shopping? **OR** Can I help you do the shopping? but not Can I help you with the going to the store? Also, Can I help you with the dishes? **OR** Can I help you wash the dishes?
④ *Can* may replace *could* here.
Practice Use *can* to make offers of assistance. Use *help you* or *for you* in your sentences. Be aware of the difference in meaning between Can I carry your books for you? and Can I help you carry your books?

127 Work to Do

① **OR** What do we have to do next? **OR** What's there to do next?
④ *That* in line four refers to make the hotel reservations in line two.
⑥ *Need to* is slightly less urgent than *have to*. *Need to* suggests a personal decision, while *have to* might also be a duty imposed upon a person. In this dialogue *have to* and *need to* are virtually interchangeable.
Practice *Must* is not often used in American English to indicate necessity, but it is usually equivalent to *have to*. Try *must* in this dialogue. Note that there are two non-interchangeable negative forms: *do not have to* and *must not*—the former expresses what need not be done, and the latter warns or forbids.
Communication Name some things that may be necessary to do to prepare for a

Teaching/Study Notes

trip or a party. Use the impersonal *you* and the modal *have to*. ♦ You have to get a visa. You have to send out invitations. ❖ What are some things you *have to* do every day? ♦ I have to brush my teeth. ❖ What don't you have to do today? ♦ I don't have to go to the dentist. I don't have to eat lunch in the cafeteria.

128 Popular Sights
① **OR** Be sure not to miss the art museum. **OR** You mustn't miss the art museum. **OR** You must see the art museum. **OR** You just have to see the art museum (slightly feminine). **Or** You've got to see the art museum. ❖ *Can't* in line one expresses the meaning *must not* or *do not*.
③ *Should* can be used here, but with a milder, less urgent meaning. Note the stress on *have to*: You *have to* see the university. **OR** You've got to . . .
Practice *Can't* with the meaning *must not* is often used to express a regulation. ♦ You can't smoke here. You can't be late for class. You can't park here.
Communication What tourist attractions are *musts* in your home town? ❖ What are some rules or regulations at school or at home? Use *can't*. ♦ We can't chew gum in class.

129 It Must Be Hers
② That's not --D--'s jacket. **OR** That can't be --D--'s jacket.
③ **OR** Then it has to be --C--'s. **OR** Then it's got to be --C--'s.
④ Has got to be and must be may replace has to be in this line.
Practice Students should be familiarized with parts of clothing for use in substitutions: *belt, collar, cuff, hood, shoulder, sleeve, zipper*.

130 Should and Had Better
③ *Should* is more appropriate than *had better* here, because *should* is used to express preference for one of two or more reasonable alternatives. *Had better* is generally used when there is only one good or reasonable course of action in the mind of the speaker.
⑤ **OR** You'd better not take Chinese. ❖ You'd better is the contracted form of you had better.
Practice Note that the contracted *had* is sometimes not heard when it is used with *it*. Thus, *it'd better* very often sounds like *it better*. Some careless speakers also drop the contracted form with other pronouns. ♦ *I better* go home now may be heard instead of the correct form *I'd better* go home now. ❖ *Had better* is often used as a warning or threat, even if the situation is not under the speaker's control. ♦ It'd better not rain tomorrow! He'd better not give us a test today! I'd better get a good grade in this class! Try it. Make warnings or express strong hopes using *had better*. ❖ Use *should* and *had better*. ♦ T: She has a headache. S1: She should lie down and rest. S2: She'd better take an aspirin. *Should* or *had better* can be used according to the speaker's feelings, or intentions, or perceptions regarding options.

Teaching/Study Notes

131 An Idea
② *Should* and *ought to* are interchangeable in this dialogue.
⑤ The *why*-question may be used to offer a suggestion, as it does here.
Practice What are some things you don't have to do, but which you should do? ❖ Give advice using the *why*-question form. ▶ T: <u>I don't have enough money for lunch</u>. S: <u>Why don't you borrow some money</u>?

132 Why, Then?
③ Lines three and five are the same in meaning. Notice how *then* in line three replaces the *if*-clause: <u>Why are you crying if you're not hurt</u>?
Practice Make similar constructions with *if*-clauses in *why*-questions. ▶ <u>Why do you eat in the school cafeteria if you don't like the food? Why did you lend him your car if you don't trust him</u>?

133 A Full Schedule
① Note the use of both the simple present tense and the present continuous here. ❖ Also, <u>She's jogging every day</u>. **OR** <u>She goes jogging every day</u>. Also, <u>She's taking judo lessons . . .</u>. **OR** <u>She takes judo lessons . . .</u>. Note the habitual nature of these activities.
② **OR** <u>When does she go jogging</u>? Expressions: *find time to do something*, *have time to do something*, *make* or *take time to do something*. See **Appendix 25** for additional expressions with *go + v-ing*.
④ **OR** . . .<u>find time for judo</u>.
Practice Make questions in the past or present or with the continuous with *be + going to* and the adverbs *before* and *after*. ▶ S1: <u>Do you wash your face after you eat breakfast or before you eat breakfast</u>? S2: <u>Before I eat breakfast. How about you</u>? S1: <u>After breakfast</u>. S3: <u>Are you going to go to the gym before lunch or after lunch</u>? S4: <u>After lunch</u>. ❖ Use *have time to* and *have time for*. ▶ S1: <u>Do you have time to eat breakfast before you come to school</u>? S2: <u>Sometimes I have time for breakfast before I come to school</u>. **OR** <u>I always take time to eat breakfast</u>.

134 Two Jobs
② <u>She's working two jobs</u>. **OR** <u>She has two jobs</u>.
④ *Better* in line four is the comparative form of *well*.
⑤ Teaching. **OR** <u>She likes teaching better</u>.
Practice Use a *v-ing* or an infinitive after *like*. ▶ S1: <u>Do you like cooking</u>? S2: <u>No, I don't like to cook</u>. S3: <u>Do you like taking the bus to school</u>? S4: <u>Yes, I like to take the bus to school</u>. ❖ Tell what you don't like. Use <u>v + -ing</u>.
▶ I don't like walking to school.

135 Now and Then
② **OR** <u>I *can't stand* cooking</u>. **OR** <u>I *can't stand* to cook</u>.

-292-

Teaching/Study Notes

④ Note that the past tense of *used to* is expressed in the first sentence in line four with *did*, so the form *use to* need not be inflected for past tense.
Communication Are there some activities or things which you like now but didn't use to like? ♦ I didn't use to like to study English, but I do now. I didn't use to like coffee, but now I do.

136 Welcome News

① Although *yes/no*-ques word order is used in line one, the sentence is really a comment or an opinion, and it seeks positive confirmation. ❖ Other adjectives that can be followed by a *that*-clause include: *disappointed, excited, surprised;* Also, the following may be used with a *that*-clause: *It's nice that. . ., It's a good thing that. . ., It's a terrible thing that. . ., It's good to hear that. . ., It's disappointing to hear that. . .*
③ I was happy to hear that . . .. **OR** It's nice to know that . . ..
Practice Combine verb + *that*-clause with adj + *that*-clause. ♦ I think (that) it's nice that he didn't give us a test. **OR** (see dialogue 111 adj + *of* + obj) I think it was nice of him not to give us a test. **OR** I don't think it was nice of him to give us a test. ❖ Practice modifying the adjective. ♦ I think it was *kind of* sad that he didn't pass the exam. He was *kind of* disappointed that she got married. ❖ Make questions. ♦ Don't you think it's great that ------ is getting married? Aren't you disappointed that . . .? Weren't you surprised to hear that . . .?

137 A Good Story

① *It* refers to a movie.
④ The historical present tense is used here to talk about the events of a story that can be re-read or viewed again.
⑤ The subject of Sounds interesting is *that* or *it*. ♦ It sounds interesting.
⑦ I want to see it. **OR** I want to read the book. ❖ The verb *tell* is used here in the pattern v + ind obj + d obj (see dialogues 80 and 81). *Tell* is introduced in reported speech in dialogue 165.
Practice Try extending line six. ❖ Try the dialogue in the past tense. Start the conversation with: A: I saw an interesting movie last week. B: What was it about? A: It was about a young couple.

138 No Free Time

④ **OR** I wasn't able to go to my son's graduation . . ..
Practice Ask questions with *can*. ♦ S1: Can you speak Russian? S: No, I can't. **OR** Yes, I can. ❖ Make invitations and excuses. ♦ S1: Would you like to play badminton with us after class? S2: I would like to, but I'm afraid I can't. I have to go straight home after class. S3: Would you be interested in going to a movie Saturday night? S4: Thanks, I'd like to. But I can't, I'm afraid. My parents are going out tonight and I have to baby-sit.

Teaching/Study Notes

139 A Name in the News
① Use the given name and family name here. The use of the indefinite article with a name means *a person named* ------.
③ **Or** How well did you know her?
Communication What are some things you used to do, but which you don't do now? ♦ I used to live in Mexico, but now I don't.

140 Might and Might Not
② I might not. **OR** Maybe not. **OR** I may not. **OR** Maybe I won't go. **OR** I might not go. **OR** Probably not. ❖ The negative *might not* can be taken for a *no* reply.
③ **OR** Why aren't you going to class this evening?
④ **OR** I might not be able to. ❖ Note the use of *will* here to ask about intention without being too intrusive. ♦ Do you think *you* will? *You* receives additional sentence stress.
⑤ *Maybe* is usually used with *will* when the subject is the first person pronoun, not with *be going to* + v. ♦ Maybe I'll go *not* Maybe I'm going.
Practice Use *I don't know* and *might* and make negative replies to offers. ♦ Do you want to play tennis tonight? S2: I don't know. I might have to study for a test.

141 Comparing Hotels
② **OR** Compared with the Grand Hotel it is expensive. **OR** It's more expensive than the Grand Hotel. ❖ An object or a person is *compared with* or *compared to* someone or something.
④ **OR** But it's not the most expensive hotel in town.
Practice Use *compared with*. ♦ T: Is your hometown large? S: Compared with this town it is. **OR** Compared with this town it isn't. ❖ Make similar sentences.
♦ Compared with **A** I am tall, but compared with **B** I am short.

142 On a Diet
② **OR** I'm trying to lose weight. **OR** I'm dieting.
④ Use *less* with noncount nouns and *fewer* with count nouns. Use *more* with both count and noncount nouns.
Practice Use *less* and *fewer* with nouns. ♦ T: potatoes S: fewer potatoes T: ice cream S: less ice cream ❖ Note *less of* and *more of* can be used when they are followed by a determiner + noun, or a noun phrase. ♦ I'm going to eat less of my favorite ice cream. I should eat more of our garden vegetables. **But,** I'm going to eat less ice cream and more garden vegetables.

143 Bigger, Not Better
① **OR** Which is roomier, your new car or your old car?
② **OR** No. My old car is roomier than my new car. ❖ a little bit **OR** quite a bit
Practice See also dialogue 70 for practice with *as* + adj + *as* pattern.

Teaching/Study Notes

144 More and Less
① **OR** Is that novel interesting?
② The comparative form of adjectives with *more* is introduced in dialogue 66.
④ Note that *less* is often used with multi-syllable adjectives, and the <u>not as</u> + adj + <u>as</u> pattern is more frequently heard with adjectives of one syllable. ♦ <u>not as *fresh* as</u> is more common in spoken English than <u>less *fresh* than</u>.
Practice See **Appendix 26** for adjectives which take *more* and *less* in comparative forms. ❖ Make comparisons using <u>less + adj</u> or <u>not as + adj + as</u> ♦ T: <u>This city and your home town.</u> S: <u>My home town is less polluted than this city.</u>
T: <u>Lesson two and lesson seven.</u> S: <u>Lesson two was not as fun as lesson seven.</u>

145 Different Opinions
① Opinions are compared in this dialogue, not facts.
② Note that *most boring*, or *most uninteresting* could be used here in place of *least interesting*. If *most boring* is used in line two, line three would be <u>More boring than Professor --D--</u>?
Practice Other pairs of adjectives that could be used in the substitutions: *most beautiful - ugliest; best - worse; strictest - most easy going ; most delicious - least delicious; best tasting - worst tasting.* ❖ Try the conversation using *the least interesting* in line one, *the most interesting* in line two, *more interesting* in line three, and *less interesting* in line four.

146 Products
① *Much* is used with noncount nouns: *as much wheat as*
② **OR** <u>No, it didn't.</u>
③ *Many* is used with count nouns: *as many cars as*
④ *It* and *they* are both used in this dialogue as a pronoun for the U.S. *It* is usually used to refer to countries, but the impersonal *they* pronoun is also heard, often in reference to the government of a country.
Practice Use *as much/many as* in questions. ♦ S1: <u>Did you go skiing this year as many times (</u>or <u>*as often) as* you went last year</u>? S2: <u>No, I went more times last year.</u> S3: <u>Do you have as much homework as I have</u>? S4: <u>I have more homework than you have.</u> **OR** <u>Yes, in fact I have more homework than you have.</u> S5: <u>Does this class have as many students as the French class</u>? S6: <u>No, the French class has more students.</u>

147 Carefully
② *as . . . as* forms of adverbs are introduced in this dialogue, and comparative forms of adverbs are practiced; *better* was introduced in dialogue 77.
Communication Ask classmates questions using adverbs with *as . . . as*. ♦ S1: <u>Does your mother speak English as well as your father.</u> S2: <u>My mother speaks English better than my father.</u>

Teaching/Study Notes

148 World Traveler

① **OR** Have you *ever* been to Acapulco? *Ever* should be used in a question, not normally in a reply.

② Note that the past tense, not the present perfect, is used to describe an action at a point of time in the past. I was in Acapulco last winter.

Practice Try the conversation using the third person singular in place of the second person singular. ♦ Has ------been to Alaska? ❖ Play "Scavenger Hunt." (See **T/S Notes** on dialogue 110.) Find someone in your class who has been downtown this past week; . . . has never been to Washington D.C.; . . . has been to the same movie two times, . . . has had a birthday within the last month, etc. ❖ Listen to the two phrases: has he ever . . . and has she ever. . .? Listen again and again until the differences can be easily heard perceived.

Communication Ask about familiar places. ♦ T: Have you (ever) been to Los Angeles? S: Yes, I was there last year. T: Have you been to Disneyland? S: No, I haven't been there. ❖ Guessing Game. S1: Have you ever been to Australia? S2: (guessing) No, but you have. **OR** No, and you haven't either. **OR** Yes, and you have too. **OR** Yes, but you haven't. S1: You're right. I haven't. **OR** You're wrong. I have. ❖ Play "True or False." One student makes a statement using the present perfect with *be* and classmates guess whether the statement is true or false. ♦ S1: I have never been to the hospital. S2: True. S1: Yes, it's true. S3: I have been to Paris. S4: False. S3: No, that's true.

149 The Menu

① The present perfect form of *have* is introduced in this dialogue. ❖ The article *the* is used here because **A** and **B** are looking at the same items on the menu. The colloquial verb is *have* or *try*, not *eat*.

④ Is it good? *not* Is it delicious? *Delicious* is rarely used in a *yes/no*-question, because *delicious* is used to describe the ultimate quality. For the same reason, the adjective *beautiful* is avoided in affirmative *yes/no*-questions.

⑤ **OR** It's OK. **OR** No, it isn't.

⑥ **OR** How's the tuna pie here?

⑦ *Them* is required in place of *that* if a count noun is used in line six.

Practice Ask classmates additional questions with the perfect form *have had*. ♦ Have you ever had a pet? Have you ever had a broken leg?

Communication What have you had to eat at the school cafeteria? Was it good?

150 A Compliment

② . . . for some time. **OR** ...for a while.

④ *For* is used to call attention to an amount of time in the past, present, or future. ♦ I'll be here *for ten more minutes*. I lived abroad *for two years*. *Ago* is used to express an amount of time that has elapsed since an event occurred. ♦ I came here *ten minutes ago*. They left for Europe *a month ago*. Note that *in* (see

Teaching/Study Notes

dialogues 42 and 44 for use of *in* with expressions of time) may be used to refer to a point in the past. We came here *in* 1990.
Practice Ask and answer questions with time expressions using *ago, for,* or *in*.
♦ S1: When did you get that sweater? S2: I got this sweater three months *ago*. I've had it *for* three months. **OR** S1: How long have you had those shoes? S2: *For* about two months. I bought them *in* June.

151 A Little Longer

① The use of *be going to + be* v-*ing* stresses the on-going nature of the activity.
② **OR** I'm going to stay here until I finish typing this letter. Note that the verb *finish* may be followed by v-*ing* here.
③ **OR** How long will it take you to finish typing that letter?
④ **OR** I'll be finished in a little while. ❖ Other possible time expressions: Not much longer. Pretty soon.
Practice Ask about quantities of time. ♦ How long will it be before we have a test? How much longer are you going to stay in Canada?

152 A Word of Advice

③ Try line three with *be sure (not) to*. ♦ Whatever you do, be sure not to go to that new restaurant across the street. Note that *be sure not to* may be stronger than *don't*. The advice can be made gentler with the verb *suggest*: I suggest that you don't go to that new restaurant across the street. See dialogue 185 for practice with *suggest*.
Practice Think of additional reasons (line five) for not recommending the new restaurant across the street.

153 A Dream

① Note that the idioms are *have a dream*, and *have a nightmare*. ❖ Other adjectives that could be used here in substitutions include: *frightful, wonderful, curious, bad, terrible.*
③ **OR** I dreamed that I climbed . . ..
⑥ **OR** Then what happened?
Practice Expand the dialogue by adding one or two additional lines. Answer the question in line six, telling what happened next. ❖ This topic is also suitable for practicing the past continuous (see dialogues 120 and 123) and the past passive (see dialogues 200, 201, and 203).

154 First Things First

① *I guess* is typically followed by *will* when describing one's own intentions with a lack of enthusiasm or conviction. The use of *going to* with *guess* would suggest the activity may be involuntary. ♦ I guess we're going to have a test tomorrow.
❖ go and play tennis, **OR** go to play tennis; also heard: go play tennis.

Teaching/Study Notes

② **OR** <u>Before you do your homework</u>? **OR** <u>You're going to play tennis before you do your homework</u>?
③ Note the use of *will* here to express assurance.
④ *Should* could be used in place of *had better*, but with a slightly weaker connotation (see dialogue 130). ❖ *After* gets stressed in this sentence to contrast it with *before* in line two. Both *after* and *before* may be followed by <u>v + -ing</u> (as in lines two and four), or they may be followed by a clause (see for example dialogue 133).
Practice Tell true things about yourself using *before* and *after*. ▶ <u>After having breakfast today, I read the newspaper</u>. **OR** <u>After I had breakfast, I read the newspaper</u>. ❖ See dialogue 133 for more practice with the adverbs *before* and *after*.

155 International Trade
① **OR** <u>What country . . .</u>? ❖ The superlative is used with quantity in this dialogue. Use *least* with noncount nouns and *fewest* with count nouns; use *most* with both count and noncount nouns.
Practice Use a chart or graph to talk about other countries (for purposes of practice, however, real and accurate statistics are not essential, and have not been used in the dialogue). Other possible substitutions include: *manufacture aircraft; harvest rice* or *wheat, construct houses, cultivate land, grow potatoes, plant tobacco.*

156 Since When?
① **OR** <u>Do you still practice the violin every day</u>?
③ A change in the verb t in line one requires a corresponding change in line three.
④ The action described should be one which is of very short duration. An activity that requires an extended period of time, such as *study*, will not work here.
▶ <u>. . . not since I *became* a doctor</u>, but not <u>. . . not since I *studied* medicine</u>.
Practice Use *since* in statements. ▶ <u>I like your house *since* you painted it</u>. **OR** <u>Are you driving to school since you got your license</u>?

157 Not Yet
① *Yet* is optional, but the use of it stresses the negative in the sentence.
② **OR** <u>No, I haven't</u>.
④ **OR** <u>After I've watched the news</u>. ❖ Though the present perfect is appropriate here, the simple present is often used in its place. ▶ <u>I'll prepare my lesson after I watch the news</u>. ❖ *Will* in line four expresses assurance and suggests that the speaker intends to perform the activity to comply with a request. The use of *going to* would suggest the action is the speaker's desire or intention.
Practice See **Appendix 19** for a list of verbs which form the past participle with the suffix *-ed*. Refer to the list to practice the present perfect. ▶ T: <u>prepare</u> S: <u>I've prepared my lesson</u>. **OR** <u>I haven't prepared my lesson yet</u>.

-298-

Teaching/Study Notes

158 Passing Time
② *Until* is used in reference to a point in time. Lines two and five offer two examples of *until* with time expressions.
④ The reply <u>No</u> means <u>No, not until 3:30</u>.
Practice Use *until* in sentences. ♦ <u>Class doesn't end until 3 o'clock. I'm going to stay here until the class ends.</u>

159 Duties
③ *Already* may precede the past participle (line three), or come at the end of an utterance.
⑤ Note the use of <u>*have* + *just* + past participle.</u> ♦ <u>Haven't you just recently been to Europe?</u> (See line four, dialogue 103 for an example with the simple past tense.)
❖ *Finish* is often followed by <u>v + -*ing*</u>. ♦ <u>I haven't finished using the computer yet.</u>
Practice Irregular past participle forms are introduced in this dialogue. See **Appendix 20** for a list of irregular verbs. ❖ Ask classmates questions with *finish*.
♦ S1: <u>When are you going to finish using the encyclopedia?</u> S2: <u>I'll finish soon.</u>
S3: <u>Have you finished sending the invitations?</u> S4: <u>No, I haven't.</u>

160 Lucky
① <u>How would you like to . . .?</u> This pattern may also be used to make a suggestion. Line one is not a suggestion, however.
② Note that *must not* cannot be substituted for *doesn't have to* in line two.
③ **OR** <u>Does he? Really?</u>
④ **OR** <u>I wouldn't mind *having to get up* at 5:30 every morning, . . .</u>. ❖ Note that <u>wouldn't want to have to</u> may be used in a reply, but is generally not used in a question; <u>would like to have to</u> may be used in a question, as in line one.
⑤ **OR** <u>I wouldn't either.</u>
Practice Make similar sentences: <u>I'm glad</u> (or <u>I'm lucky</u>) <u>I don't have to walk to school.</u> <u>I wouldn't like to have to eat in the school cafeteria every day.</u> <u>I would hate to have to wear a uniform to school.</u> <u>I don't mind having to walk to school.</u>
Communication Ask classmates questions with *have to*. ♦ S1: <u>How would you like to have to work after school every evening?</u> S2: <u>I wouldn't like to have to.</u> **OR** <u>I wouldn't want to have to.</u> **OR** <u>I wouldn't mind it.</u> **OR** <u>I wouldn't mind having to work after school every evening.</u> S3: <u>Do you like to have to come to school in the morning?</u> S4: <u>No, I don't.</u> ❖ What don't you like to have to do? Tell the class.

161 Experiences
① **OR** <u>What's riding in a helicopter like?</u>
Practice Play "Scavenger Hunt." Find someone who. . .<u>has never ridden a subway,</u> <u>. . .has celebrated a birthday within the last month,</u> <u>. . .has cheated on a test</u>, etc.
See also **T/S Notes** for dialogues 110 and 148 for examples of the Scavenger Hunt.

Teaching/Study Notes

Communication Classmates ask each other questions. ♦ Have you ever bought something on credit? Have you ever met a famous person? Make similar questions using the present perfect.

162 A First Time

③ The present perfect cannot be used in line three. ❖ OR Was that the first time (that) you had ever been there?
⑤ Note the stress on *is*. Because of the stress on *is*, the contracted form with *it* is not possible. ♦ It *is* a nice restaurant.
Practice Talk about past experiences. ♦ S1: I went to a professional soccer game yesterday. S2: Hadn't you ever been to a professional soccer game before? S1: No, I hadn't. OR No, I'd never been before.

163 Ordinary Activities

① OR Do you ever take the bus to work? Here the question with *ever* can be expressed with the simple present or present perfect. ❖ Note that *work* in line one is a noun. ❖ Note the use of the article: *the* bus, not *a* bus, because the speaker is referring to a specific bus line.
④ *Before* in line four refers to the time expression *this morning* in line three. Note that the past pfct is used here, because **B** in line four is asking about the portion of an experience that extends up to a point in the past. The question could also be: Hadn't you ever taken the bus to work before you took the bus this morning?
⑤ *in* a long time, **OR** *for/in* quite a while.
Practice Ask classmates questions about their past experiences. Use the past perfect. ♦ Before you went to France, had you ever been to Europe? Had you ever studied English before you took this class?

164 That's News to Me

② Note that although the action described in line two has not begun yet (it doesn't begin until next week), the verb *was starting* is in the past tense because the clause is introduced by a past tense form of a verb: *thought*.
④ Because of the past form *knew*, the verbs that follow it are put into the past tense form, although the implication of past time may not apply. Thus, he had a new car is past in form only, not in meaning. ❖ Although Did you know in line one is the past form, there is a tendency for the past tense of the verb in questions not to influence the tense of the *that*-clause. However, the same past tense form in a statement —I didn't know—does influence the v in the clause. ♦ *I didn't know* you could cook. *I didn't know* you had a brother. *Could* and *had* are present in meaning, but past in form. A past or present pfct v in a clause preceded by a past t form is expressed with the past pfct. ♦ You have lived overseas becomes I didn't know you had lived overseas. Also, You broke your leg becomes I didn't know you broke your leg. **OR** I didn't know you had broken your leg.

Teaching/Study Notes

Practice If the past or present perfect is used in line one, line four requires the past perfect. ♦ A: <u>Did you know that --C-- *has graduated* from school and that he's going to start a new job next month</u>? B: <u>I thought he was going to go to graduate school</u>. A: <u>I don't know</u>. B: <u>Well, I knew he *had graduated* from school, but I didn't know he was going to start a new job next month</u>. ❖ Make short replies using the proper tense. ♦ T: <u>I didn't know you *could cook*</u>. S: <u>Yes, I *can*</u>. T: <u>I didn't know you *had lived* in France</u>. S: <u>Yes, I *have*</u>. T: <u>I didn't know you *had* a twin sister</u>. S: <u>Yes, I *do*</u>. ❖ Answer questions. ♦ T: <u>Did you know he *has* a new car</u>? S: <u>Yes, I knew he *had* a new car</u>. **OR** <u>No, I didn't know he *had* a new car</u>.

165 At the Supermarket

① Line one includes the indirect quote <u>. . . to get some eggs</u>. The direct quote would be "Get some eggs." ❖ Note that *some* and *any* are used for both plural count nouns and noncount nouns. A singular noun may be used here, however. ♦ <u>a cake</u>, **OR** <u>a loaf of bread</u>.
② **OR** <u>Only eggs</u>?
③ <u>Let's see . . .</u> is used to fill a pause in conversation and has no lexical meaning here.
④ The pattern <u>v + obj + *to* v</u> has previously been introduced in dialogue 86. ❖ Note that *tell* must always have an object. *Tell* is generally used when the object needs to be specified. ❖ **OR** <u>She said to get some apples</u>?
⑤ **OR** <u>She said not to get any</u>.
Practice Put imperative sentences into reported speech forms. ♦ T: <u>Come to class on time</u>. S: <u>Our teacher told me (*or* us) to come to class on time</u>. **OR** <u>Our teacher said to come to class on time</u>. T: <u>Don't be late</u>. S: <u>Our teacher told me (*or* us) not to be late</u>. **OR** <u>Our teacher said not to be late</u>. T: <u>Don't forget your homework</u>. S: <u>Our teacher told me (or us) not to forget my (our) homework</u>. **OR** <u>Our teacher said not to forget my (our) homework</u>.

166 Exports and Imports

① The *by*-phrase is omitted in the passive when the agent is unimportant, unknown, or, as in line one, superfluous or irrelevant. The passive is well-suited for this sentence. The *they*-passive could also be used in line one: ♦ <u>Do they mine coal in Japan</u>?
⑤ **OR** <u>What does Japan export</u>? ❖ The adverb of agent with *by* is included here because it is essential for understanding the sentence.
Practice Use the passive voice when an action takes preference over the agent or when many people or an anonymous or unknown individual or agent performs the action. ♦ <u>The Olympics were seen by millions</u>. ❖ Additional verbs that may be used to form the present passive in substitutions for this dialogue include: *caught in, exported to/from, frozen in, imported to/from, made in, manufactured in, mined in, printed in, processed in, produced in, published in, shipped to/from*.

Teaching/Study Notes

167 What Am I?
④ OR <u>Yes, but not usually.</u> OR <u>Not normally.</u>
Practice Note the use of the present passive in the dialogue. Additional verbs that might be used in the passive in substitutions include: *carry, move from place to place, play with, wear.* ❖ Limit the number of guesses in *What am I?* to a reasonable number depending on the ability, level, and number of students in the class.

168 Putting Things Off
① *Yet* is optional in line one, but the use of it emphasises the negative.
② OR <u>No, not yet.</u>
③ *Yet* is sometimes heard with the past tense. ♦ <u>Did you clean your room yet</u>? More correctly, however, *yet* should be used with the present perfect: <u>Have you cleaned your room yet</u>?
⑥ OR <u>Watching television.</u> This is the first use of the present perfect continuous. If the reply to the question consists of several activities, then the past tense may be used. ♦ <u>I read the newspaper, wrote a letter, and watched the news on TV.</u>
Practice Use the present perfect with *since*. ♦ T: <u>They arrived here this morning.</u> S: <u>They've been here since this morning.</u> T: <u>I came in October.</u> S: <u>I've been here since October.</u> ❖ Make sentences with the present perfect continuous. ♦ <u>I've been reading this book since last week. My sister has been living here for a year.</u> ❖ Ask classmates questions using the present perfect continuous. ♦ <u>What have you been doing for the last five minutes? How long have you been going to school here</u>?

169 Teacher and Parent
④ OR <u>Has he been paying attention in class?</u>
Practice The dialogue can also be used in the affirmative to talk about a good employee or a good student. ♦ <u>He has been doing his homework. She has been getting along well with other employees.</u> ❖ Use *since*. ♦ <u>I've been living here since May. We've been jogging every day since July.</u> ❖ Make questions with the question words *how long, what, who, why.* Use the pres pfct continuous. ♦ <u>Why haven't you been walking to school? Since when have you been taking judo lessons? How long have you been studying English? Which class have you been teaching?</u>

170 First Experiences
④ Notice the difference between the past perfect in the question in line one and the present perfect in the question in line four. ❖ *Until* cannot replace *before* in line one, but *before* can replace *until* in line four.
Practice Use *until* or *before* with the past perfect. Use true information. ♦ <u>Until I took this class, I had never met our teacher. Until I turned 18, I had never driven a car.</u>

Teaching/Study Notes

171 Except for One Thing

① How's your new job? **OR** (more colloquially) How's your new job going?
② *except + that* clause, **OR** *except for the fact + that* clause ♦ . . . except for the fact that I have to get up so early.
③ **OR** But otherwise you like it?
④ *except for* + noun ♦ I like this class except for the tests. I ate everything except for the salad.
⑤ *Except for* + present participle ♦ He did all the work except for painting the ceiling. ❖ **OR** *Aside from* having to get up so early. *Aside from* can replace *except for* in lines four and five.
Practice Make sentences with *but otherwise*. ♦ I don't like the weather here, but otherwise I like this city. I like the weather here, but otherwise I don't like this city.
❖ Use *otherwise*. ♦ We'd better hurry, otherwise we'll be late. Don't forget your homework, otherwise the teacher will get angry. ❖ Use *except that* and *except for*.
♦ I like this city except for the weather here. This is a nice place except that it gets very cold in the winter.

172 Please Guess

① *I am* cannot be contracted here. Only embedded *wh*-questions with *be* and *have* are used in this dialogue; embedded *yes/no*-questions and *wh*-questions with other verbs are introduced in dialogue 173.
③ Note the way in which *do you think* is embedded in the question. Also possible: How old *would you say* I am? and How old *would you guess* I am?
⑥ **OR** Oh, is that right? Line six should be said with a lack of interest.
Practice Use *do you think* in questions. ♦ T: How far is the station? S: How far do you think the station is?

173 Information, Please

③ Embedded *yes/no*-question: Do you know if + declarative word order. ♦ Is it on schedule? Do you know if it's on schedule? Also, Does the hotel have a coffee shop? Do you know if it has a coffee shop?
④ **OR** Yes, it is on schedule. **OR** No, it's not on schedule.
Practice Change the *yes/no*-questions into questions with Do you know if . . .
♦ T: Was she late for class? S: Do you know if she was late for class? T: Does the college have a swimming pool? S: Do you know if the college has a swimming pool? ❖ Other phrases for introducing indirect questions include: Would (Do) you happen to know . . ., I'd like to find out . . .. Can (Could) you tell me . . .; also, try: I was just wondering . . . ♦ S1: Do you know where the . . . is? S2: No, I don't. Why? S1: Oh, I was just wondering where it was. Note that the past form *was wondering* requires that the clause with the indirect question also use a past form of a verb. (See also dialogue 164 for examples of the past tense with present meaning.)
Communication Ask classmates for information about your school or about a city

Teaching/Study Notes

or about other topics. Use <u>Does anybody know...</u>? ◆ <u>Does anybody know how old this school is</u>? <u>Does anybody know if there is going to be a test on Friday</u>? ❖ Play the game "Who Am I Thinking Of?" Students guess the name of the famous person that the teacher or a selected student is thinking of. Students ask *yes/no*-questions, prefacing them with <u>I'd like to know</u>... or <u>Please tell me</u>... ◆ <u>I'd like to know if you are a politician</u>. <u>Please tell me if you speak Spanish</u>.

174 Looking Ahead
② **OR** <u>That's a long way off, but</u>...
Practice Other nouns that can follow <u>n + be + to v</u> pattern include: *ambition, desire, dream, goal, hope, intention, job, plan*. Ask and answer questions using <u>n + be + to v</u> pattern. ◆ T: <u>What is your dream</u>? S: <u>My dream is to become a pilot</u>.
Communication Talk about friends or family members and tell the class their ambitions. ◆ <u>My father's ambition is to become a famous novelist</u>.

175 Relating News
④ The present form of *say* allows the indirect quote to keep the original tense of the direct quote. ◆ Direct quote: "<u>I'm enjoying my stay in Europe</u>." Indirect quote: <u>She says that she's enjoying her stay in Europe</u>. Direct quote: "<u>I went to Paris</u>." Indirect quote: <u>She says she went to Paris</u>. Direct quote: "<u>I've been to London</u>." Indirect quote: <u>She says she's been to London</u>.
⑤ **OR** <u>Does she say anything about school</u>?
⑥ <u>Here</u>. **OR** <u>Here, you read it</u>.
Practice Indirect or reported speech is also used to tell what has been written. <u>It says here (that)</u>... is often used to introduce an indirect quote from written material, such as a newspaper. ❖ Use reported speech and report what is written in a letter from a famous person. ◆ S1: <u>Is that a letter from the president</u>? <u>What does he say</u>? S2: <u>He says he's going to visit us next week</u>.
Communication Make indirect quotations of what someone said. ◆ <u>The prime minister said that he was going to speak at the United Nations</u>. **OR** <u>It says in the newspaper here that the president is not going to attend the conference</u>.

176 Which Person?
③ <u>Which one is it...</u>? **OR** <u>Who is it...</u>? ❖ A relative clause with the present tense form of *have* can be reduced using *with:* <u>The one *with* the red sports car</u>? **OR** <u>The one *that has* the red sports car</u>?
⑤ **OR** <u>The one with the yacht</u>?
⑦ **OR** <u>The president of the computer company</u>? ❖ <u>*a computer company*</u> **OR** <u>*the computer company*</u>.
Practice The relative pronouns *who* and *that* may both be used to refer to persons. *Who* is not used to refer to objects. ❖ The dialogue uses only relative clauses with *be* or *have*. Note that short phrases with *be* + adj can be reduced to <u>adj + *one*</u>. ◆ <u>The</u>

Teaching/Study Notes

one who is tall. OR The tall one. ❖ Look at several pictures of similar objects, such as cars or houses. Use relative clauses to identify the one you like. ♦ I like the car with the sunroof. I like the house that has the swimming pool.
Communication Talk about dreams or wishes. Use relative clauses with rel pron, or use reduced relative clauses. ♦ I'd like a car that has a ski rack. I'd to have a house with a large garden.

177 Telling a Friend
③ . . . he hadn't found it is in the past perfect tense because the verb *tell* is in the past tense. Also heard: He didn't tell you that he didn't find it?
④ OR . . . I saw him just a few minutes ago.
Practice Review past forms of modals for use with reported speech. ♦ *will* → *would; have to/must* → *had to; should* → *should; can* → *was/were able* or *could; may* → *might; might* → *might.*

178 Someone Intelligent
② OR Someone who is intelligent. ❖ OR A person who is from a good family.
③ Both the relative pronouns *who* and *that* can be used to refer to persons.
Practice The sentences with prepositional phrases in the substitutions can be reduced. ♦ Someone who is in good health. OR Someone in good health. Also, Someone who is from Japan. OR Someone from Japan. ❖ Note: Someone who is intelligent may be reduced to Someone intelligent, but A person who is intelligent may be reduced only to an intelligent person.
Communication Do you know an unusual person? ♦ I know someone who gets up at 3AM every day. I have a friend who never goes to class. Make similar sentences about people you know. ❖ Talk about qualifications. ♦ T: What kind of person should a teacher be? S: Someone who likes to help people. ❖ Use *anyone, someone* and relative clauses. ♦ S1: Do you know anyone who can speak Chinese? S2: Yes, I do. OR I don't anyone who can speak Chinese, but I know someone who can speak Japanese.

179 Getting Used to Things
① OR Do you like your new job?
② OR I'm still getting used to the short lunch breaks.
Communication What are some things you can't get used to at school? Are you living in a new city or country, or do you have a new car? What aren't you used to? OR What are you still not accustomed to?

180 Wondering
① The idiom *I hear . . .* is commonly used to casually inform someone of an event.
② OR That's what I hear too.
Practice See dialogues 172 and 173 for additional practice with embedded ques.

Teaching/Study Notes

Communication What do you wonder about? ♦ I wonder where I'll be at this time next year. I sometimes wonder if I will pass this class.

181 See That Man?
① . . .that man beside the door is reduced from . . .that man who is beside the door. See reduced clauses with prepositions in dialogue 178.
② **OR** Which man?
③ The one wearing. . . is reduced from The one who is wearing. . .
④ The one with the baseball cap? is reduced from The one who has the baseball cap?
⑤ **OR** The one facing us . . ..
⑥ What *about* him? *About* is stressed.
Practice Students call on classmates using reduced relative clauses instead of names. Then they ask questions about classmates using relative clauses. ♦ S1: The student wearing the blue sweater. S2: Yes? S1: Who is the student sitting next to the door? S2: Her name is ------.

182 Some Time Ago
① **OR** How long has it been since you played tennis.
Practice Talk about past activities. ♦ S1: When was the last time you flew in an airplane? S2: Two months ago. **OR** I haven't flown in an airplane for two months. **OR** I haven't flown in an airplane since I came here.

183 Modern Art
① **OR** What would you say that is? **OR** What does that look like to you? **OR** What do you think that is supposed to be?
② I'd = I would. ❖ **OR** It looks like a man playing the piano to me.
Practice "Would you say" can be used to solicit opinions. ♦ How old would you say it is? How far would you say the station is from here? Make similar questions that seek an opinion or an estimation.
Communication Students draw abstract images on the blackboard. Classmates use present participles in phrases to try to guess what the drawings depict. ♦ Is it a man fishing? A person eating something?

184 Pointing Someone Out
① **OR** . . .whom I told you . . .. Although *whom* is more strictly correct as the relative pronoun here, *who* is often heard, and it is accepted in spoken English when it is not preceded by a preposition.
② What man? **B** is trying to recall a person whom **A** told **B** about.
③ You know . . .. **OR** Don't you remember? ❖ The relative clause cannot be reduced here.
④ **OR** The one who is getting off the bus?

-306-

Teaching/Study Notes

185 Good Advice
④ OR <u>I suggested to him that he get a part-time job</u>. OR . . . <u>that he should get a part-time job</u>.
Practice Other verbs that take the subjunctive include: *demand, insist, propose, require.* See also **Appendix 13**. ❖ Subjunctive forms of *be:* <u>I *be*</u>; <u>you *be*</u>; <u>she/he/it *be*</u>; <u>they *be*</u>; <u>we *be*</u>. Subjunctive forms of have: <u>I</u>, <u>you</u>, <u>he</u>, <u>she</u>, <u>it</u>, <u>we</u>, <u>they</u> *have*; Subjunctive forms of other verbs: <u>I</u>, <u>you</u>, <u>he</u>, <u>she</u>, <u>it</u>, <u>we</u>, <u>they *go*</u>. Note that the only change in verbs, other than in *be,* occurs in the third person singular form. ❖ The dialogue may be continued if line five is replaced with the question: <u>Why did you recommend that he not work at ------ Department Store</u>? Line six might provide the reason. ♦ <u>Because they don't pay very well</u>.

186 Interruption
① <u>Sorry for. . .</u> is a casual apology. <u>I'm sorry for the interruption</u> and <u>I'm sorry that I interrupted you</u> are more formal expressions of apology.
④ OR <u>I said I wanted to go to Mexico</u>.
Practice Use reported speech in questions. The teacher or a student makes a short presentation on a simple topic to the class. Students ask each other questions about the presentation. ♦ S1: <u>Where did ------ say he was going</u>? S2: <u>He said he was going to the shopping center</u>. S1: <u>What time did he say he was coming back</u>? S2: <u>He didn't say</u>.

187 Assistants
② *Must* may be used here, but *have to* is predominant in American English. Also, *have got to* may be used. See dialogue 96 for practice with *have got to.*
③ Causatives *have* and *get:* <u>have someone do something (for you)</u> or <u>get someone to do something (for you)</u>.
Practice Make sentences using the causative *have*. What would you like to have someone do for you? ♦ <u>I'd like to have someone make breakfast for me every day</u>. ❖ Other causatives are *make, force,* and *let*: <u>make someone do something</u>; <u>force someone to do something</u>; <u>let someone do something</u>. ❖ Make polite requests with the *get* causative. ♦ <u>Could I get you to close the door, please</u>? OR <u>Could I get you to please hand me the stapler</u>? The request with the *get* causative expresses some authority.
Communication Tell what someone doesn't let you do. ♦ <u>My father doesn't let me drive his car at night</u>.

188 Hurry!
③ OR <u>It'll be 7:30 when we get to the airport</u>. By the time (that) replaces *when* in line three. <u>By the time (that)</u> provides more emphasis than *when.* ❖ See dialogue 108 for practice with *either.*
Practice Use *by this time* (*tomorrow, next year,* etc.) with the future perfect. ♦ <u>By</u>

Teaching/Study Notes

this time next year, I will have graduated from this school. By 4 o'clock today, I will have finished my report. ❖ Use *by the time (that)* with a clause with *will*.
▶ By the time we get to the restaurant, I will be very hungry.

189 Tour Guide
① OR What time did she say to be in the hotel lobby? OR Did she tell us what time to be in the hotel lobby?
④ *Anything about* + gerund or noun ▶ She didn't say anything about having lunch. OR She didn't say anything about lunch.
Practice Use *anything about* + noun or gerund or clause. Make questions. ▶ Did our teacher say anything about giving us a test? Did you tell her anything about my party?

190 Choices
② OR The one from Scotland. Note that *be* may be dropped in a relative clause with a prepositional phrase, but not in one with an adjective. ▶ The one that is French may be reduced only to The French one. However, The one that is from France may be reduced to The one from France.
Practice Make reductions. ▶ T: The book that is old. S: The old book. T: The book that is on the shelf. S: The book on the shelf.
Communication Ask classmates about their preferences. Use *which* + noun and *prefer*. ▶ Which city do you prefer: this one or your hometown? Which way do you prefer to go home: by car or by bus?

191 Doctor's Advice
③ *Will* and *might* may be used in combination with *be able to*. ▶ Do you think you'll be able to go to work on Monday? ❖ In colloquial English, *might* is not normally used in a *yes/no*-question. However, *might* is commonly used in *yes/no*-questions when it is preceded by *Do you think* . . . ▶ Do you think I might be able to go work on Monday?
④ OR You ought to be able to. ❖ *Should be able to* suggests a condition or expresses a reservation, as for example: If you don't have a fever, you should be able to go to work on Monday. (Conditional forms are introduced beginning with dialogue 218.)
Practice Modals that can follow *will, might,* and *should* include *have to* and *be able to. Be able to* can also follow *have to*. Make statements or questions using modal combinations. ▶ Will we have to have a test next week? I might not be able to come to class tomorrow. I might have to go to the dentist. I should be able to finish my assignment by noon.

192 Regrets
① Perfect form with modals: modal + *have* + pp.

Teaching/Study Notes

Communication Tell something you regret doing or not doing. ♦ I should have gotten a hair cut last week, because now I'm too busy. I shouldn't have skipped breakfast this morning, because now I am very hungry. ❖ Do you have any regrets or second thoughts? ♦ S: Sometimes I think that (maybe) I shouldn't have bought a new car. T: Why? S: Because it was very expensive.

193 Here and There

④ The relative pronoun and preposition, in this case *in which*, may sometimes be used in place of *where*, however the result is usually formal. ♦ Isn't Tokyo the city in which his son lives?
Practice Make clauses with *where*. ♦ T: Paris S1: That's where I was three years ago in June. OR S2: Isn't that where you lived for a year? T: Barcelona S3: That's where the summer Olympic Games were held in 1992. OR S4: That's where I want to go some day.
Communication Talk about famous places. Uses clauses with *where*. ♦ T: Do you know anything about Chicago? OR What do you know about Chicago? S: I know Chicago is where the world's tallest building is. S2: I know that's where Mr. ------ is from. S3: Chicago is where I lost my passport last year.

194 A Short Conversation

⑤ What did he say to that? OR What was his response to that?
Practice Work in pairs and make questions and replies similar to the following example. ♦ S1: Did ------ tell you that she was going to spend the summer in France? S2: No, she told me that she had a summer job here.

195 Most and Least

① Note: the observations made by **A** are subjective, not objective—opinion rather than fact; subjective opinions are required in the substitutions also. ❖ Note the use of *ever* in a relative clause; *ever* may be used in a clause and in questions, but not normally in a declarative sentence. ♦ He's the tallest person I have ever seen (clause), but not I have ever seen a very tall person.
② The meaning of line two could be that **B** does not consider this movie interesting, or literally, that while this movie may be interesting, **B** has seen more interesting ones.
③ **A** concedes the movie may not be the most interesting, but it is certainly *among* the most interesting movies he or she has ever seen.
Practice Use subjective opinions rather than facts in the substitutions. ❖ Use *ever* in relative clauses in questions with the superlative. ♦ S1: What is the largest city you've ever visited? S2: Shanghai is the largest city I have ever visited. ❖ Ask questions using superlative forms and *wh*-questions. ♦ What is the tallest building in this city? Who is the most famous sportsman (or one of the most famous sportsmen) in your country?

Teaching/Study Notes

196 A Good Job
① *The* is optional with *most* in line one. ❖ **OR** What do you like about your job the most?
② **OR** The thing I like most about my job is not having to come to the office before 9 o'clock. **OR** The thing which I like most..., ❖ Note that the complement of *be* does not have to be a *that*-clause. ♦ The thing I like most about my job is *its good salary and benefits*. (Second substitution.)
③ **OR** What do you like (the) least about your job.
④ The part of my job.... **OR** The thing about my job.... Both of these expressions can be used with *job*, but *the part of* may not be compatible with other topics. For example, it would not be natural to use it with objects or persons.
Practice More examples: What do you like most about working at ------ Department Store? What do you like most about being a teacher? And, Do you like working at ------? What do you like about it? What don't you like about it?
Communication Ask for opinions about various topics. What do you like most about this city? What do you like the least about school? What do you find the most interesting about your job?

197 Maybe
① **OR** I wonder why ----- didn't come to the party last night. See embedded *wh*-questions in dialogues 172 and 173 for additional examples.
② **OR** Maybe he couldn't get a ride. **OR** Maybe he wasn't able to get a ride.
③ **OR** He might not have been able to get a ride. **OR** Maybe he wasn't able to get a ride. ❖ **OR** Or he might have been studying for a test.
Practice Try the conversation again with line one in the present continuous. ------ isn't coming to the party tonight. I wonder why. Make necessary changes in lines two through four. ❖ Use *maybe* or *might* in response to *I wonder why*.
♦ T: ------ canceled her wedding plans. I wonder why. S1: She might have fallen in love with someone else. S2: Maybe she couldn't afford to get married. Make responses to the following: T: ------ quit his job. I wonder why. T: ------ quit school. I wonder why. T: I wonder why ------ is taking French lessons.

198 Not Necessarily
① The meaning of *must* here is supposition, not necessity. ❖ Other examples with *must*: He must be going on a date tonight. He must have failed the test. He must not have gotten up on time this morning.
② **OR** Why do you think they are having a sale? ❖ Idiom:... *make one think*...
❖ *They* in line two refers to that store. The plural pronoun may be used to refer to companies and businesses.
⑤ I guess not here is a concession. ❖ **OR** I guess it doesn't.
Practice Try the following variation of the dialogue. **A**: You like English, don't you? **B**: What makes you think I like English? **A**: Because you always look happy

-310-

Teaching/Study Notes

in class. **B**: Just because I look happy in class, that doesn't necessarily mean I like English. **A**: No, I guess not.
Communication Make some observations. ♦ Just because a person is tall, it doesn't necessarily mean that he is good at basketball. Just because a person speaks Chinese, that (*or* it) doesn't necessarily mean he or she can read Chinese.

199 What's This For?
Practice Although it cannot be smoothly substituted in this dialogue, the impersonal *you* can also be used to describe the purpose of something. ♦ You use it to wash clothes. **OR** You wash clothes with it. The passive with *to* + v is also possible, although it does not work smoothly in substitutions for this dialogue. ♦ It's used to wash clothes.

200 Snapshots
④ **OR** That was taken in Paris when I was traveling in Europe.
Communication Students bring to class photographs of a trip or other event in their lives, and they talk about the photographs with their classmates. ♦ Where was this photograph taken? What were you doing when this photograph was taken? Who took this picture?

201 Changes
① *They* may be used here with a passive-like meaning when the real subject is not emphasized. This use of *they* is called the *they*-passive.
Practice Other verbs that may be used in the dialogue substitutions include: *constructed, demoted, divided, made (made president, etc.), promoted, razed, rearranged, refurbished, remodeled, removed.* ❖ Use the *they* passive. ♦ T: He was made president. S: They made him president. T: The building was remodeled. S: They remodeled the building. ❖ In addition to *they*, *someone* can also be used when the subject is a single person and is unknown or unimportant. ♦ Someone stole my car.
Communication Students mention changes they have observed recently. Use both the *they*-passive and the passive form of verbs. ♦ The campus library is being remodeled. The director of the department has been promoted. They've installed air-conditioning in the library.

202 Something to Say
④ **OR** Wasn't the weather terrible yesterday?
Practice Tag questions are useful for conversation openers with strangers or acquaintances. Consider appropriate conversation openers for the following situations: • at a wedding reception, • on a tour, • at a dinner party. Make tag questions using various verb forms including the present perfect, continuous tenses, and modals.

Teaching/Study Notes

203 Everything's Ready
① OR Have you typed those reports? The passive is used in line one as a means for someone with authority to ask indirectly about **B**'s progress.
Practice Use the present perfect with the passive. ♦ S1: I can't take my car to school today. T: Why? S1: The tire hasn't been changed yet. S2: I can't buy another car. T: Why? S2: Because my first car hasn't been paid for yet. ❖ Note: Has the book been read yet? is not a likely passive sentence in English when the real subject is *you*.

204 The Work Is Done
① OR I hope you've . . . .
Practice Use the present perfect with the passive. Express surprise. ♦ S1: The car has been put in the garage! S2: I know. I put it in the garage. S3: The kitchen has been painted! S4: I know. I painted it! ❖ Use *someone* in place of the passive. ♦ S1: Someone put the car in the garage! S2: I know. *I* put it in the garage.

205 Finishing Up
① *Be finished* can be followed by *v-ing* or by *with* + noun or noun clause. ♦ They'll be finished painting the room today. When will you be finished with your homework?
② The passive with a modal is used in line two: can't be painted
⑥ OR They ought to be finished . . . . OR Everything should be finished by tomorrow. Although *should be* + pp expresses expectation in line six, the pattern can also be used to express an opinion.
Communication Offer opinions with *should be* + pp. ♦ I think a foreign language should be required in elementary schools. I think tomorrow should be declared a holiday. I don't think people should be permitted to park their cars here.

206 A Reminder
① Please remind me . . . can also be followed by a *that*-clause. ♦ Please remind me that I should turn left when I get to the school.
③ The object of *remind* —*to turn left*— is omitted here.
Practice Use *when*-clauses with *remind* and *forget*. ♦ T: Don't forget to call your parents when you get home. S: Yes, please remind me to call my parents when I get home. T: Don't forget to get some gas when you come to a station. S: Yes, please remind me to get some gas when I come to a station. ❖ Practice *Please remind* + obj with a *that*-clause, and *Please remind* + obj with an infinitive phrase. ♦ Please remind ------ that we don't have class tomorrow. OR Please remind me not to forget to pay the rent tomorrow.

207 Things That Annoy
① *When* in this dialogue introduces a condition and the conjunction is sometimes

Teaching/Study Notes

replaced by *if* in conversation; *when*, however, is more common. (Conditions with *if* are introduced in dialogue 218.)
② **OR** Yes, except when it's windy. See dialogue 241 for practice with *except when*.
④ Hmm. **OR** I see.
Communication Ask classmates about their personal preferences using *when*.
♦ Do you mind walking to school when its raining? ❖ State personal preferences.
♦ I don't like to cook when I have to hurry, but I like to cook when I have lots of time.

208 This One or That One?

① The relative clause may be reduced in the passive: the one *that was* painted by Picasso ♦ the one (*that was*) painted by Picasso.
② The use of the relative clause in a *wh*-question puts additional emphasis on the question word. Which one is it that was painted by Picasso? Also possible: Which is the one painted by Picasso? **OR** Which one was painted by Picasso?
④ **OR** Then I guess I like the one by Miro. **OR** I like the one by Miro.
Practice Other passive participial phrases that may be used in the substitutions include: *cooked with, made with, marked down in price, photo (was) taken by, reduced in price, remodeled this year, repaired by, written by.* ❖ Additional examples of reduced relative clauses in the passive: He was wearing shoes made in Italy. Cars made in the future will be powered by solar energy. ❖ Make relative clauses with the pattern used in line two. ♦ T: Who called last night? S: Who was it that called last night? T: What hotel are we staying at? S: What hotel is it that we are staying at? T: Why can't he come to the party? S: Why is it that he can't come to the party?

209 Complainers

① *That*, the object of *like*, refers to a past event here and is more appropriate than *it*. If the activity is habitual, *it* may be more appropriate: I don't like it when the teacher gives us a test and he doesn't tell us about it in advance. **OR** . . . gives us a test without telling us about it in advance.
② **OR** You know what makes (or *gets*) me angry? **OR** Do you know what I don't like?
④ **OR** . . . calls on me in class *and* I'm looking out the window.
Practice Notice the use of the pronouns *that* in line one of substitution one, *it* in substitution two, and *this* in substitution three. They refer, respectively to the past (*that*), habitual behavior (*it*), and the present (*this*).
Communication Talk about things you like. Use *when* as a conj. ♦ I like it when we have a holiday. I like it when we watch a movie in class. ❖ Express other feelings or opinions you have using the conjunction *when*. ♦ I don't feel good when I see someone unhappy. It bothers me when I get behind in class. I get afraid when I get lost. I'm happy when I can play with my children.

Teaching/Study Notes

210 A Few Favors
① The idiom *by any chance* makes the question gentler in tone and suggests that the speaker intends to impose upon **B**.
② **B** might also reply in an informal style: Yes. Why?
③ The expression do you suppose you could. . . helps to make a request gentler or more polite in tone.
Practice Try the following dialogue. A: Could I ask you a favor? B: Sure. What is it? A: Could you drive me home from school? B: Sure. ❖ Practice asking for favors. Use Could I ask you a favor? or Could you please do a favor for me? or Do you think you could do something for me?

211 Supposing
① *Be supposed to* is somewhat of an indirect way of indicating necessity or responsibility, but it also suggests that the requirement has been imposed upon the subject. One could say Don't we have to clean this mess up before class begins? but the connotation is slightly different from line one. Also possible: Aren't we to clean this mess up . . .? This usage, however, is slightly formal and *be supposed to* is more common in conversational English.
② The person referred to here and in line three probably said: "This has to be cleaned up before class begins," or "I want this cleaned up before class begins."
Practice *Be supposed to* is also used to refer to general rules and regulations, as for example, We're not supposed to smoke in this building. **OR** You're supposed to take your shoes off and leave them by the door.
Communication Talk about rules or regulations at your school, at work, or in society in general. Use *be (not) supposed to* + v.

212 Shortcomings
① Note that responses to What do you think of. . .? usually indicate personal preference—like or dislike: I like it. **OR** It's OK. **OR** I don't think much of it. The questions What do you *think about* . . .? and What's your opinion of . . .? often require a more serious reply that takes into consideration the various factors influencing an opinion or view.
② *Even though* can often be replaced by *although* or *though*, however the additional emphasis provided by *even though* is necessary in line two. *Even though* can be replaced by *in spite of the fact that,* but it cannot be replaced by *even if* in this sentence. In the following example, *even though* may be replaced by *although*, though with less emphasis. ▶ Even though it's a long way from my home, I prefer to walk to school.
④ The intensifier *so* in line three is not repeated in line four.
Communication Make comments using *even though*. ▶ I like my job *even though* the pay is very low. I don't like my room *even though* it has a nice view of the lake. I like this class *even though* we have difficult tests.

Teaching/Study Notes

213 Really?
① OR I hear that ------ and ------ were married . . .. OR I was surprised to hear . . .
③ OR That's wonderful. *Great* in line three refers to the fact that they got married and are going to France on their honeymoon.
Practice The *get* passive usually occurs with process verbs as opposed to stative verbs. ♦ He got married yesterday. OR He was married yesterday. **But**, The news was heard by everyone, **not** The news got heard by everyone. ❖ The *get* passive can also be used to express what the speaker views as unfortunate or unfavorable. ♦ The house got hit by lightning. My bike got stolen. ❖ The past participles of some verbs commonly used with the *get* passive include: *arrested, broken, burned, caught, chosen to..., damaged, divorced, elected, finished, fired, hired, hit, hurt, injured, invited, laid off, lost, married, promoted, put (into, etc.), selected, started, sued, thrown out, transferred.* ❖ Practice forming the *get* passive. ♦ T: They were married. S: They got married. T: He's being promoted. S: He's getting promoted.

214 How Not to Get Along
② *Agree on* or *agree about* ❖ Note that *s + should* may replace the infinitive phrase: . . . on what to have . . . ♦ on what they should have . . . ❖ *Couldn't* may replace *didn't* in line two.
④ OR . . . on how to cook the main dish.
⑤ That's too bad is an idiom; *too* cannot be replaced with *very* here. The expression: That's unfortunate could also be used here. *Too* cannot modify unfortunate here.
Practice Use infinitive phrases. ♦ T: I don't know what I should do. S: I don't know what to do. T: I don't know who (whom) I should invite to the party. S: I don't know who (whom) to invite to the party.
Communication Use *agree with* + obj + *on* or *about*. Make true statements. ♦ I don't always agree with my parents on what time I should be home at night. I don't always agree with my sister about which TV program to watch. I don't always agree with my wife about who (whom) to invite for dinner. ❖ Do you ever argue or disagree with your friends? What do you argue or disagree about? ♦ Sometimes we disagree about which movie we should see, or about where to meet.

215 When and While
① OR Have you done your homework?
③ OR Have you cleaned your room?
⑥ OR I'll clean it *after* I finish (or, *have finished*) reading this article. ❖ Compare the use of the conjunction *when* here with its use in dialogues 206, 207, and 209, in which it is not possible to replace *when* with *after*.
Practice Use *while* in sentences. ♦ I sometimes listen to classical music while I do my homework. My brother almost always reads the newspaper while he is eating breakfast.

Teaching/Study Notes

216 Smooth Talker
② OR <u>He convinced me to drive him to the ski grounds tomorrow.</u>
③ Also, with the *get* causative: <u>He got me to lend him my skis.</u>
Practice Use *would* as it is used in line six. ❖ T: <u>------ is good at talking people into doing things.</u> S: <u>He would make a good salesman.</u> T: <u>------ is good at skiing.</u> S: <u>She would make a good ski instructor.</u>

217 How Come?
④ Note that question word order with *how come* is different from question word order with *why*. Review questions with *how come* in dialogue 82.
⑤ OR <u>The reason (that) she doesn't like it is that . . .</u>. OR <u>She doesn't like it because a waiter here spilled coffee on her once.</u>
Practice Ask classmates questions. Students should reply using *the reason why* or *the reason that*. ▶ S1: <u>Why were you late for school today?</u> S2: <u>The reason why</u> (or <u>that</u>) <u>I was late for school is that I missed the bus.</u> ❖ *The reason* may also be used with the prep *for*. Make sentences like those in the following models.
▶ <u>What was the reason for his leaving early? The reason for his leaving early was that he had a headache.</u>

218 Conditions
② The *unless*-clause replaces the negative *if*-clause. Also possible: <u>If I don't have to work overtime.</u>
⑤ OR <u>Not unless you're going.</u>
Practice Use *unless* to express conditions. T: <u>If you don't buy my ticket, I'm not going to the theater with you.</u> S: <u>I'm not going to the theater with you unless you buy my ticket.</u>
Communication Use *unless* to express true feelings or conditions. ▶ <u>I wouldn't eat in the school cafeteria unless I didn't have time to go to a restaurant.</u>

219 Dreamers
① OR <u>any movie star who (whom) you wanted (to meet), . . .</u> ❖ Note that *any* in this line means none in particular—without limitation.
② Line two is a confirmation question.
Practice Try the conversation with the following suggested line-one substitutions: <u>If you could be any animal you wanted, what would you like to be?</u> OR <u>If you could play any instrument you wanted, what would you like to be able to play?</u> OR <u>If you could have any kind of pet you wanted, what would you like to have?</u>
Communication Ask questions similar to the following: <u>If you could ask Abraham Lincoln one question, what would you like to ask him?</u> <u>If you could be in the Olympic Games, what sport would you like to play?</u> <u>If you could have anything to eat you wanted, what would you like to have?</u> ❖ Make questions using the past conditional. ▶ <u>If you could have been born in any country, where would you like to</u>

Teaching/Study Notes

have been born? If you could have been a famous 19th century writer, who would you like to have been?

220 Giving Permission
② *Provided that* or *provided* or *providing*.
④ *Provided that* cannot replace *if* in line four.
Practice Ask questions. Make replies with *provided that* or *providing*. ♦ S1: Would you ride in the space shuttle if you had a chance? S2: Yes, provided that I had lots of life insurance. S1: Are you coming to class tomorrow? Yes, providing that I get up on time.

221 An Excuse
① Although the sentence is declarative in form, the exclamatory nature of the sentence makes it clear that the sentence solicits a reason or excuse for not being in class.
④ The past conditional with an unreal condition is introduced here. The past perfect is used in the *if*-clause, and *would have* or *could have* is used in the main clause.
Practice Use *if* with the past conditional. ♦ S1: I lost my passport. S2: If you had kept it at home, you wouldn't have lost it. S3: Tomorrow is ------'s birthday. S4: If I had known that, I would have bought him a present.
Communication Tell classmates something you would have done differently if you had known something. ♦ I would have studied last night if I had known we were having a test today.

222 Wouldn't You?
④ In unreal conditions, the verb is put into the subjunctive; thus, *is leaving* in line three becomes *were leaving* in line four. Subjunctive forms of *be* are: I, you, he, she, it, we, they *were*; however, *was* may be heard, as in *. . . if I was leaving . . .*.
❖ *Wouldn't you be?* is a short form of *Wouldn't you be happy if you were leaving for Europe tomorrow?*
Practice Additional adjectives that could be used in substitutions include: *scared, unhappy, upset,* and other adjectives of emotion. The adjective *lucky* may not be used in the substitutions in this dialogue because it is not an emotion. ❖ Practice *yes/no*-questions with *if*-clauses. ♦ S1: Would you be disappointed, if you were leaving for Europe tomorrow? S2: No, I'd be excited.
Communication What would make you happy? Upset? Angry? ♦ I'd be happy if tomorrow were a holiday. I'd be upset if we had a test today.

223 Unbelievable
① *In order to* may be replaced with *to* in line one.
③ An *if*-clause and an impersonal *you* with the future conditional form are used here instead of an *in order to*-clause as in line one.

-317-

Teaching/Study Notes

Practice Give some familiar conditions using *in order to* or *to*. ♦ You have to be 18 to get a driver's license in my country. You have to get an A on the test in order to pass the course. ❖ Use the future conditional with *if*-clauses to express real conditions. ♦ If you want to pass this class, you have to get an A on the test.

224 Reasons
① Line one asks about something which is expected of **B**, or something which **B** might be obliged to do.
② OR No. I would have studied if I had been feeling well. A clause with *but* replaces the *if*-clause in line two. *But* may be replaced by *only* in this line.
③ OR I would have too if I hadn't fallen asleep after dinner. *But* may replace *only* in line three. *Only* as a conditional conjunction is normally used only in spoken English.
Practice Use *but* or *only* with the conditional. ♦ T: I would go to the beach with you if I could swim. S1: I'd go to the beach with you only I can't swim. ❖ Note *but* and *only* in the conditional are usually used as replies or responses to questions. Make replies with *but* or *only*: ♦ T: Did you buy a Mother's Day present for your mother? S: No, I would have but I didn't have any money. ❖ Note that the pattern I would, but . . . is useful for introducing excuses. ♦ S1: Aren't you coming to my party? S2: No, I'm sorry. I would, but I have to work.

225 Just in Case
③ It might. OR It might be.
④ OR I doubt that it will be warm.
Practice Use *(just) in case*. ♦ Let's study hard tonight, just in case we have a test tomorrow. Let's take our tennis rackets, just in case we get out of class early today. ❖ Give advice using *just in case* and *don't you think you should*. ♦ Don't you think you should take your umbrella, just in case it rains?

226 Would You?
② OR . . . if I hadn't consulted my wife first.
Practice Use *without + v-ing*. ♦ T: ------ sold his house, and he didn't consult his wife first. S: ------ sold his house without consulting his wife first. T: ------ went to a wedding, and he didn't have an invitation. S: ------ went to a wedding without (having) an invitation. ❖ Make questions. Use *without + v-ing* or noun phrase. ♦ Would you ride in a boat without a life jacket? Would you take a test without studying for it?

227 A Good Thing
② *Glad* gets extra stress to express disbelief.
Practice Try the conversation in the past tense. A: It's a good thing I had a cold yesterday. B: You're *glad* you had a cold? A: Yes, because I if didn't have (or

Teaching/Study Notes

hadn't had) a cold, I would have had to go to school. And if I had gone to school yesterday, I would have had to take the English test.
Communication Make true statements with *glad*. Use *if*-clauses. ♦ I'm glad tomorrow is a holiday. If it weren't a holiday, I wouldn't be able to go camping. I'm glad we didn't have a test. If we had (*or* had had) a test, I might have failed it.

228 Free Advice
③ To make a suggestion slightly more gentle, use: Maybe you'd better . . . . **OR** Don't you think you'd better . . . . ♦ Maybe you'd better call a taxi . . . . **Or** Don't you think you'd better call a taxi if you want to get there on time?
⑤ I would if I were you. **OR** I'd call a taxi if I were you.
Practice Use *If I were you, I'd. . . .* ♦ S1: If I were you, I'd take my umbrella. S2: Why? S1: It looks like it's going to rain today.
Communication What would you do if you were ------ (a person familiar to all the class)? ♦ If I were the prime minister, I'd lower taxes. If I were our teacher, I wouldn't give any tests.

229 Thanks
② **OR** Oh, that was no trouble at all.
③ **OR** Without your help, I wouldn't have gotten the job.
Practice The substitutions work well when **B** helps or gives assistance to **A** in some way; thus, Thanks for baking me a cake doesn't work; nor does Thanks for inviting me to the party.
Communication Use *if it hadn't been for* or *if it weren't (wasn't) for* ♦ If it weren't (wasn't) for the elevator, we'd have to walk up five flights of stairs to class. If it hadn't been for the rain yesterday, I could have played golf.

230 Unaware
④ **OR** . . . I would have told you it was closed.
Communication Tell some things you might not have done if you had had certain information. ♦ If I had known it was going to be warm today, I wouldn't have worn my sweater. If I had known you were allergic to chocolate, I wouldn't have bought you that box of candy.

231 Afterthought
③ The past conditional is used here to express unreal or contrary to fact conditions.
④ Oh, you never know suggests that maybe things might not have worked out as expected. ❖ **OR** If you had invested in the stock market, you might have lost all your money.
Practice Use lines one through three of the dialogue as a model and make a conversation with the future conditional. ♦ **A**: Sometimes I think I should sell my car. **B**: Why? **A**: Because if I sell my car, I can buy new camping equipment.

Teaching/Study Notes

Communication Make true statements with *sometimes I think*. ♦ Sometimes I think I should quit my part-time job. Sometimes I think I should have taken French instead of English.

232 Do You Mind?

① *Since* may replace *as long as* in line one, but not in line four.
④ *If* may replace *as long as* in line four but, not in line two without a change in meaning.

Practice Use the first person singular pronoun as the subject in the main clause in line one in substitutions in order for the dialogue to work smoothly. ❖ *I was wondering if . . .* may also be used to ask for permission. ♦ I was wondering if I could use your bicycle. I was wondering if I could leave work a little early today. Make requests for permission using Do you mind if and I was wondering if.

233 Working Together

① Notice the difference between *see* + *if* in line one and *see* with embedded question in line five. In line one *see if* means try; in lines four and five *see* with an embedded question means find out. The embedded question with *see* (find out) may, of course, be an *if*-clause, as in the following example. ♦ Please see if the teacher is going to give us a test tomorrow. (Please find out if the teacher is going to give us a test tomorrow.)

Practice Requests can be made with *see*. Would you mind seeing what time the bus leaves for the airport? OR Could you see what time the bus leaves for the airport? ❖ Make offers with *see if* meaning try. S1: I can't find my pen. S2: I'll see if I can find it. S1: I don't understand this math problem. S2: I'll see if I can help you with it. ❖ Make sentences with *see if* and *let's*. ♦ Let's see if we can get home before 5. (Let's try to get home before 5.) Let's see if we can find something to eat in the refrigerator. (Let's try to find something to eat in the refrigerator.) Let's see what's on TV. (Let's find out what's on TV.) Let's see if there's anything in the refrigerator. (Let's find out if there's anything in the refrigerator.)

234 It Depends

④ *Whom* as the relative pronoun is more correct than *who* in line four, because the relative pronoun is the object of *with;* however, *who* is more typical of conversational English. ❖ OR It depends on with whom I am traveling for one thing. Although this usage is correct, the two prepositions sound awkward together.

Practice Ask questions. Make responses using: *it depends on . . . .* ♦ S1: What are you going to do after class? S2: It depends. S1: On What? S2: It depends on how much homework I have. If I don't have a lot of homework, I'm going to play tennis.

235 Nagging

① OR I wish you would have done your homework before you went to the movie.

Teaching/Study Notes

Practice Note that the subjunctive is used with *wish*. The past forms of verbs are used to express present tense wishes, and past perfect forms are used to express past tense wishes. ▶ I wish you would do your homework. I wish you had done your homework.

Communication What do your parents, brother or sister, or spouse wish that you would or would not do? ▶ My wife wishes I would make dinner on Sundays. ❖ What does someone hope you will do or hope you won't do? ▶ My brother hopes I will lend him my car.

236 The Truth of the Matter

① An *if*-clause may replace *then* in line one: . . . because if I went back to school, I'd have to give up my job. This dialogue works smoothly when the *because*-clause in line one is affirmative.

④ *Even if* introduces an emphatic condition. *Even if* is often used in a *yes/no*-question as a confirmation question.

Practice Use *even if.* ▶ T: I'm going on a picnic tomorrow. S: Even if it rains? T: No, if it rains I'm not going. **OR** Yes, even if it rains.

237 Decision Making

① *If* may replace *whether or not* in line one.

② *Decide* may be followed by an infinitive phrase or a *that*-clause. ❖ **OR** I've decided that I'm going to take a trip.

Practice Also possible in line one are: Have you made up your mind whether or not . . .. Have you made a decision as to whether or not . . .. ❖ Use embedded *wh*-questions to ask about someone's plans for the weekend, for the summer, for this evening, or for another time. ▶ S1: Have you decided what you will do tonight? S2: Yes, I've decided to go to a movie. S3: Have you decided what movie you will see? S2: Yes, I've decided to see ------. S4: Have you decided who you will go with? S2: No, I haven't.

238 Hope for the Best

① *Hope* is used when there is a real possibility for something to be realized. *Wish* is used when there is no real possibility for something to be realized.

③ **OR** I wish she weren't going to give us a test. *Wasn't* may replace *weren't* although the subjunctive *weren't* is more strictly correct.

Practice Express wishes. ▶ I wish I could take a long trip. I wish I had enough money to buy a good camera. I wish I were 18 years old. ❖ Express ambitions or desires with *hope.* ▶ I hope it doesn't rain tomorrow. I hope I get a letter today. I hope I win the marathon race.

239 Wishes

① The subjunctive form of the verb *own* is used in line one. The past forms of verbs

Teaching/Study Notes

are used to express present tense wishes, and past perfect forms of verbs are used to express past tense wishes. Note that in line one of the second substitution the subjunctive form of *be* is *were*, though *was* is often heard in conversation.
Practice Express wishes with the negative. ♦ <u>I wish I didn't have to get up at 6:30 in the morning. I wish this class weren't (*or* wasn't) difficult.</u> ❖ State what you don't wish. ♦ <u>I don't wish I had a cat.</u>

240 Exceptions
④ <u>except that</u> **OR** <u>except for the fact that</u>.
⑤ **OR** <u>It sounds like you had a good time.</u>
Practice Make sentences with *except for the fact that*. ♦ <u>I like this school except for the fact that it is so far from my home.</u>
Communication Make true sentences with *except for when*. ♦ <u>I don't mind washing dishes except for when we have company. I like to go fishing except for when it's cold.</u>

241 Hardly Ever
③ Note that the response to line two is negative. <u>She does</u>? is not a natural reply.
Practice Note that *especially* can be used in the same position as *except*. Use *especially* or *except* in reply to questions. ♦ T: <u>Do you like to cook?</u> S: <u>Yes, especially when I can cook for guests.</u> T: <u>Do you like your classes?</u> S: <u>Yes, except when we have tests.</u>

242 In a Hurry
① The passive with *would like* and *want* requires a transitive verb, as in lines one and two.
Practice *Would like* and *want* in the passive are also commonly used to offer assistance. ♦ <u>Would you like your car washed?</u> A reply might be <u>No, thank you. I don't want (or need) my car washed today.</u>

243 Tennis or Swimming?
① **OR** <u>Which would you rather do: go to the pool or play tennis?</u>
Practice Practice sentence stress. Repeat the question with emphasis on *you*.
♦ S1: <u>What would you like to do?</u> S2: <u>I don't know. What would *you* like to do?</u>
S1: <u>What time do you want to leave?</u> S2: <u>I don't know. What time do *you* want to leave?</u>
Communication Ask classmates about their preferences. Use *would rather* in questions and in replies. ♦ S1: <u>What</u> (*or* <u>Which</u>) <u>would you rather do: play tennis or go to a movie?</u> S2: <u>I'd rather go to a movie than play tennis.</u> **OR** <u>I'd prefer going to a movie.</u> S1: <u>Would you rather see *The Sound of Music* or *The Third Man*?</u> S2: <u>I'd prefer to see *The Third Man*.</u> S1: <u>When would you rather go: before lunch or after lunch?</u> S2: <u>I guess I'd rather go after lunch than before lunch.</u>

Teaching/Study Notes

244 Instructions

① Note that while *tell* is commonly used in the passive, the passive form of *say* is used only in a few expressions. *Say* occurs in this dialogue only in the active voice.
④ He said I should make graphs. . . . **OR** He said to make graphs. . . .
⑥ **OR** No, he said to make graphs. . . . Note that the passive with *tell* is stronger than the active forms *he said* or *he told me to*.
Practice What were you often told to do (or to not do) by your parents or teachers when you were a small child? ♦ I was often told by my teacher not to talk in class. I was often told by my parents to hurry.

245 Getting Things Done

① The passive-causative form in lines one and two is *to have something done*.
③ **OR** When do you leave for your ski trip?
⑤ The passive-causative form in line five is *to get something done*.
Practice Make sentences with *to have something done* and *to get something done*.
♦ I had my tire repaired yesterday. I'm going to get my hair cut tomorrow.

246 Whether or Not

② *If* may be used in place of *whether or not* in line two.
④ *If* may replace *whether or not* in the first clause, but not in the second clause. However, *should* may be used instead of the infinitive in the second clause.
♦ . . . then I'll decide whether or not I should read it.
Practice Talk about difficult decisions. Use *whether or not*. ♦ I can't decide whether or not to buy new a car. I'm not really sure whether I should get a part-time job after school or not.

247 Determination

④ *Whether or not* cannot be replaced by *if* in line four.
Practice Express strong determination using *whether or not*. ♦ I'm going to the beach tomorrow whether it's warm or not. I'm not going to school tomorrow whether we're having a test or not. ❖ Strong determination can also be expressed with *even though*. Try it. ♦ I'm not going to miss the test even though I don't feel well.

248 Because

① *So (that)* is used in a clause of purpose with *be, have to, will, be able to, can, will, will be able to*, and the negative and past forms of these verbs.
Practice Answer questions with *so (that)* or *because*. ♦ T: Why are you leaving early today? S1: So that I'm not late for my dentist appointment. **OR** S2: Because I have to go to the dentist. ❖ Make suggestions and give replies with *so that*.
♦ S1: Let's bring our lunch to school tomorrow? S2: Why? S1: So that we don't

Teaching/Study Notes

have to eat in the cafeteria.
Communication Talk about yourself or someone you know. Use *so that*. ♦ I am taking the bus tonight so that I can get home early. My friend uses a tape recorder in class so that he doesn't have to take notes.

249 Trying to Recall

① Note that rising intonation is used in line one as a means of indicating that the speaker wants information repeated.

③ *Again* may also be used with the question to make it obvious that the speaker wants information repeated. ♦ And who was it that we borrowed that tent from again? *Again*, however, does not work well with the question in line one because *again* would sound awkward immediately after an adverb of time.

⑤ **OR** I thought it was him.

Practice Make questions to get a repetition of information. ♦ T: When did we go camping? S: When was it that we went camping? T: Who called us last night? S: Who was it who called us last night?

250 Mysteries

② **OR** Why does he want to buy a yacht?
③ **OR** That's what *I*'m wondering. (*I* is stressed.)
④ *You* in the subject position here, and in line five, is the impersonal pronoun.
⑤ **OR** You might think so.
⑥ *Would* may be used in line six. I wonder why he would want to buy a yacht.
Practice Use *even* in sentences. ♦ My brother's been to Paris three times and he's never even seen the Eiffel Tower. ----- has lived in Mexico for seven years and he can't even say "thank you" in Spanish.

Appendix

Appendix

Appendix 1 Major intonation patterns

statement: It's a bracelet.   No, he isn't.
No, she doesn't.   He sells cars.

request: Stand over there.   Try on that coat.

yes/no-question: Is it a necklace?   Are you from Beijing?
Do you like English?   Have you been to Acapulco?

wh-question: What's this?   Where's the art museum?
How about the tickets?   What do they have?

or-question: Is this your book or mine?
Which do you like better, basketball or hockey?

tag question: Yes, it is, isn't it? (comment)
That's your teacher, isn't it? (confirmation)

lists: A camera, shoes, clothes, books, and an umbrella.
I like to read, play tennis, and listen to music.

Appendix

Appendix 2 Pronunciation: -*s* suffix

- when a word ends in /s, z, ʃ, ʒ, tʃ, dʒ/, the -*s* suffix is pronounced /əz/.

- when a word ends in a vowel sound or in a voiced consonant sound that is not a sibilant, the -*s* suffix is pronounced /z/.

- when a word ends in a voiceless sound which is not a sibilant, the -*s* suffix is pronounced /s/.

/əz/	/z/	/s/
classes	apples	asks
dishes	children's	gifts
mixes	father's	it's
oranges	gloves	likes
sandwiches	goes	notebooks
suitcases	letters	personal effects
teaches	papers	photographs
watches	shoes	presents

Appendix 3 Pronunciation: -*ed* suffix

- when a verb ends in a /d/ or a /t/ sound, the -*ed* suffix is pronounced /əd/.

- when a verb ends in a voiced sound other than /d/, the -*ed* suffix is pronounced /d/.

- when a verb ends in a voiceless sound other than /t/, the -*ed* suffix is pronounced /t/.

/əd/	/d/	/t/
decided	arrived	baked
graduated	called	finished
interrupted	cleaned	liked
started	enjoyed	looked
suggested	married	stopped
tasted	played	talked
visited	stayed	watched
wanted	studied	worked

Appendix

Appendix 4 verb + *to* verb: *I like to study.*

afford	continue	hate	manage	say
agree	decide	have	mean	seem
appear	demand	help	need	start
arrange	desire	hesitate	offer	tend
ask	expect	hope	plan	try
begin	forget	intend	prefer	use
care	get	learn	pretend	want
choose	guarantee	like	promise	wish
claim	happen	love	refuse	

Appendix 5 verb + obj + *to* verb: *I advise you to study hard.*

advise	command	get	permit	tell
allow	convince	help	persuade	train
ask	depend on	hire	prepare	trust
authorize	encourage	instruct	remind	urge
beg	expect	invite	request	want
challenge	forbid	like	require	warn
choose	force	order	teach	

Appendix 6 noun + *to* verb: *I have permission to leave early.*

agreement	failure	need	promise	threat
arrangement	guarantee	permission	refusal	wish
decision	hesitation	plan	request	
desire	intention	preparation	tendency	

Appendix 7 verb + *(that)* clause: *I think (that-)the test was easy.*

acknowledge	assume	confess	dream	guarantee
admit	believe	decide	emphasize	guess
agree	bet	declare	estimate	hear
allege	boast	demonstrate	expect	hint
announce	charge	deny	explain	hope
answer	claim	determine	feel	imagine
argue	complain	discover	find	imply
assert	conclude	doubt	forget	indicate

Appendix

infer	mention	protest	remark	show
insinuate	notice	prove	remember	state
insist	observe	read	repeat	stress
judge	point out	realize	reply	suggest
know	presume	recall	report	suppose
learn	pretend	recognize	reveal	think
maintain	promise	regret	say	understand
mean	propose	relate	see	write

Appendix 8 verb + ind obj + *(that-)*clause:
I admitted to him that I didn't study. He told me that I was failing.

admit (to)	emphasize (to)	promise	say (to)
announce (to)	explain (to)	protest (to)	shout (to)
answer	guarantee	prove (to)	show
assure	hint (to)	read (to)	state (to)
bet	imply (to)	relate (to)	stress (to)
boast (to)	indicate (to)	remark (to)	suggest (to)
comment (to)	inform	remind	teach
complain (to)	mention (to)	repeat (to)	tell
convince	notify	reply (to)	write (to)
declare (to)	persuade	report (to)	
demonstrate (to)	point out (to)	reveal (to)	

Appendix 9 noun + *(that-)*clause: *I have the feeling that it's going to rain.*

agreement	claim	doubt	guess	recollection
argument	conclusion	dream	hope	rule
assumption	decision	expectation	inference	suspicion
belief	denial	fear	judgement	understanding
charge	discovery	feeling	observation	

Appendix 10 verb + verb-*ing*: *She began studying yesterday.*

admit	begin	deny	favor	keep on
advise	cease	detest	finish	like
anticipate	consider	dislike	give up	love
appreciate	continue	enjoy	hate	mind
avoid	delay	face	imagine	miss

Appendix

omit	prefer	regret	resist	stop
postpone	recollect	remember	risk	suggest
practice	recommend	resent	start	try

Appendix 11 verb + ind obj + d obj **or** verb + d obj + *to* ind obj:
I'll lend you my dictionary. I'll lend my dictionary to you.

address	give	owe	relay	supply
advance	grant	pass	rent	take
allow	hand	pay	sell	teach
bring	issue	phone	send	tell
deny	lend	present	serve	throw
drop	loan	promise	ship	trade
extend	mail	quote	show	whisper
feed	offer	read	sing	write

Appendix 12 verb + ind obj + d obj **or** verb + d obj + *for* ind obj:
Please buy me a pen. Please buy a pen for me.

bake	dig	make	read
boil	do	mix	reserve
build	find	order	save
buy	fry	pack	sew
call	get	paint	shoot
catch	guarantee	peel	sing
cook	land	play	vote
cut	leave	pour	
dial	light	quote	

Appendix 13 verb + *(that-)*clause + subjunctive:
He insists that we be on time for class.

advise	direct	propose
arrange	forbid	recommend
ask	insist	request
beg	intend	require
demand	order	suggest
desire	prefer	urge

Appendix

Appendix 14 v + v-*ing* or v + *to* v:
We continued playing. We continued to play.

begin	like	start
choose	neglect	remember*
continue	prefer	try*
hate	propose	*gerund and infinitive
intend	stand	have different meanings

Appendix 15 v + obj + n: *We appointed him president.*

appoint	elect	take
choose	name	vote
designate		

Appendix 16 v + obj + compl adj or noun: *We considered him a friend.*

believe	find	keep	picture	rate
call	imagine	leave	pronounce	think
consider	judge	make	prove	

Appendix 17 v + obj + compl: *They built the house in an hour.*

apply	cut	hole	serve	take
build	drink	laugh	set...free	use
burn	drive	like	slice	want
buy	eat	paint	spin	wear
chop	get	prefer	spread	
color	have	sell	stain	

Appendix 18 v + obj + v: *Have him do it for you. Watch him practice.*

causatives	observation	
have	feel	observe
let	hear	overhear
make	notice	see, watch

Appendix

Appendix 19 High-frequency regular verbs

1: *-ed* suffix pronounced /d/

admire	control	imagine	praise	spell
advertise	copy	improve	pray	spoil
advise	cover	inquire	prefer	stay
agree	criticize	insure	prepare	study
amuse	damage	interfere	pressure	suffer
allow	dare	issue	prize	surprise
anger	declare	join	quarrel	telephone
annoy	delay	kill	question	threaten
answer	deliver	lean	receive	tie
apologize	describe	learn	refer	travel
appear	deserve	level	refuse	try
argue	destroy	live	remain	use
arrange	disappear	love	remember	view
arrive	discover	mail	remove	warn
assure	disturb	manage	repair	wave
bargain	dream	manufacture	reply	weigh
beg	dry	marry	require	welcome
believe	earn	measure	rescue	whisper
blame	employ	mention	reserve	whistle
borrow	encourage	model	resign	wonder
breathe	enjoy	move	return	worry
burn	enter	multiply	rob	
call	entertain	nail	roll	
calm	equal	name	row	*also has an irregular form
care	examine	narrow	rub	
carry	excuse	obey	sail	
change	exercise	oblige	save	
charge	exist	observe	seize	
claim	fail	occupy	serve	
clean	fan	occur	sew	
clear	fill	open	share	
close	flow	owe	shave	
compare	follow	own	shine*	
concern	fool	pause	show	
consider	fry	plan	shower	
confuse	gather	play	sign	
contain	handle	postpone	smile	
continue	hire	pour	solve	

Appendix

2: -ed suffix pronounced /t/

ache	curse	knock	purchase	thank
advance	dance	lack	push	touch
approach	develop	laugh	race	trick
ask	discuss	like	reach	type
attack	distinguish	lock	reduce	walk
bake	drop	look	remark	watch
bark	escape	mark	risk	wipe
block	establish	mix	rock	witness
brush	express	notice	sacrifice	work
camp	finish	pack	scratch	wrap
chase	help	park	search	wreck
check	hope	pass	shop	
cook	introduce	pinch	slip	
cough	joke	promise	stamp	
crack	jump	pronounce	stop	
cross	kick	punish	tax	

3: -ed suffix pronounced /əd/

add	decide	grant	persuade	respect
admit	defeat	guard	pet	rest
accept	defend	hate	point	reward
applaud	demand	hesitate	present	select
appoint	depend	hunt	pretend	start
arrest	desert	imitate	prevent	suggest
assist	direct	include	print	suspect
associate	divide	indicate	profit	taste
attempt	doubt	insult	protect	test
attend	educate	intend	rate	trade
attract	effect	interrupt	recommend	translate
avoid	elect	invent	record	trust
blind	expect	invite	regard	visit
burst	experiment	lift	regret	vote
celebrate	explode	limit	remind	wait
collect	extend	list	rent	want
complete	fade	neglect	repeat	waste
connect	float	omit	report	wound
correct	flood	paint	represent	
count	fold	permit	resist	

Appendix

Appendix 20 High-frequency irregular verbs

Group 1: present, past, and past participial forms are the same
▶ *put*   present: put   past: put   pp: put

bet	cost	let	shed	thrust
bid	forecast	put	shut	upset
broadcast	hit	quit	spit	
burst	hurt	rid	split	
cast	knit	set	spread	

Group 2: past and past participial forms are the same
▶ *hear*   present: hear   past: heard   pp: heard

present	past and pp	present	past and pp
bend	bent	kneel	knelt
bind	bound	lay	laid
bleed	bled	lead	led
breed	bred	lean	leaned
bring	brought	leap	leaped/leapt
build	built	learn	learned/learnt
burn	burned or burnt	leave	left
buy	bought	lend	lent
catch	caught	light	lit
creep	crept	lose	lost
deal	dealt	make	made
dig	dug	mean	meant
dream	dreamed/dreamt	meet	met
feed	fed	mislead	misled
feel	felt	misunderstand	misunderstood
fight	fought	pay	paid
find	found	read	read
flee	fled	say	said
fling	flung	seek	sought
get	got	sell	sold
grind	ground	send	sent
hang	hung	shine	shone
have	had	shoot	shot
hear	heard	sit	sat
hold	held	sleep	slept
keep	kept	slide	slid

Appendix

present	past and pp		present	past and pp
smell	smelled or smelt		strike	struck
speed	sped		sweep	swept
spell	spelled or spelt		swing	swung
spend	spent		teach	taught
spill	spilled or spilt		tell	told
spin	spun		think	thought
spit	spat		understand	understood
spoil	spoiled or spoilt		win	won
stand	stood		wind	wound
stick	stuck		wring	wrung
sting	stung			

Group 3: past and past participal forms are different
▶ *give*   present: give   past: gave   pp: given

present	past	past participal
be	was/were	been
beat	beat	beaten
become	became	become
begin	began	begun
bite	bit	bitten
blow	blew	blown
break	broke	broken
choose	chose	chosen
come	came	come
do	did	done
draw	drew	drawn
drink	drank	drunk
drive	drove	driven
eat	ate	eaten
fall	fell	fallen
fly	flew	flown
forbid	forbad(e)	forbidden
forget	forgot	forgotten
forgive	forgave	forgive
freeze	froze	frozen
give	gave	given
go	went	gone
grow	grew	grown
hide	hid	hidden

Appendix

present	past	past participal
hide	hid	hidden
know	knew	known
lie	lay	lain
mistake	mistook	mistaken
ride	rode	ridden
ring	rang	rung
rise	rose	risen
run	ran	run
saw	sawed	sawn/sawed
see	saw	seen
sew	sewed	sewn/sewed
shake	shook	shaken
show	showed	shown
shrink	shrank	shrunk
sink	sank	sunk
speak	spoke	spoken
spring	sprang	sprung
steal	stole	stolen
undertake	undertook	undertaken
wake	woke	woken
wear	wore	worn
weave	wove	woven
withdraw	withdrew	withdrawn
write	wrote	written

Appendix 21 Two-word verbs

Intransitive verbs

back up	cheer up	die out	give up
blow away	clear out	dig in	go off
blow out	come to	drive off	grow back
boil away	come up	drop off	grow up
break down	cool off	dry off	hang up
break up	count down	dry up	heat up
build up	cry out	end up	help out
burn out	cut back	fall over	hold back
calm down	die away	fall through	hurry up
catch on	die down	get across	keep away
catch up	die off	get up	keep out

Appendix

lock up	pull through	sign off	start out
lose out	pull up	sing out	stretch out
melt away	quiet down	sit up	take off
move up	rest up	slow down	tire out
pack up	roll over	speak up	turn out
pass away	run off	speed up	turn up (appear)
pass by	save up	split up	wake up
pass on	show off	spread out	wear down
pass out	show up	stand up	wear out
pull over	shut up	start off	work out

Transitive verbs
A dash indicates the verb is both separable and inseparable; an elipsis indicates the particle is separated from the verb in the indicative. The other verbs are inseparable.

accuse ... of	break out	carry — off	cool — off
act — out	break up	carry — out	count on
add ... to	break — up	carry — through	cover — up
agree on	bring — about	cash — in	cross — off
agree with	bring — back	catch on to	cross — out
approve of	bring — down	catch up with	crowd — out
argue with	bring — in	check — off	cry about
arrive at	bring — off	check — out	cut — back
arrive in	bring — on	check — over	cut — off
ask ... for	bring — out	cheer — up	cut — out
• • •	bring — up	chop — down	cut — up
back — up	brush — off	clean — away	• • •
beat — down	build — up	clear — out	dash — off
beat — off	burn — down	clip — out	decide on
become of	burn — out	come across	die from
believe in	buy — off	come apart	dig — out
belong to	• • •	come from	do — in
block — off	call — back	come out	do — over
blow — away	call for	come up with	draw — up
blow — down	call — in	comment on	dream about
blow — off	call — off	compare ... to	dream of
blow — out	call on	compare ... with	dress — up
blow — up	call — out	complain about	drink — up
break — down	call — up	congratulate ... on	drive — back
break into	calm — down	consent to	drop — off
break — off	care for	consist of	drop out of

Appendix

- drown — out
- dry — off
- dry — out
- dry — up
- eat — up
- empty — out
- escape from
- even — off
- even — out
- • • •
- fall down
- fall for
- fall from
- fall through
- fasten — down
- fence — off
- fight — off
- figure — out
- fill — in
- fill — out
- fill — up
- find — out
- finish — off
- finish — up
- fix — up
- flag — down
- force — down
- foul — up
- • • •
- get — across
- get along with
- get back from
- get in
- get into
- get on
- get ... out
- get out of
- get ... over with
- get — through
- get ... up
- give — away
- give — out
- give — up
- go away
- go for
- go in
- go out
- go out for
- go over
- go through
- go with
- grow — back
- • • •
- hand — down
- hand — in
- hand — out
- hang on to
- hang — up
- happen to
- have on
- head — off
- hear about
- hear from
- hear of
- heat — up
- help — out
- hold — back
- hold — off
- hold — out
- hold — over
- hold — up
- hunt — down
- • • •
- insist on
- interfere with
- • • •
- jot — down
- • • •
- keep ... away
- keep ... back
- keep ... down
- keep ... off
- keep on
- keep — on
- keep ... out
- knock — out
- know about
- • • •
- laugh at
- laugh — off
- lay — aside
- lay — away
- lay — down
- lay — out
- lean on
- leave — out
- let — down
- let — off
- let — out
- let — up
- listen to
- live on
- live with
- lock — up
- look after
- look around
- look at
- look for
- look in on
- look into
- look alike
- look out for
- look — over
- look — up
- • • •
- major in
- make — up
- mark — down
- mark — off
- measure — out
- melt — away
- mix — up
- move — into
- move — out
- • • •
- narrow — down
- note — down
- • • •
- object to
- open — up
- • • •
- pack — away
- pack — up
- pass — off
- pass — on
- pass — over
- pass through
- pay — back
- pay for
- pay — off
- pick — out
- pick — up
- pin — down
- play — back
- play — down
- point at
- point — out
- pour — out
- pull — off
- pull — out
- pull — over
- pull — up
- push — in
- put — across
- put — aside
- put — away
- put — back
- put — down
- put — off
- put — on
- put — out
- put ... through
- put — up
- • • •
- read — back
- read — over
- rely on
- remind ... of

Appendix

rinse — off	shoot — down	take — in	turn — down
rip — out	show — off	take — off	turn — in
roll — over	shut — down	take — on	turn — off
roll — up	shut off	take — out	turn — on
round off	sign — up	take — over	turn — over
round — up	sign up for	take — up	turn — up
rub — away	sit in on	talk about	• • •
rub — off	slow — down	talk — over	use — up
rule — out	smile at	taste like	• • •
run away from	sort — out	tear — away	vote for
run — down	speak with	tear — down	vote — down
run for	split — up	tear — off	• • •
run into	spread — out	tear — out	wait for
run — into	stand for	tell — off	wait on
run out of	stay out of	thin — out	wake — up
run over	stir — up	think about	wash — down
• • •	stop at	think of	wash — off
save — up	stop for	think — over	wash — out
see about	straighten — out	think through	watch out for
see — off	straighten — up	think — up	wear — down
send — away	stretch — out	throw away	wear — out
send — off	succeed in	throw — down	win — back
send — out	sum — up	throw — off	wipe — away
set — aside	sweep — away	throw — out	wish for
set — down	• • •	tighten — up	work for
set — off	take after	try — on	work on
set — out	take — back	try — out	worry about
shake — off	take charge of	try out for	wrap — up
shave — off	take — down	turn — back	write — down

Appendix 22 Nouns: count and noncount

Food

Fruit

count			noncount	
apples	coconuts	papayas	coconut	papaya
apricots	grapefruit	peaches	grapefruit	pineapple
avacados	lemons	pears	kiwi fruit	watermelon
bananas	limes	plums	lemon	
blueberries	mangoes	raspberries		
cherries	oranges	strawberries		

Appendix

Meat and Poultry

count		noncount	
chicken livers	sausages	bacon	ground lamb
chicken wings	spare ribs	braised turkey	ham
hamburgers	steaks	chicken	hamburger
porkchops		fried chicken	roast turkey
roasts		ground beef	steak

Vegetables

count

artichokes	cucumbers	onions	tomatoes
beans	endives	peas	turnips
beets	green pepers	potatoes	vegetables
Brussels sprouts	leeks	pumpkins	
carrots	mushrooms	radishes	

noncount

asparagus	celery	spinach
broccoli	corn	squash
cabbage	lettuce	
cauliflower	okra	

Bakery Products and Desserts

count		noncount
buns	date bars	bread
cakes	doughnuts	cake
cookies	muffins	ice cream
cream puffs	pies	pie
crepes	souffles	pudding
croissants	sweet rolls	
cupcakes	turnovers	

Beverages

count	noncount	
milk shakes	coffee	punch
sodas	hot chocolate	tea
	lemonade	vegetable juice
	milk	
	orange juice	

Appendix
Seafood

count		noncount
clams	mussels	crab
crabs	oysters	fish
fish	scallops	lobster
lobsters	shrimp	shrimp

Cooking

count		noncount		
eggs	baking powder	flour	pepper	shortening
	baking soda	honey	salad oil	sugar
	butter	margarine	salt	syrup

On the Menu

count	noncount	
appetizers	baked chicken	rice pilaf
baked potatoes	broiled trout	salad
enchiladas	casserole	sauerkraut
french fries	chicken curry	soup
lobster tails	fried rice	spaghetti
omelets	lasagna	toast
pancakes	macaroni and cheese	tuna pie
salads	meat loaf	veal stew
sandwiches	pizza	
stewed tomatoes	potato salad	

The nouns in the following categories are all noncount.

Abstractions

admiration	information	safety
advice	intelligence	space
assistance	knowledge	traffic
crime	life	trouble
fun	love	truth
help	patience	work
honesty	peace	
hope	relaxation	

Appendix

Subjects of Study

art	engineering	math	science
Chinese	geography	medicine	sociology
economics	history	music	

Other Substances

bread
grass
nylon
rice
rubber
sand
water

-ing Forms

camping
clothing
cooking
playing tennis
shopping

Generic Terms

equipment
fruit
furniture
jewelry
mail
money

Activities/Sports

fun
hiking
play
shopping
tennis
work

Natural Phenomena

air	smoke
fire	snow
heat	sound
light	wind
rain	

Some words may be either count or noncount depending on their meaning. Some of them are:

business	glass	room
change	life	space
fish	paper	youth

Certain non-plural words ending in *s* are also noncount:

economics
news
physics
tennis

Appendix

Appendix 23 Quantifiers

bag	— groceries
bar	— butter, candy, soap
bottle	— orange juice, salad dressing
bowl	— cereal, rice, soup
box	— cake mix, cereal
bunch	— bananas, grapes
can	— soup, vegetables
carton	— eggs, milk
cube	— ice, sugar
cup	— coffee, soup, tea
dish/plate	— appetizers, sandwiches
ear	— corn
glass	— ice water, milk, tomato juice
head	— cabbage, lettuce
jar	— instant coffee, strawberry jam
list	— telephone numbers
loaf	— bread
lump	— sugar
package	— paper, meat
pad	— paper
pair	— glasses, pants, shoes
piece	— bread, cake, candy, furniture, paper, pie
pile	— books, grass, junk
pound/100g	— beef, butter
roll	— aluminum foil, paper
sack	— flour, rice
sheet	— paper
slice	— bread, ham, toast
spoonful	— jam, sugar
stalk	— celery
stick	— butter, gum
tube	— toothpaste

Appendix 24 Expressions with *be:* be + noun/adjective/adverb phrase

be a chance of	be about to
be a nobody	be absent from
be a question of	be acceptable to
be able to	be according to

-344-

Appendix

be acquainted with
be afraid of
be afraid to
be all for something
be all in
be an authority on
be an opportunity for
be angry at something
be angry with someone
be annoyed at something
be annoyed with someone
be any doubt about
be anxious to
be ashamed of
be astonished at
be aware of
be away from
be back in (period of time)
be bound to
be busy + v-*ing*
be busy with
be capable (incapable) of
be careful of/with
be careless about/of
be cautious of/with
be certain of
be close to
be comparable to/with
be content with
be contrary to
be cured of
be cut out for
be delighted with
be dependent on
be different from
be difficult for/to
be disappointed in/with/by
be disgusted with
be displeased with
be divorced from
be due to
be eager for/to

be easy for/to
be enthusiastic about
be equal to
be essential to
be excited about
be familiar with/to
be famous for
be fed up with
be frightened by
be good at
be good for
be grateful to
be happy with/about
be hard of hearing
be hard up
be impatient with/for
be important to
be indifferent to/towards
be inferior to
be interested in
be jealous of
be kind to
be like
be mad at
be made from/of
be married to
be named after
be opposed to
be pressed for time
be profitable
be proud of
be put down
be relevant to
be rid of
be satisfied with
be scared of
be sensitive to/about
be short of/on
be sick of
be similar to
be sorry for
be stuck up

Appendix

be sure of
be surprised by/at
be suspicious of
be taken by surprise
be thankful for/to
be the matter with

be thrilled by
be tired of
be used to
be useful to
be well-known for
be willing to

be + prepositional phrase

be after someone
be at ease (with)
be at home
be at one's best
be at war with
be behind the times
be behind time
be for something or someone
be in charge of
be in favor of
be in love with
be in season, fashion
be in the know
be in the way
be in touch/contact with
be next (in line)
be on (TV, radio)
be on call
be on edge
be on fire
be on good terms with
be on one's way (to)
be on sale

be on the job
be on the road
be on the telephone
be on to a good thing
be out
be out of
be out of date
be out of funds/money
be out of line
be out of luck
be out of order
be out of place
be out of the question
be out of time
be over
be short of
be up against
be up and about
be up in the air
be up to doing something
be up to someone (to do something)
be up to something
be within the law

Appendix 25 Idioms and Expressions

a good deal
above all
according to
after hours
again and again
all in all

all night/day long
all together
as a matter of fact
as far as I know
as good as
as usual

Appendix

as you know
ask a favor of someone
as a question
ask for permission from
ask the way
at all
at all times
at any moment
at first
at least
at no time
at once
at the expense of
at the moment
at times
• • •
back and forth
bear in mind
bear left/right
book a ticket/a flight
break the ice
break the news
by ear
by heart
by means of
by order of
by the way
by way of
• • •
call it a day
can't stand/bear something
change one's mind
clear the table
close the meeting
come off it
(not) come to much
• • •
declare war on
do one's best
do one's hair
do someone a favor/a good turn
do something about something

do something in no time
do something the last minute
do well in
do without someone/something
down and out
down to earth
drive out of
drop in on
Dutch treat
• • •
each other
every now and then
every so often
• • •
fail to see the point
fall in love with
far from
feel like + v-*ing*
feel sorry for
feel well/sick
feel worn out
find fault with
fire someone
foot the bill
for a while/a minute
for all I can
for all I know
for example
for good
for one thing
for the purpose of
for the sake of
for the time being
form an opinion
from (place) to (place)
from time to time
• • •
get accustomed to
get acquainted with
get along with
get angry with
get away with

Appendix

get back from
get billed for
get divorced from
get even with
get fired
get going
get hired
get hit
get in touch with
get interested in
get it into one's head
get lost
get mad at someone
get married to someone
get on in the world
get on someone's nerves
get one's own way
get over with
get rid of
get robbed
get sick
get someone to do something
get sued
get the point
get through with
get tired of
get to the point
get told off (for something)
get used to
give birth
give someone a hand
give way to
go ahead with
go behind someone's back
go boating
go broke
go climbing
go dancing
go downtown
go Dutch
go easy
go fishing

go for a walk/a hike/a swim
go hiking
go home
go in for something
go native
go on a diet
go on a picnic/a trip
go on (a) vacation
go out of one's way
go riding
go shopping
go sightseeing
go skiing
go swimming
go to a great expense
go to a lot of trouble
go to a party
go up in the world
grow out of

• • •

hang on to (something)
have a good time
have a minute
have a reason for
have a talent for
have a way with
have a word with someone
have ability in/as
have access to
have an appointment with
have an easy time of it
have an opportunity to
have charge of
have confidence in
have experience in
have faith in
have fun
have had it
have had its day
have influence over
have it in for
have one's way

Appendix

have patience with
have repairs done
have something done
have something on one's mind
have something to do with
have spare time
have the last word
have time off
have to do with
have trouble + v-*ing*
here and there
hold the line
How about...?
How come...?
• • •
I'll tell you what.
in a way
in case of
in contrast to/with
in exchange for
in fact
in good health
in good shape
in need of
in one's opinion
in other words
in place of
in short
in some ways
in spite of
in that case
in the case of
in the dark/distance
in the event of
in the long run
in time
it's about time...
it's too bad...
it stands to reason that/why...
• • •
just because
just for this once

keep a promise
keep a secret
keep a straight face
keep an eye on something
keep (something in mind)
keep in touch with
keep one's fingers crossed
keep one's word
keep to oneself
keep track of
keep up with
keep up with the Joneses
kill time
know something by heart
know what's what
• • •
learn (something) by heart
learn (something) the hard way
(the) line is busy
little by little
live up to
look forward to
look up to
lose face
make a living as/at/by
make a long story short
make a mistake
make a name for oneself
make a point
make a promise
make a speech
make an agreement with
make believe
make both ends meet
make fun of
make haste
make oneself at home
make peace with
make room for
make small talk
make someone feel at home
make something work

Appendix

make the bed
make the best of something
make up for lost time
make up for something
make up one's mind
make up to someone
make up with someone
mind one's own business
miss out on something
move out of
• • •
need practice in
never mind
nothing doing
• • •
of course
off and on
on account of
on behalf of
on one's way
on purpose
on time
on the other hand
on the way
on vacation
once in a while
once more
once or twice
one of these days
one way ticket
open an account
(the) other day
out of order
out of (something)
out of the way
out of town
over and over
own up to
• • •
(a) package tour
pass an examination
pass away

pay attention to
play a trick on someone
play baseball/golf/tennis
(a) play on words
(a) poor excuse
pretty much
put an end to
put off until
put someone at ease
put someone to shame
• • •
quite a bit
• • •
raise a question
raise an objection
receive an education
red tape
round trip
(a) round trip ticket
run a temperature
run out/short of something
• • •
say the word
see eye to eye
see for oneself
see out of
see the light
see the point
see the world
seem like
set fire to
set the ball rolling
set the table
slip one's mind
speak out
speaking of
spend the night
spend time + v-*ing*
stand a good chance of
stand firm/fast
stand up for something
start the ball rolling

Appendix

stay over night
stick up for someone
So what?
speak out on something
speaking of
take a call
take a drive/a walk/a hike
take a hint
take a left/right
take a look at something
take a photograph/a picture
take a thing for granted
take advantage of
take an interest in
take care of
take hold of
take one's time
take part in
take pride in
take sides
take the place of someone
take turns
tell a lie

time and again
travel first class
turn the corner
• • •
under the circumstances
under the weather
up to date
up to/until now
up to the minute
• • •
wait up for someone
what about...?
What for?
What's the matter?
What's the point?
What's up?
What's wrong with...?
with the exception of
work a machine
work on something
work over time
• • •
You're welcome.

Appendix 26 Adjectives requiring *more* and *less* in the comparative, and *most* and *least* in the superlative

accessible
ambitious
annoying
believable
boring
busy
careful
comfortable
common
convenient
delicious
different
difficult
exciting

expensive
friendly
honest
idealistic
interesting
modern
serious
studious
talented
time-consuming
tiring
troublesome
trust-worthy
well-behaved

Appendix

Appendix 27 Common past participles used as adjectives: *The door is <u>broken</u>.*

broken	finished	lost	separated
closed	honored	murdered	spoken
completed	injured	organized	
defeated	interested	recorded	

Index

Dialogues

A
Afterthought — 231
Another Roll? — 92
Assistants — 187
At a Bookstore — 29
At a Sale — 59
At Airport Customs — 3
At Dinner — 80
At the Supermarket — 165
Austrian — 7

B
Baby, The — 100
Because — 248
Belongings — 24
Bigger, Not Better — 143
Busy People — 69
By Coincidence — 116
By Yourself? — 64

C
Carefully — 147
Causes — 118
Changes — 201
Choices — 190
Comparing Hotels — 141
Complainers — 209
Compliment, A — 150
Conditions — 218
Correcting Someone — 103

D
Decision Making — 237
Delicious Cake — 46
Determination — 247
Different Opinions — 145
Difficult Language, A — 66
Dining Experience, A — 97
Dining Out — 87

Do You Know Him? — 25
Do You Mind? — 232
Doctor's Advice — 191
Doing Things — 60
Doing Well — 76
Downtown — 2
Dream, A — 153
Dreamers — 219
Duties — 159

E
Everybody's Things — 13
Everything's Ready — 203
Except for One Thing — 171
Exceptions — 240
Excuse, An — 221
Experiences — 161
Exports and Imports — 166

F
Feeling Ill — 96
Few Favors, A — 210
Finishing Up — 205
First Experiences — 170
First Things First — 154
First Time, A — 162
Flour and Eggs — 18
Fond Memories — 123
For Me? — 20
For You — 111
Free Advice — 228
From China — 5
Fruit and Vegetables — 15
Full Schedule, A — 133

G
Getting Around — 83
Getting Better — 77
Getting Things Done — 245

Dialogue Index

Getting Used to Things — 179
Gift Suggestions — 52
Giving Permission — 220
Good Advice — 185
Good Job, A — 196
Good Movies — 70
Good Story, A — 137
Good Thing, A — 227
Gossip — 58
Great Trip, A — 98
Guess My Occupation — 115

H

Happy to Help — 126
Hardly Ever — 241
Hello! — 6
Helping Others — 95
Her Car — 47
Here and There — 193
Hope for the Best — 238
Hopeful — 88
Housework — 114
How About Jam? — 45
How Come? — 217
How Not to Get Along — 214
How Often? — 51
Hurry! — 188

I

I Think So Too — 84
Idea, An — 131
In a Hurry — 242
In the Refrigerator — 17
In Your Shirtpocket — 11
Information, Please — 173
Instructions — 244
International Trade — 155
Interruption — 186
Is It Expensive? — 48
Is This Yours? — 31
It Depends — 234
It Must Be Hers — 129

J

Just in Case — 225

K

Keeping Busy — 90
Korea, Not Japan — 49

L

Last Night — 113
Late for Work — 63
Let's Go to a Movie — 74
Little Longer, A — 151
Looking Ahead — 174
Looking for Things — 28
Lost and Found — 39
Lucky — 160

M

Maybe — 197
Me Neither — 108
Menu, The — 149
Might and Might Not — 140
Modern Art — 183
More and Less — 144
More Salad? — 93
Most and Least — 195
Most Expensive, The — 68
Mysteries — 250

N

Nagging — 235
Name in the News, A — 139
New Restaurant, A — 36
Newer Than That — 65
No Free Time — 138
Not Necessarily — 198
Not Yet — 157
Now and Then — 135

O

Occupations — 26
Offering Help — 86

Dialogue Index

On a Diet — 142
Once in a While — 50
Ordinary Activities — 163

P
Passing Time — 158
Pastimes — 75
Permission — 125
Photo Album — 21
Photographs — 19
Picnic Plans — 55
Plans — 61
Please Guess — 172
Pointing Someone Out — 184
Popular Sights — 128
Predictions — 85
Products — 146
Putting Things Off — 168

Q
Quantities — 73

R
Really? — 213
Reasons — 224
Regrets — 192
Relating News — 175
Reminder, A — 206
Request, A — 81
Right Now — 62

S
Same or Different?, The — 117
Saturday and Sunday — 110
Schedules — 42
See That Man? — 181
Self-Introduction, A — 78
Shopping List, A — 72
Short Conversation, A — 194
Shortcomings — 212
Should and Had Better — 130
Similar People — 109

Since When? — 156
Size and Shape — 71
Small Talk — 35
Smile! — 54
Smooth Talker — 216
Snapshots — 200
Some of Them — 94
Some Time Ago — 182
Someone Intelligent — 178
Something to Say — 202
Spinach — 23
Starting Tomorrow — 91
Suggestions — 14
Supposing — 211

T
Take Ten Guesses — 16
Teacher and Parent — 169
Telephone Conversation, A — 121
Telling a Friend — 177
Tennis or Swimming? — 243
Thanks — 229
That Goes Here — 38
That's My Bag — 10
That's News to Me — 164
These Things — 8
Things That Annoy — 207
Things to Do — 107
This One or That One — 208
To the Kitchen — 57
Tomorrow — 122
Tomorrow's Activities — 124
Too Tired — 119
Tour Guide — 189
Tourist Attractions — 79
Travel Experiences — 99
Travel Information — 44
Travel Time — 112
Truth of the Matter, The — 236
Trying to Recall — 249
Two Jobs — 134
Two Places for Rent — 34

Dialogue Index

Two Tours — 43

U, V
Unaware — 230
Unbelievable — 223

W, X
Wants and Desires — 53
Wednesday the 19th — 41
Weekend, The — 89
Weight Watcher — 105
Welcome News — 136
Well, I Can! — 106
What Am I? — 167
What Do They Do? — 104
What Is It? Guess! — 1
What Kind? — 37
What Time Is It? — 40
What to Whom?, The — 102
What's It Like? — 33
What's This For? — 199
When and While — 215
Where Are You From? — 27
Where Were You? — 120

Where's the Hotel? — 9
Whether or Not — 246
Which One? — 32
Which Person? — 176
Who Am I Thinking Of? — 56
Who Did It? — 101
Who Has It? — 22
Whose? — 30
Why? — 82
Why, Then? — 132
Window Shopping — 4
Wishes — 239
Wondering — 180
Word of Advice, A — 152
Work Is Done, The — 204
Work to Do — 127
Working Together — 233
World Traveler — 148
World's Longest, The — 67
Would You? — 226
Wouldn't You? — 222

Y, Z
Yours or Hers? — 12

Expression

A

ability, expressing: 138, 140, 191, 205
accepting offers: 93
accustomed to, telling what one is: 179
acknowledging something: 47, 70, 198
acquaintance, making an: 78
acquaintance, talking about an: 25, 109, 111, 164
activities, describing customary: 50, 63, 69, 75, 115, 133
activities, describing daily: 133, 134
activities, describing habitual: 50, 63, 69, 75, 115, 133
activities, indicating the time of: 158, 188, 215
activities performed: 166, 167, 199, 200, 201, 203, 204, 205, 213, 242, 244
activities, presently occurring: 60, 62
activities, reporting past events/: 98, 99, 100, 101, 103, 108, 110, 113, 114, 120, 123, 201, 215
activities, scheduled, *see* scheduled events/activities
admiring something: 4, 150
advice, offering: 130, 131, 152, 154, 185, 187, 192, 228
advice, soliciting: 130
age: 71
agreement, expressing: 46, 74, 84, 107, 124
allow, *see* permission
alternatives, expressing: 32, 107, 208, 243
amount, *see* quantity
amount of time, *see* quantity of time

anticipating events: 85, 122, 188
apologizing: 186
appointments, *see* scheduled events/activities
appreciation, *see* gratitude
asking for directions: 2, 9
assistance, declining: 126
assistance, offering: 86, 126
assistance, requesting: 86, 95, 126
assumption, making an: 60, 198
assurance, expressing: 205

B

brand names: 37
buy, *see* cost

C

causation, expressing: 187, 242, 245
cause, *see also* reasons
causes, indicating: 118
causes, inquiring about: 118
certainty, expressing: 129
choice, making a: 32, 130, 178, 190, 208
choice, offering a: 32, 190, 208
claiming things: 10, 12, 24, 30, 31, 32, 94
clarifying information: 102, 103, 186, 189, 213, 249
classifying things: 37
clothing, talking about: 33, 56, 59, 121
coincidence, expressing: 116
colors: 10, 16, 30, 71
comparisons, making: 34, 43, 65, 66, 67, 68, 70, 77, 105, 109, 116, 117, 134, 141, 142, 143, 144, 145, 146, 147, 155, 160, 195, 196
complaining: 209

Expression Index

compliment, paying a: 4, 150
concession, making a: 212
condition, reference to a former state or: 135, 139
conditions, expressing: 218, 219, 220, 221, 222, 223, 224, 225, 226, 227, 229, 230, 231, 232, 236, 239
confirming information: 47, 78, 102, 103, 186, 189, 213, 223, 249
consequences: 132, 188, 227, 228
continuity, expressing: 156
contradicting someone: 7, 26, 49
conversation, opening a: 6, 46, 202
conversation, reporting a: 175, 177, 186, 189, 194, 244
conviction, expressing: 88, 122
correcting someone: 7, 26, 49
cost, expressing: 29, 48
country, *see* national origin
customary activities, describing: 50, 63, 69, 75, 115, 133, *see also* habitual/daily activities

D

daily activities, describing: 133, 134
dates: 41, 44
days: 41, 44, 69
decisions, making: 236, 237, 246
deduction, expressing: 129, 198
denying something: 101
describing objects: 10, 29, 33, 34, 47, 71, 117, 129, 167, 183, 190
describing people: 16, 47, 56, 109, 121, 176, 178, 181, 183
desires, expressing: 53, 193
determination, expressing: 91, 247
dimensions: 71
directing someone to do something: 54, 59, 154, 159, 244
direction, expressing: 9, 43, 57
direction, expressing geographic: 27

directions, asking for: 2, 9
directions, giving: 2, 9 (*see also* instructions, giving)
disagreement, expressing: 7, 26, 49, 214
dislikes, *see* likes
doubt, expressing: 106
duration of time, expressing: 151, 156, 182

E

emphasizing questions: 249
evaluation, making an: 48, 76
events, anticipating: 85, 122, 188
events, describing a sequence of: 61, 113, 133, 137, 153, 154
events/activities, discussing scheduled: 41, 42, 43, 44, 69, 158
events/activities, reporting past: 98, 99, 100, 101, 103, 108, 110, 113, 114, 120, 123, 201, 215
exception, expressing: 171, 240, 241
excuses, asking for: 82, 118
excuses, giving: 82, 118
expectation, expressing: 191, 211
experience, relating: 148, 149, 157, 159, 161, 162, 163, 168, 169, 170, 182
explanation, requesting an: 234
expressing . . . *see individual items*

F

favors, asking: 210
feelings, expressing personal: 136
finding places: 2, 9
finding things: 11, 13, 18, 28, 95
food, talking about: 15, 17, 18, 23, 36, 45, 55, 72, 73, 80, 87, 92, 93, 97, 105, 142, 149, 165
former state or condition, reference to a: 135, 139

Expression Index

frequency, expressing: 50, 51
future intentions, indicating: 121

G
geographic direction, expressing: 27
geographic location, expressing: 5, 27, 148
giving directions: 2, 9
gratitude, expressing: 1, 14, 229
greeting someone: 6

H
habitual activities, describing: 50, 63, 69, 75, 115, 133
health, talking about: 77, 96, 191
help, *see* assistance
hope, expressing a: 88, 174, 204, 235, 238
hypothetical situation: 219, 222, 226, 227, 231

I
identifying objects: 1, 3, 10, 30, 31, 32, 47, 65, 129, 167, 208
identifying people: 19, 21, 47, 56, 111, 176, 181, 184
imposing on someone: 232
information, clarifying: 102, 103, 186, 189, 213, 249
information, confirming: 47, 78, 102, 103, 186, 189, 213, 223, 249
information, providing: 173
information, providing personal: 5
information, requesting: 172, 173
information, requesting personal: 5
instructions, giving: 54 (*see also* directing someone to do something)
instructions, reporting: 165, 244
intentions, indicating: 55, 57, 58, 61, 62, 64, 69, 87, 89, 90, 91, 106, 164, 236, 237
intentions, indicating future: 121
interest, expressing: 180
introductions, making: 78

J, K
jobs, *see* occupations

L
likelihood, expressing: 122, 131
likes/dislikes, expressing: 23, 35, 52
location, geographic, expressing: 5, 27, 148
location, referring to: 193
location/position, expressing: 2, 9, 11, 22, 28, 29, 38, 39

M
measurement, *see* dimensions
money, *see* cost

N
national origin (nationality), indicating: 5, 7, 27
necessity, expressing: 96, 127, 128, 138, 140, 160, 191
need, *see* necessity
negation, expressing: 1, 7, 26

O
objects, claiming, *see* claiming things
objects, describing: 10, 29, 33, 34, 47, 71, 117, 129, 167, 183, 190
objects, identifying: 1, 3, 10, 30, 31, 32, 47, 65, 129, 167, 208
obligation, expressing: 131, 160, 211
occupations, talking about: 26, 104, 115, 134, 196
occurring activities, presently: 60, 62
offering something: 92, 93
offers, accepting: 93
offers, declining: 92, 93

Expression Index

opening a conversation: 6, 46, 202
opinion, expressing an: 84, 149, 183, 212
opinion, soliciting an: 70, 149, 183
ownership/possession, indicating: 8, 10, 12, 13, 14, 22, 24, 30, 31, 32

P

past, *see also* former
past events/activities, reporting: 98, 99, 100, 101, 103, 108, 110, 113, 114, 120, 123, 201, 215
past reference (*be*): 15, 39
pastimes, talking about: 50, 75
people, describing: 16, 47, 56, 109, 121, 176, 178, 181, 183
people, identifying: 19, 21, 47, 56, 111, 176, 181, 184
people, talking about: 20
permission, declining: 125
permission, granting: 125, 220
permission, requesting: 125
personal feelings, expressing: 136
personal information, providing: 5
personal information, requesting: 5
persuading: 216
places, finding: 2, 9
plans, indicating: 58, 61, 89, 90, 174
plans, making: 124
polite requests, making: 80, 81, 86
position, *see* location/position
possession, *see* ownership
possibility, expressing: 140, 197
prediction, making a: 85, 88
preferences, indicating: 23, 35, 52, 135, 190, 207, 208, 212, 234, 243, 247
presently occurring activities: 60, 62
prices, *see* cost
probability, expressing: 60, 89
proposal, making a: 74, 90
provisions, indicating: 220

purpose, indicating: 57, 199

Q

quantity, expressing: 17, 18, 45, 72, 73, 94, 95, 142, 146
quantity of time, indicating: 112, 150, 151, 182
questioning judgement: 250

R

ranking things: 66, 68, 145, 195
reasons, requesting: 82, 118, 132, 217, 221, 231, 248
reasons, stating: 82, 118, 119, 132, 217, 221, 224, 227, 231, 236, 248
recommendations, making: 128, 152
relating experience: 148, 149, 157, 159, 161, 162, 163, 168, 169, 170, 182
relatives, talking about: 21
reporting a conversation: 175, 177, 186, 189, 194, 244
reporting instructions: 165, 244
reporting requests: 165, 244
requesting information: 172, 173
requesting personal information: 5
requests, making: 206, 210, 232, 233, *see also* directing someone to do something; instructions
requests, making polite: 80, 81, 86
requests, reporting: 165, 244

S

scheduled events/activities, discussing: 41, 42, 43, 44, 69, 158
selecting, *see* choice
self-introductions, making: 78
sequence of events, describing a: 61, 113, 133, 137, 153, 154
size, *see* dimensions
speculation, expressing: 60, 197

Expression Index

story, relating a: 137
suggestions, declining: 74
suggestions, offering: 14, 52, 74, 79, 107, 119, 124, 185
suggestions, soliciting: 74, 107, 124
supposition: 211
surprise, expressing: 58, 116

T

telling time, *see* time, indicating the
time, expressing duration of: 151, 156, 182
time, indicating quantity of: 112, 150, 151, 182
time, indicating the (telling time): 40
time, requesting the: 40
time of activities, indicating the: 158, 188, 215
transportation, discussing: 83, 112

U, V

urging someone to do something: 128
used to, telling what one is: 179

W, X, Y, Z

wish, expressing a: 235, 238, 239
wondering about something: 180, 197, 250

Grammar

A
a, an, see **articles**
a vs *the*, see **articles**
able, see **modals:** *be able to*
about: 71
across from: 9

adjectives
adj of nationality: 7
adj + adj + n: 32, 33
adj + n: 4, 10, 16, 30, 31, 32, 33
adj + *of* + obj (+ *to* v): 111
adj + *that*-clause: 136
adj + *to* + obj: 111
adj + *to* v: 126, 136(+ *that*-cl),
be + adj: 4, 6, 7, 10, 15, 33
comparative and superlative forms
- *-er (than):* 65, 66, 67, 68, 141, 143, 144, 145, 195
- *more (than):* 66, 68, 141, 143, 144, 145, 195
- *less (than):* 144, 145, 195
- *as* + adj + *as:* 70, 143
- *as* + adj + n + *as:* 70
- *-est:* 67, 68, 145, 195
- *most:* 68, 145, 195
- *least:* 145, 195
see also *alike, compared with, different, the same, similar*
superlative in rel clause: 195
dem adj: 3(sing), 4(sing), 8(pl), 31 see also dem pron
possessive adj: 10, 13, 21, 24, 30, 31
too + adj + *to* verb: 119
see also **quantifiers**

adverbs
agent: 166, 167, 208, 213
comparison and superlative forms:

- *-er (than):* 77(*better*), 134(*better*), 147
- *more (than):* 147
- *(not) as* + adv + *as:* 147
- *most:* 196
- *least:* 196
see also *alike, compared with, different(from), like(prep), the same(as), similar(to)*
degree: 29(*only*), 36(*very*), 40 (*almost*), 48(*extremely, kind of, not very, pretty, quite, rather, really, very*), 51(*or so*), 68(*much*), 75(*a lot*), 76(*fairly, rather*), 77(*much*), 105(emphatic *that*), 109(*a lot*), 123(emphatic *that*), 143(*a little bit*)
direction: 9, 27, 43, 57, 83, 112
frequency: 50(*always, never, once in a while, usually*), 51(*every day, frequently, hardly ever, often, once a year, sometimes*), 75(*again, always* with pres cont), 115(*usually*), 161(*never*)
intensifiers, see adv of degree
manner: 54(*natural, still*), 76(*well, badly, poorly, satisfactorily*), 77(*well*)
means: 83(*by*), 112(*by*)
place: 2, 3, 5, 7, 9, 10, 11, 22, 27, 28, 29, 38, 39, 42, 62(wo),
see also prepositions of place/direction
time: 15(today), 40(telling time), 41(*on*/days, dates), 42(*in, at*), 44(*at, on, in the afternoon, tomorrow, etc.*), 61(*first, then*), 62(*now, right now*), 69(*Saturdays,* etc.), 81(*right now*), 85(*next year,*

-365-

Grammar Index

etc.), 89, 91, 150(*ago*), 154(*before/after* + v-*ing*), 156(*still*), 157 (*yet*), 158(*until*), 162(*before*), 163(*before, in* with duration), 168(*since, yet*), 179(*still*), 182 (*ago, for*), see also prep of time
see also individual items

after: 133, 154, 157
again: 75, 78
ago: 150, 182
alike: 117
all right: 47
almost: 40
already: 159
always: 75
and: 3, 5, 6
another: 92, 95, 104
any, quant
    adj: 17, 18, 44, 45, 93
    pron: 18, 44
any more: 93
any of: 94
anymore: 135, 156
anyway: 212(*but...~*), 225

articles
    a/an: 1, 2, 3, 4, 41
    a/an vs *the:* 2, 41
    the: 2, 9, 41, 149

as...as, see **adj, adv, quant**
as long as: 232
as much/many...as, see **quant**
at(prep of time): 40, 42, 44
auxilliary verbs, see **modals**

B
back, see *in back of*

be,
    contracted: 1, 2, 3, 4, 5, 6, 7, 17

pres pfct: 148
past pfct: 162
simple past tense: 15, 39, 97
simple pres tense: 1, 2, 3, 4, 5, 6, 7, 8, 9, 10

be able to, see **modals**
be finished + v-*ing, ~ with:* 205
be going to + v: see **continuous**
be in a hurry to have something done: 242
be interested in: 90
be like(in comparisons): 109
be(get) used to: 179(+ v-*ing* or n), see also *used to*

because: 82, 118, 248
because if: 231
because then: 236
before: 133, 151, 154, 162(pfct), 163(pfct), 170
behind: 9
beside: 9
besides: 119, 236
better, see **adv/adj** compar, **modal** *had better*
both(of): 43, 109

but: 8, 34, 224
but...anyway, see *anyway*

by,
    prep of agent: 166, 167, 208, 213
    prep of means: 83, 112
    prep of place: 11
    prep with measurements: 71
    prep with object: 64
by the time, conj: 188

C
can, see modals
cardinal numbers, see **quantifiers**

Grammar Index

care for, care to: 93

causatives
  convince: 216
  get: 187(*get* + obj + *to* v), 245
    (passive, *get something done*)
  have: 187(*have* + obj + v), 242
    (passive), 245(passive, *have something done*)
  passive: 242, 245
  persuade: 216
  talk someone into something: 216

clauses
- *if*-clause: 132(reason), 233 (*see if*-clause), see also clause of condition, embedded ques
- concession: 212(*even though, but...anyway*), 247(*even though*)
- condition: 218, 219, 220, 221, 222, 223, 224, 225, 226(reduced), 227, 228, 229, 230(*if I had known*), 231, 232, 236(*even if*), 238, 239
- exception: 171, 240, 241
- place: 193
- purpose: 57(*to* + v phrase), 248
- reason: 82, 118, 132(*if*), 217, 232, 236, 248, 250
- relative: 176(*be/have;* reduced), 178(*be/have;* reduced), 181(reduced), 184(reduced), 190(reduced), 195(superlative), 208 (passive; reduced)
- result: 118, 129
- time: 133, 151, 156, 182, 188, 200, 206(imper), 207, 215
  pro-clause with *so:* 84, 88, 210, 211
  that-clause: 84, 87, 88, 106(*know ~* past with pres meaning), 130(in *wh*-ques), 136(adj + [*to* v] + *that*-cl), 154(*guess ~, think ~*), 164(*Did you know ~?*), 172(in *wh*-ques), 175(*say ~*), 177(*tell* + obj + *that*-cl), 183(in *wh*-ques + *that*), 194(*say ~, tell* + obj + *that*), 196(compl of *be*), 204(*hope*), 235(*hope, wish*), 237(*decide*), 238(*hope ~, wish ~*)
  where-clause: 193

compared with: 141
comparison, see **adjectives, adverbs, quantifiers**

conditional, see also **conjunctions**
  future: 218, 220, 223, 228(modal *had better*)
  past: 221, 222, 224, 227, 229(*if it hadn't been for...*), 230(*...had known...*), 231, 238
  present: 219, 222, 226, 227, 228, 236, 238, 239
  reduced: 226(*without* + v-*ing*)
  with modal: 219

conditional conjunctions, see **conjunctions**

conjunctions
- concession: 171(*otherwise*), 212 (*even though, but...anyway*), 247 (*even though*)
- condition: 218(*unless, if*), 219 (*if*), 220(*provided, if*), 221(*if*), 222 (*if*), 223(*if, in order to*), 224(*only, but*), 225(*in case*), 226(*if*), 227 (*if*), 228(*if*), 229(*if*), 230(*if*), 231 (*because if*), 232(*as long as*), 236(*even if*), 238(*if*), 239(*if*)
- exception: 171(*except that*), 240 (*except for the fact that, except that*) 241

-367-

Grammar Index

- place: 193*(where)*
- purpose: 223*(in order to)*, 248
- reason: 82*(because)*, 118*(because)*, 217*(why, the reason why)*, 232*(since, as long as)*, 236*(because then, so)*, 248*(so that, because)*, 250*(so that)*
- result: 118*(so)*, 129*(so)*
- time: 133*(after, before)*, 151 *(before, until)*, 156*(since)*, 157 *(after* with pfct), 158*(until)*, 168 *(since)*, 170*(before/until)*, 182 *(since)*, 188*(by the time)*, 200 *(when)*, 206*(when)*, 207*(when)*, 209*(when)*, 215*(while, when)*, 250
see also *after, and, as long as, before, both, but, either, how, if (see if), in case, in order to, like, neither, only, so, then, though, until, what, when, where, whether or not, while, why*

connectives, see **conjunctions**

continuous
be going to + v: 58, 59, 61, 62, 69 (contrasted with simple pres), 87(contrasted with *will*), 89(contrasted with *will*), 90(intention), 91, 151*(going to be* + cont)
future: 121, 122
modals: 198
past: 120, 123, 164
present: 55(future), 56, 57 60, 62, 69(vs *be going to,* simple pres t) 75(habitual/customary activity + *always*), 82, 90, 133(vs simple pres t), see also *be going to* + v
see also short replies

contractions
be: 1, 2, 3, 4, 5, 6, 7, 17

do: 14, 16, 18, 23, 25, 26
have: 96
not: 1*(be)*, 7*(be)*, 14*(do)*, 16*(do)*, 18*(do)*, 23*(do)*, 25*(do)*, 26*(do)*
will: 87
would: 92
could, see **modals**
count nouns, see **nouns**

D

days of the week: 41, 69
decide: 236(~ + *to* v), 237(~ + *to* v; ~ *that;* ~ *if;* ~ ques word, *whether or not*), 246(~ *whether or not to*)
dem adj, see **adjectives**
dem pron, see **pronouns**
depend on: 234
determiners, see **articles, quantifiers, adjectives**
different, different from: 117

do
contracted, see **contractions**
emphatic *do:* 117, 212
pro-verb: 14, 16, 18, 23, 25, 26, 29, 34, 35, 36 see also **short replies** and *yes/no-*ques and *wh-*ques
do someone a favor: 210

E

either: 35(rejoinder), 108(rejoinder)
else with ques word
what else: 175
embedded imperative, see **imper**
embedded ques: 172(*wh*-ques), 173(*yes/no-, wh-*ques), 180(*wonder* + *wh-, yes/no-*ques), 186, 189(with reported speech), 193, 233(with *see*), 237(with *decide whether or not*)

enough(of): 73, see **quantifiers**

-368-

Grammar Index

-est, superlative forms, see **adj, adv**
even: 250
even if: 236
even though: 212, 247
ever: 50, 51, 148(pfct), 149(pfct), 195(pfct, super) see also **questions**
every: 51, 63
everyone: 60
except
~ *for:* 171, 240; ~ prep: 241;
~ *that:* 171, 240; ~ *to* v: 241
~ *when:* 241

extremely: 48

F
favor, do someone a: 210
few, a: 45, 94
fewer: 142
fewest: 155
find time + to v: 133
finish: 151(*finish* + v-*ing*), 159, 205
(*be finished* + v-*ing; be finished with* + n)
first: 61, 113

for with obj pron: 20, 111
for with amount of time: 182
for + v-*ing:* 199

from(preposition of place): 5, 7, 27
from with obj pron: 20

future, see **modal** *will*, **simple pres t, present continuous**
future conditional, see **conditional**
future perfect, see **perfect forms**

G
gerund: 75, 196(gerund phr), 229
get, see **causatives, passive** with
get (*get* passive),

get someone to do something: 187, see **causatives**
get something done, see **causatives**
get used to, see *be used to:* 179
go idioms, see **Appendix**
going to + v, see **continuous**
guess + that-clause, see **clauses**

H
had better, see **modals**
had to (past of *have to*), see **modals**
half of: 94

have
contracted: 96
simple past: 97
simple pres tense: 14, 16, 18, 22, 29, 34, 36, 44
with pfct t: 149, 150

have + for + n: 97
have got + n: 96
have got to + v: 96 see **modals**
have + obj + *to* v: 127
have. . .on: two-word sep v: 56
have someone do something: 187, see **causatives**
have something done: 242, 245 see **causatives, passive**
have time + to v: 133
have + to v: 97
have to, see **modals**

he, see **pronouns**
help(~ + obj + v): 95, 126
her, poss adj, obj pron, see **adj,** and **pron**
hers, possessive pron, see **pron**
herself, refl pron, see **pron**
him, obj pron, see **pron**
himself, refl pron, see **pron**
his, poss adj/pron, see **adj, pron**

-369-

Grammar Index

historical present, see **simple pres t**
hope: 88, 204, 235, 238
hope vs *wish:* 235, 238
how, conj: 214
*how, wh-*ques, see **questions**
how about + n, *wh-*ques, see **questions**
*how long, wh-*ques, see **questions**
*how much longer, wh-*ques, see **questions**
*how much time, wh-*ques, see **questions**
how + adj, *wh-*ques, see **questions**
how + adv, *wh-*ques, see **questions**
*how come, wh-*ques, see **questions**
how much/many + n, *wh-*ques, see questions
*how often, wh-*ques, see **questions**

I

I, see **pronouns**
if, see **conj, cond,** embedded ques, clauses
it, see **pronouns**

imperative
   affirmative: 54, 59, 81, 86, 159
   embedded imperative: 165, 244
     see **reported speech**
   in passive with reported speech: 244
   neg: 54
   with two-word verbs: 54

impersonal pronoun, see **pronouns**

in,
   prep of place: 3, 11, 22
   prep time: 42, 44
in a long time: 163
in back of: 9
in case: 225
in order to: 223

indirect object, see **object pronouns**
indirect ques, see **embedded ques**
indirect speech, see **reported speech**
infinitive phrase, see **phrases**
infinitive replacement of *should:* 214, 244
instead: 140
interested in, be: 90
intonation, see **questions:** *yes/no*-ques, **Appendix 1**
irregular verbs, see verb tenses, **Appendix 20**
it, subject/object pron, see **pron**
it would be nice if: 238
itself, refl pron, see **pron**

J

just: 103, 159
just like: 71

K

kind of: 48, 115
kitty-corner from: 9
know: 106(in *that*-cl + past t), 164(in *that*-cl + past t)

L

last time, the: 182
least, see **adj, adv, quant**
less, see **adj, quant**
let (allow) + obj + v: 125
let's (suggestion): 74, 119, 124
like: 71(prep), 109(prep), 160(conj)
little, a, see **quantifiers**
little bit, a: 143
lot, a: 75, 109

M

many: see **quantifiers**
   as many...as: 105
may, see **modals**
maybe: 25, 30, 140, 197

Grammar Index

me, obj pron, see **pron**
might, see **modals**
mind + v-*ing:* 160
mine, poss pron, see **pronouns**

modals
 be able to: 140(ability/with *may*), 191(with *will, should*), 197(with *might* with pres pfct)
 can: 125(permission), 126(offer/ request), 128(necessity), 138 (ability), 205(passive)
 could: 80(polite request), 106(past of *can*), 107(opportunity), 126(polite request), 138(past of *can*), 197(past of *be able*), 219(in cond)
 had better: 130(advice/contrast with *should*), 154(command), 228 (in cond cl), 242(passive)
 have got to: 96(necessity)
 have to: 127(necessity), 128(recommendation), 129(deduction, certainty), 138(necessity/past tense: *had to*), 140(with *might*), 160(with *want to, would like to*), 191*(will* + *have to),* 242(passive) see also *must, need to*
 may: 125(permission), 140(probability/with *be able to*)
 might: 140(possibility/with *have to, be able to*), 197(pfct, *possible* vs *maybe,* + *be able to*)
 must: 129(deduction), 198(deduction, cont, pfct)
 ought to: 131(advice)
 shall: 124
 should: 107(suggestion), 130(advice/contrasted with *had better*), 131(advisability), 191(expectation, + *be able*), 192(pfct), 205(passive), 214(replace infin phr), 216, 244(replace infin phr)
 will: 85(prediction), 86(request), 87(intention; after *think*), 88 (assurance, after *think*), 89(after *think,* vs cont), 92(offer), 121(promise/assurance), 122(prediction), 154 *(guess + will,* intention), 188, 191 *(+ be able to, ~ + have to),* 204, 205(passive)
 would: 80(polite request), 107, 216 (hypothetical), 250(expectation)
 would care to/for: 93(offer)
 would be glad/happy to: 126*(would + be + adj + to v)*
 would mind, 160(~ + v-*ing*),
 would like: 92(offer), 242(with passive)
 would like to: 124(desire), 160(~ + *have to*)
 would rather: 243

mood, see **imper, pass, subjunctive**
more: 73, 92, 93
more see also **adj, adv, quant**
most, see **adjectives, adverbs, quantifiers**
much: 68(adv), 105*(as much as)*
must, see **modals**
must, a: 128
my, poss adj, see **adj**
myself, reflexive pron, see **pron**

N
nationality, see **adjectives**
negatives
 no: 1, 2, 7, 26
 not:
  with *be:* 1, 7, 17*(there + be)*
  with *do:* 14, 16, 18, 26
  in rejoinder: 49, 103
 not (in rejoinder): 49, 103
 not yet: 40
 see also **contractions**

Grammar Index

need, need to: 127
neither: 108(rejoinder)
neither of: 109
never: 161(pfct), see adverbs of frequency
next to: 9, 11
no, see **negatives**
nominative (subj) pron, see **pronouns**
noncount nounts, see **nouns**
not, see **negatives**

nouns
  gerund noun: 75, 196
  noncount: 15, 17, 18, 23, 36, 45, 72, 92, 93, 105, 146
  noun with *of* relational prep: 29
  noun possessive *'s:* 8, 12, 21, 24, 30
  noun + *be* + *to* v: 174
  plural: 3, 8, 11, 12, 13, 14, 15, 17
  singular: 1, 2, 3

now: 62
numbers, see **quantifiers**

O

object, see object pronouns
object pronouns, see **pronouns**
of, relational prep: 29
  adj + *of* + obj (+ *to* v): 111
often: 51
on,
  prep of place: 11, 22
  prep of time: 41, 44
on top of: 11
one, ones, see **pron**
one of: 94
only: 29, 224(conj)
or: 12, 129
or-ques, see **questions**
or so: 51
ordinal numbers, see **quantifiers**
opposite: 9

other: 104
other(s), the: 95, 104
others: 104
otherwise: 171
ought to, see **modals**
our, poss adj, see **adjectives**
ours, poss pron, see **pronouns**
ourselves, refl pron, see **pronouns**
over there: 2

P

part of: 94
participial phrases, see **phrases**
particle + v, see **two-word verbs**

passive
  causatives: 242, 245
  continuous: 201, 203
  future (see modal *will*)
  get passive: 213
  get something done: 245
  have something done: 242, 245
  modals: 204(*will*), 205(*will, should, can*), 242(*have to, had better*)
  passive-like forms: 242(*would like, want*), 245(*have, get*), see also *they* passive
  past: 200, 201, 203, 208, 213
  perfect forms: 201, 203, 204
  present: 166, 167, 199
  rel clause with passive: 208
  reported speech with *tell* and imper: 244
  supposed to: 211(~ + *to* v; ~ + *to be* pp)
  they passive: 201
past conditional, see **conditional**
past perfect, see **perfect forms**
past tense, see **simple past tense**

perfect forms
  future pfct: 188

-372-

Grammar Index

modals: 188*(will)*, 192*(should)*, 197*(might)*, 198*(must)*
past pfct: 162*(be,* with *before)*, 163(other verbs, adv *before)*, 170*(before, until)*
present pfct: 148*(be*/contrasted with past t, *ever)*, 149*(have, ever)*, 150*(have)*, 157(reg v), 159(irreg, with *just)*, 161*(never)*, 162(contrasted with past pfct), 163(contrasted with past pfct), 182, 195(with super, adv *ever)*
pres pfct cont: 168, 169, 197

persuade someone to do something: 216
phrasal verbs, see **two-word verbs**

phrases
for + v-*ing:* 199
gerund phrase: 196, 229*(thanks for* + v-*ing)*
infinitive phrase: 214(replaced with *should)*, 244(replaced with *should)*
participial phrase: 181, 183, 184, 208(past)
prep phrase: 176(reduced rel cl, *with)*, 178*(with)*, 190(reduced rel cl), 199*(for* + v-*ing)*, 226*(without* in cond cl), 241 *(except)*

polite requests, see **imper, modals**
possessive *'s,* see **nouns**
possessive adj, see **adjectives**
possessive pron, see **pronouns**
prefer(to): 243

prepositions
agent*(by):* 166, 167, 208, 213
direction: 43*(to)*, 57*(to)*, 83*(to)*, 112*(to)*

exception: 171, 241
means: 83*(by)*, 112*(by)*
measurement: 71*(by)*
of(relational): 29
place: 3*(in)*, 5*(from)*, 7*(from)*, 9*(across from, behind, beside, in back of, kitty-corner from, next to, opposite)*, 11, 22*(in, on)*, 27*(from)*, 38, 39
prep phrase: 171, 176(reduced rel cl, 178(reduced rel cl), 190(reduced rel cl), 199, 226, 241
reflexive: 64*(by)*
starting: 91
time: 40*(at)*, 41*(on)*, 42*(in, at)*, 44*(at, in, on)*, 158*(until)*, 168 *(since)*, 182*(for)*
verb + prep, see **two-word verbs**
with: 64 see also prep phrase
with objects: 20*(for, from)*, 64 *(by, with)*, 80*(to)*, 81*(to)*, 111 *(for, of, to)*, 125*(with)*
without: 226

present continuous, see **continuous**
present conditional, see **conditional**
present perfect, see **pfct forms**
present tense, see **simple present tense**
pretty: 48(adv)
pro-clause, see **clauses**
pro-forms see **pro-verb,** pro-clause
probably: 60, 89
progressive forms, see **continuous**

pronouns
another: 95, 104 see also *other(s), the other(s)*
any, see **quantifiers**
dem: 2(sing), 3(sing), 4(sing), 8(pl), 10(sing), 19(sing), 21(sing), 31
everyone: 60

Grammar Index

he, see subject pron
her, see obj pron
hers, see poss pron
herself, see refl pron
him, see obj pron
himself, see refl pron
his, see poss pron
I, see subj pron
impersonal: 29*(you, we)*, 201*(they)*, 250*(you)*, see also *one, ones*
it, see subj/obj pron
its, poss pron
itself, see refl pron
me, see obj pron
mine, see poss pron
myself, see refl pron
nominative, see subject pron
object: 19, 20, 24, 25, 80, 81
one, ones: 28(sing), 31, 32, 44, 104, 176, 190
other(s): 104
other(s), the: 95, 104
ours, poss pron
ourselves, refl pron
possessive: 12, 13, 30, 31, 32
quantity: see **quantifiers**
ques word as pron, see rel pron
reflexive: 64
relative: 176(s, *who, that*), 178(s, *who, that*), 181*(who, that)*, 184(prep + *whom*, obj of cl), 190*(which, that)*, 195*(that* with super), 208(s, *that, which*)
she, see subject pron
some, see **quantifiers**
someone: 178(rel cl)
subject (nominative): 1*(it)*, 2*(it)*, 3*(it)*, 5, 6, 7, 14, 16, 25
theirs, see poss pron
them, see obj pron
themselves, see refl pron
they, see subj pron, impersonal pron
us, see obj pron
we, subj pron, impersonal pron
what as obj pron: 102
whatever: 152
where: 193
you: see impersonal/subj/obj pron
yours, poss pron
yourself, see refl pron
yourselves, see refl pron
pretty, adv of degree: 48
pro-verb *do:* 14, 16, 18, 23, 25, 26, 29, 34(rejoinder), 35(short reply), 36(short reply)
provided(that): 220

Q
quantifiers
another: 92, 95, 104
any(of): 17(adj), 18(pron/adj), 44 (adj/pron), 45(adj), 94
any more: 93
both(of): 43, 109
comparative and superlative forms
more: 142, 146(~ *than*)
fewer: 142, 146(~ *than*)
less: 142, 146(~ *than*)
as much (of). . . as: 105, 146
as many (of). . . as: 105, 146
the most: 155
the least: 155
the fewest: 155
enough(of): 73
every: 51(frequency), 63
few of, a: 45, 94
half of: 94
little of, a: 45, 94
more(of): 73, 92, 93*(some more)*
neither(of): 109
noncount noun quantifiers: 72, 73, 92
numbers: 14(cardinal), 41(ordinal)

Grammar Index

numbers as pre-articles: 94
one of: 94
other(s): 104
other(s), the: 95, 104
part of: 94
rest(of), the: 94
some(of): 17(adj), 18(pron), 45 (adj), 94
some more: 93

question word in cl: 209, 214, 217
questions, see also **short replies**
 else in *wh*-ques: 175*(what else)*
 embedded questions: 172(*wh*-ques, *be/have*), 173(*wh*-ques, *yes/no*-ques), 180, 186(*wh*-ques), 189(reported speech), 193, 233*(see),* 237*(decide + whether or not, if)*
 indirect ques, see embedded ques
 intonation, see *yes/no*-ques
 negative questions, see *yes/no*-ques
 or-questions, see *yes/no*-ques
 reported questions, see **reported speech**
 tag ques:
  be: 46, 47
  have: 47
  other verbs: 101(past), 202
  modals: 86(*will,* request), 124 (*shall* with *let's*), 202
  perfect: 157, 202
  passive: 202
 that-clause in ques: 130, 164, 172, 183

wh-questions
 again in ques for confirmation: 78
 be(past): 39
 be(pres) 3, 4, 6, 9, 11, 18, 21, 27, 28, 29, 30, 32, 33, 36, 37, 40, 41
 cont: 55, 57, 60, 61, 76, 82, 83
 emphasis on question word: 249

have: 22, 36, 37, 73, 97
modals: 124, 160
other verbs(pres): 38, 42, 50, 51, 53*(want),* 77, 112
other verbs(past): 98, 99, 110, 113
pfct: 150, 168, 182
question words
 how: 6*(be),* 36*(be),* 77, 83(cont), 110(past), 160(modal)
 how about + n: 11*(be),* 13, 14
 how + adj/adv: 71, 76
 how come: 82(cont)
 how long(time): 112, 150(pfct), 151*(how much longer),* 182(pfct)
 how much/many + n: 73*(have)*
 how much time: 112
 how often: 51
 what: 3*(be),* 4*(be),* 29*(be),* 36 *(have),* 50(other v), 53(other v), 55(cont), 60(cont), 61 (cont), 79, 89, 97, 99, 110 (past), 124 (modals), 168(pfct cont), 183(*that*-cl)
 what + n: 41(day, *be*), 71(color), 113
 what about + n: 174, 181(~ + obj)
 what day: 41*(be)*
 what else: 175
 what for: 199*(what . . . for)*
 what kind (of): 37*(be, have)*
 what . . . like: 33*(be)*
 what's it like to . . . : 161
 what + n 41(day, *be*), 71(color), 113
 what time: 40*(be),* 42*(do)*
 when: 41*(be),* 42*(do)*
 where: 9*(be),* 11*(be),* 18*(be),* 27*(be),* 28*(be),* 38(other v), 39*(be* past), 57(cont), 98, 99

Grammar Index

which + n: 32*(be)*, 134, 190
who: 21*(be)*, 22*(have)*, 55(subj, cont), 102(obj)
whom: 102(prep + ~)
whose: 30*(be)*
why: 82(cont), see also *how come*

yes/no-questions
 ever in *yes/no*-ques: 50, 51, 148, 149
 intonation ques: 7*(be)*, 19, 26*(do)*
 negative ques: 65*(be)*, 103*(do)*
 or in *yes/no*-ques: 12*(be)*, 129
 past t of *be:* 15
 pres t of *be:* 1, 2, 5, 7, 8, 10, 12, 13, 17*(there + be)*, 44*(there + be)*, 45*(there + be)*
 with continuous: 56, 61, 62, 82, 87
 with *have:* 14, 16, 18, 22, 29, 36, 44
 with modals: 85, 86, 92, 93
 with perfect forms: 148, 149, 162 *(before,* past pfct), 163, 168*(yet)*
 with v other than *be* or *have:*
  pres: 23, 24, 25, 35, 43, 50, 51, 52, 115
  past: 98, 103, 108

quite: 48

R
rather: 48(adv), 243(~ *than*)
 see modal *would rather*
really: 48, 63
reason why, the: 217
recommend + subjunct: 185
reflexive pron, see **pronouns**

rejoinders
 either: 35, 108
 neither: 108
 not: 49, 103
 so: 34, 116
 too: 34, 35

relative clauses, see **clauses**
relative pron, see **pronouns**

reported speech
 declarative: 175, 177, 194, 244
 imperative: 165, 244
 passive: 244
 questions: 186, 189
  also **embedded questions**
 say: 165, 175, 177, 189, 194, 244
 tell: 165, 177, 189, 194, 244
 talk: 177*(talk to)*

requests, see **imperatives,** *suppose*
rest(of), the: 94
right now: 62, 81
right there: 11

S
same, the + n: 116
same as, the: 117
say: 165, 175, 177, 189, 194, 244 see also **reported speech**
see (find out) with embedded ques: 233
see if (try): 233
shall, see **modals**
she, subj pron, see **pronouns**

short replies
 be: 2, 5, 7, 13
 cont: 55, 56
 do: 14, 16, 23, 26, 29, 35, 36
 not yet: 40, 157
 perfect forms: 149

should, see **modals**

Grammar Index

similar: 117

simple past tense
  be: 15, 39, 97, 148(vs pfct)
  have: 97
  irregular v: 99, 100, 101, 103, 110, 111, 114, 153, 164
  modals, see **modals**
  regular v: 98, 100, 111

simple present tense
  be: 1, 2, 3, 4, 5, 6, 7, 8, 9, 10, 17*(there + be)*, 18*(there + be)*, 29*(there + be)*, 44*(there + be)*, 45*(there + be)*, see also **contractions**
  have: 14, 16, 18, 22, 29, 34, 36, 44, 45(vs *there + be*)
  have got: 96 see also *have got to*
  other verbs: 23, 24, 25, 26, 35, 38, 42(future meaning), 43, 49, 50(habitual), 51, 52, 63(habitual), 69(vs pres cont), 115, 133(habitual vs pres cont), 134(habitual), 137(historical pres)

since: 156, 168, 182, 232
so(conj): 118, 129, 236
  rejoinder: 34, 116
  pro-clause: 84, 88, 210, 211,
so that: 248, 250
some, quantifier
  adj: 17, 45
  pron: 18
some more: 93
some of: 94
someone: 178
sometimes: 51
sort of: 115
start(+ v-*ing*): 91
starting: 91
still: 105, 156, 179

stop(+ v-*ing*): 91
subject pronouns, see **pronouns**

subjunctive
  certain verbs + *that:* 185*(suggest, recommend)*
  with conditional: 222, 226, 227, 238, 239
  with *wish:* 235, 238, 239

suggest + subjunctive: 185
suppose in requests: 210
suppose so: 210, 211
suppose + *that*-cl: 211
supposed to + v: 211
supposed to be + pp: 211
suppose, see **passive**
sure: 81

T
tag questions, see **questions**
talk: 177
talk someone into doing something: 216
tell: 165, 177, 189, 194, 244 see also **reported speech**
tense, see **verb tenses,** individual tenses, **modals**
thank you: 1
thanks for + n, v-*ing:* 14, 229

that, dem adj, see **adj**
  dem pron, see **pron**
  rel pron, see **pron**
  adv of degree(emphatic *that*), see **adverbs**
that-clause, see **clauses**
the, see **articles**
their, poss adj, see **adj**
theirs, poss pron, see **pron**
them, obj pron, see **pron**
themselves, refl pron, see **pron**

Grammar Index

then: 61, 113, 132
there: 10

there + be (there is/are)
 simple pres t: 17, 18, 29, 44, 45
 in contrast with *have:* 45
 there + be + to v: 79
these,
 dem adj, see **adj**
 dem pron, see **pron**
they, see **pronouns, passive** (*they* passive)
think + that-clause, see **clauses**
this
 dem adj, see **adj**
 dem pron, see **pron**
though: 90, 92
to + v, clause of purpose, see **clauses**
to, prep of direction: 43, 57, 83, 112
to, prep with obj: 80, 81, 111
today: 15
too, adv: 8, 12
 rejoinder: 34, 35
 too + adj + *to* v: 119
those
 dem adj, see **adj**
 dem pron, see **pron**

two-word verbs
 inseparable: 24, 54, 59, 177
 separable: 56, 59, 100, 114

U
under: 11
unless: 218
until: 151, 158, 170
us, obj pron, see **pronouns**
used for + v-*ing:* 199
used to + v(customary past): 135, 139
 see also *be used to, get used to* (accustomed to)

V
verb tenses
 see individual tenses: **continuous** (future, past, present cont, *be going to* + v, modals); future; **perfect forms** (present perfect, present perfect continuous, past perfect, future perfect, modals); **simple past tense; simple present tense;** see also **conditional; modals; passive; subjunctive; two-word verbs**

verbs
 v + *(for)* obj + *to* v: 112
 v + indo obj + d obj/v + d obj + *to* ind obj: 80, 81, 102
 v + ind obj + d obj/v + d obj + *for* ind obj: 111
 v + obj + *that*-clause: 177*(tell)*, 194*(tell),* 216*(convince)*
 v + obj + v: 95*(help),* 125*(let),* 126*(help)*
 v + obj + *to* v: 86*(want),* 165*(tell),* 206*(remind),* 216*(persuade)*
 v + *that*-clause, *that*-clause, see **clauses**
 v + *to* v: 52*(like),* 53*(want),* 90 *(plan),* 236*(decide),* 237*(decide)*
 v + v-*ing:* 90*(plan on),* 91*(start, stop),* 134*(like),* 151*(finish),* 159 *(finish)*
 v + particle, see **two-word verbs**
 see also **two-word verbs, verb tenses**
very: 36, 48

W, X
want: 53
want to + *have to:* 160

Grammar Index

want + obj + *to* v: 86
want + obj + pp: 242

we, see **pronouns**
well: 77
what(with clause): 209, 214
what as object: 102
what, wh-ques, see **questions**
what + n in an exclamation: 116,
   in ques: see **questions**
what about + n, see **questions**
what color, wh-ques, see **questions**
what day, wh-ques, see **questions**
what else, see **questions**
what . . . for, wh-ques, see **questions**
what's it like to. . ., wh-ques, see
   questions
what . . . like, wh-ques, see **questions**
what kind(of): wh-ques, see **questions**
what time, wh-ques, see **questions**
whatever, pron, see **pronouns**
wh-questions, see **questions**
when, wh-ques, see **questions**
when(with cl of time): 200, 206, 207,
   209, 215, 250
where, wh-ques, see **questions**
where(with cl of place): 193
whether, whether or not: 237*(decide),*
   246*(decide),* 247
while(conj): 215
which, wh-ques, see **ques**
which + n, *wh*-ques, see **ques**
which, rel pron, see **pron**
who, rel pron, see **pron**
who, wh-ques, see **questions**

whom, rel pron, see **pron**
whom(object of *to*): 102 (in ques)
   see **questions**
whose, wh-ques, see **questions**
why(with cl of reason): 217
why, wh-ques, see **questions**
will, see **modals**
   will have: see **perfect forms**
wish: 235, 238, 239
with, prep with obj: 64, 125
   in reduced rel cl: 176, 178
without in reduced cond clause: 226
wonder: 180

word order
   s + *be* + compl: 1, 2, 3, 4, 5, 6, 7, 8,
     9, 10
   s + vi: 38, 42, 43, 49
   s + vt + obj: 14, 16, 22, 23, 24, 25,
     26, 50, 52, 55
   s + vt + ind obj + d obj: 80, 81, 102,
     111
   s + vt + obj + compl: 242

would, see **modals**

Y, Z

yes/no-ques, see **questions**
yet: 40, 157, 168
you, impersonal/subj/obj pron, see
   pron
your, poss adj, see **adj**
yours, poss pron, see **pron**
yourself, refl pron, see **pron**
yourselves, refl pron, see **pron**